approaching speech/communication

Holt, Rinehart and Winston, Inc.

New York · Chicago · San Francisco · Atlanta · Dallas
Montreal · Toronto · London · Sydney

approaching speech/communication

Michael Burgoon
West Virginia University

A Leogryph Book

Project manager:	Nicholas L. Falletta
Design:	Ladislav Svatos
Photo research:	Abagail Solomon
Line art:	Vantage Art
Production:	Cobb/Dunlop

Drawings from *The Labyrinth* (Harper & Row, Publishers),
The New World (Harper & Row, Publishers),
The Inspector (The Viking Press, Inc.)
Copyright © 1960, 1965, 1968 by Saul Steinberg.
Reprinted by permission
of Julian Bach Literary Agency, Inc.

Contents

Chapter 7
page *209*

Small group communication

Chapter 8
page *241*

Public address communication

Preface

This text is designed for the introductory course in speech/communication. It attempts to develop a broad understanding of the communication process, using theoretical models as well as applications from familiar life situations. New information is included in such areas as the construction of verbal messages and nonverbal and mass communication; traditional interests such as public address and persuasion are also fully explored. Our objective throughout has been to develop in the student the resources that will enable him to evaluate messages and to create his own effective messages in a time of ever-increasing information flow.

The text is organized in three sections. Part 1 focuses on the variables in the communication process. The concepts of source, receiver, and verbal and nonverbal messages are discussed in detail. The section ends with a discussion of the obstacles to effective communication. Theoretical considerations are presented through illustrations drawn from topical areas. For example, an analysis of dogmatism and its effects on communication is developed in terms of the characters of "All in the Family." And the destructive effects of polarization are illustrated by an excerpt from James Michener's study on the confrontation between demonstrators and federal troops at Kent State.

Part 2 discusses the different speech situations—dyad, small group, public address and mass communication. The section is supported with concrete examples, such as excerpts from speeches and other practical demonstrations of the communication process at work. New research is included on therapy groups and on communication in the mass market. Part 3 is devoted to the functions of communication—persuasion, information exchange, social relations and conflict resolution.

Throughout the text special care has been given to readability and graphic format. As communicators we are aware that the way in which material is presented is nearly as important as the material itself. We feel that a textbook, particularly a communication textbook, must be interesting and motivating, not dull and "texty." And like all communicators we have striven for clarity and beauty of language in the belief that even difficult concepts can be made understandable. It is our hope that we have achieved an effective pedagogical balance between abstract concepts and practical interpretations. We have tried to keep the receiver in mind.

As part of our strategy, we have included a number of pedagogical aids. Small group and individual exercises are provided at the end of each chapter. These exercises should help personalize the information in the chapter; many are appropriate for class discussion. Each chapter also has its own annotated bibliography which includes scholarly and popular works, library references and paperbacks. The annotations often direct the student to specific chapters or sections of a work and should thus be helpful to him in research. End-of-chapter summaries are also provided for study and review. Where appropriate photos and diagrams are used to give visual support to important concepts.

Acknowledgments

The writing of acknowledgments to valued friends and trusted colleagues is among the most difficult parts of preparing a book. I cannot adequately express my appreciation for the support, influence and concern that Gerald Miller has given me over the years. It is appropriate that he served as a very helpful reviewer on this manuscript. I also offer my appreciation to Mark Knapp and John Baird of Purdue University and Larry Rosenfeld of the University of New Mexico for their reviews. James McCroskey has always believed in me and refuses to confuse the intensity of my arguments with the validity of my positions; I need that. My sometimes co-author, sometimes student, sometimes teacher, Judee Heston forces me to think about new ideas and her influence on this text is just the beginning of her contribution to the discipline of human communication. Paul Schmitt, my editor on this project, has helped in numerous ways to make this a better book. I thank all those people who care about me and human communication in whichever order.

Introduction to the communication process

Except for the biological processes which keep us alive, probably no activity is more pervasive than communication. From the moment we awake to the moment we fall asleep, the major portion of our time is spent communicating with others. It is estimated that more than 70 percent of our daily activities involve some form of verbal communication—talking, listening, reading and writing.[1] While this estimate may, at first, seem high, it does not account for numerous nonverbal communication activities such as waving hello to someone or stopping at a street corner for a red light. Clearly, man is a communicating animal. Indeed, the very quality of humanness may be defined by the communication activities in which we engage.

The pervasiveness of communication in men's lives is an indication of the many important functions which this process serves in contemporary society. No one today exists in a vacuum; we each belong to a spiraling hierarchy of groups. We are members of a family, a group of friends, a community, a state and a nation. Man's interrelatedness is a striking characteristic of twentieth century life, and his unique methods of communication make living and working together possible.

Through communication people are able to exert some control over their physical and social environment. By sharing information, man is better able to cope with forces in nature —from tilling the soil to conquering outer space. Then too, communication helps people to initiate and inhibit changes in the social system. Whether we declare war, march for peace, build a housing project or form a commune, communication is the necessary first step in achieving our goals. Of course, communication also provides personal rewards; it enables a person to become more aware of himself and others. Thus, communication helps to establish and maintain social relationships which, in turn, help a person to reach his full potential as an individual.

Despite the pervasiveness and importance of communication in our daily lives, few of us are willing to contend that we are "effective" communicators. Consider, for example, the

---

[1] David K. Berlo, *The Process of Communication* (New York: Holt, Rinehart and Winston, 1960), p. 1.

number of times during a day you say "That's not what I meant" or "What did you mean" or "I don't understand." The fact that we communicate frequently does not necessarily mean we are good at it. Examining the communication process carefully can help to make a person a more effective communicator.

The nature of the communication process

In the first months of life, an infant begins to learn the complex process of communication. Babies cry when they want food or attention, and they quickly learn that this crying behavior is a way of exerting some control over the environment. Later a child will learn to talk, and verbal communication will be added to his repertoire of gestures and sounds. But the process of learning to communicate does not stop in early childhood. People are constantly relearning and refining their means of communication so they can adapt to changing circumstances in their personal lives or in the world around them. This is what we mean when we say that communication is a process—it is not static, with an easily defined beginning, middle and end. It is a constantly changing, dynamic function, involving exchange and interaction between its various elements. Don Fabun, a communication expert, has suggested that every sentence should begin and end with the word "and" to make people aware of the on-going nature of their communication activities.[2]

To see how the different elements in a process may be constantly changing and interacting, it is helpful to examine a simple biological process such as digestion. We could list the elements of the digestive process as just the organs involved: the mouth, stomach, small and large intestines, pancreas and liver. But these elements alone do not constitute the actual process of digestion. For example, the stomach cannot digest meat proteins until the meat has been broken down in the mouth and then worked on by the enzyme pepsin. In turn, pepsin cannot perform its function without the aid of hydrochloric acid. All the elements of the digestive process must work together, interacting and changing to meet different needs. Like digestion,

---

[2] Don Fabun, *Communications: The Transfer of Meaning* (Beverly Hills, Calif.: Glencoe Press, 1968), p. 4.

the process of communication also involves change, interaction, adaptation and an on-going function.

The transactional nature of communication

Whatever your goals in life, you will eventually find it necessary—and advantageous—to learn to communicate more effectively. If you are interviewed for a job, you will have an immediate need to communicate your skills, intelligence and desire to work. If you are beginning a dating relationship, you may wish to communicate acceptance or rejection of your partner's actions. If you hold a managerial position in a corporation, you will need to communicate your business ideas to your subordinates and superiors.

All communication, regardless of the situation and number of people involved, is transactional by nature. The transaction occurs when one person called the *source* sends a message which is picked up by another person called the *receiver*. Communication only occurs when there is a relay or transfer of meaning between people.

When you talk to a friend, you are acting as the source of a message, and he is acting as the receiver. One of the first things you look for when relaying your message is the reaction of your friend. Is he interested in what you are saying? Does he seem to understand your message? You look for visual responses (a smile or eye movement, for example) and then a verbal response to your message. When the receiver reacts to a message sent by the source, he provides cues for the source about the way his message is being received. These cues are known as *feedback*, an important concept in the study of communication. Without feedback, it would probably be impossible to know if a message was received and how accurately it was received. In short, feedback enables the source of a message to know if he has accomplished his purpose in sending it.

Feedback, however, is not a one-way process. While the receiver of the message is reacting and sending signals back to the source, the source is simultaneously reacting to the feedback he is receiving and sending more feedback to the receiver. Of course, the amount of feedback varies in different communication situations; nevertheless, all communication activities involve a transaction or transfer of meaning between people.

Figure 1 Feedback may take the form of both verbal and nonverbal cues. In face-to-face situations, feedback between the interactants is usually intense and simultaneous.

The affective nature of communication

There is an old riddle that asks the question, "If a tree falls in a deserted forest, has a sound really been made?" In other words, if no one is around to hear the crash, might we suppose that the sound did not exist at all? Communication, whether it is verbal or nonverbal, cannot exist if no one is there to receive the signals. Everything we label as communication is affective because it has an impact on someone. The woman who smiles at a man at a party is communicating with him, and that communication will have some impact on the man. Just what that impact will be is difficult to predict, because the man's responses will depend on his perception, awareness and experience. In a similar way, the woman will be affected by the response which the message stimulates in the receiver. Even if the message does not get through, this lack of communication will affect the sender; the woman may try to send another message, or she may simply walk away.

While all experts agree that communication is affective, some theorists support the idea that it is impossible not to communicate. They believe that all behavior is communication and that there is no such thing as nonbehavior. Therefore, they argue that a person cannot *not* communicate.[3] While this argument may sound somewhat circular, many everyday experiences provide sound evidence to support it. For instance, when a person does not answer a question, his lack of words may

[3] Paul Watzlawick, Janet H. Beavin, and Don D. Jackson, *Pragmatics of Human Communication* (New York: W. W. Norton & Co., 1967), pp. 48-49.

Figure 2 The men in this photograph do not want to communicate with each other, yet their behavior is communicating this fact. Can people not communicate?

indicate ignorance of the answer or hostility toward the person who asked it or any number of things depending on the context of the situation. In any event, the "nonresponse" is communicating something and may actually be more eloquent than words.

The personal nature of communication

Words are important to communication because they are convenient symbols by which we can transfer meaning. A word, however, is not the thing it represents. Likewise, the meaning or "message" is not in a word but in the people who use the word. Examining a common word such as "chair" illustrates this point. What kind of "chair" do you visualize when you hear this word? Do you see a large, overstuffed living room chair, a hard wooden dining room chair, or a metal folding chair? If you heard someone say, "They gave him the chair," would you know what is meant? Would the message have the same meaning if the person being talked about was in one case a college professor and in another case a murderer?

Because meanings are in people, communication is as personal as the individuals who use it. It is impossible to separate self from the communication process because all our experiences, attitudes and emotions are involved and will affect the way we send and interpret messages. According to Kenneth Boulding, an eminent economist, every individual has an unique "image" of himself—a special way of viewing the word which is the result of all his personal experiences since childhood. A person's image of himself affects his communication activities:

> . . . our image is in itself resistant to change. When it receives messages which conflict with it, its first impulse is to reject them as in some sense untrue. Suppose, for instance, that somebody tells us something which is inconsistent with our picture of a certain person. Our first impulse is to reject the proffered information as false. As we continue to receive messages which contradict our image, however, we begin to have doubts, and then one day we receive a message which overthrows our previous image and we revise it completely. The person, for instance, whom we saw as a trusted friend is now seen to be a hypocrite and a deceiver.[4]

Of course, the purpose of any communication is to achieve shared meanings. However, the symbolic nature of communication makes this difficult to accomplish. Not only is language

---

[4] Kenneth E. Boulding, *The Image: Knowledge in Life and Society* (Ann Arbor, University of Michigan Press, 1956), pp. 8-9.

symbolic—each word carrying varied connotations for different people—but language too is a process which is constantly changing. Consider, for example, an excerpt from George Washington's inaugural speech in 1789:

> All I dare hope is that, if in executing this task I have been too much swayed by a grateful remembrance of former instances, or by an affectionate sensibility to this transcendent proof of the confidence of my fellow-citizens, and have thence too little consulted my incapacity as well as disinclination for the weighty and untried cares before me, my error will be palliated by the motives which misled me, and its consequences be judged by my country with some share of the partiality with which they originated.

Now compare this excerpt with one from President Nixon's second inaugural speech in 1973 and you will see how much our use of language has changed:

> We have the chance today to do more than ever before to make life better in America—to ensure better education, better transportation, a cleaner environment; to restore respect for law, to make our communities more liveable, and to ensure the God-given right of every American to full and equal opportunity.

Language is not the only element of communication which is subject to change. It is very doubtful that George Washington would have understood the meaning of the much-used V for victory (or for peace) sign. Such signs, gestures and behavioral cues, all integral parts of nonverbal communication, are also abstractions of reality. Each has different symbolic meanings for different people. Because communication is a personal process, a shared code of symbols is required for people to understand each other.

Defining
the communication process

Not surprisingly, there are numerous definitions of communication. However, most communication experts agree with the assumptions that have been stated so far: that communication is a dynamic process, that the communication process is a transaction which will affect both the sender and the receiver, and that communication is a personal, symbolic process requiring a shared code of abstractions. Beyond these basic assumptions, communication theorists branch off into two schools of thought: those who define communication as source-oriented and those who favor receiver-oriented definitions.[5]

Source-oriented definitions
Most source-oriented definitions include as communication all activities in which a person (the source) intentionally transmits stimuli to evoke a response.[6] Attaching the concept of intentionality to communication tends to make one view all communication activities as essentially persuasive. Furthermore, a source-oriented view of communication emphasizes certain variables of the process, such as the content of the speech or message, the way it is delivered, and its persuasiveness. In other words, this view of communication focuses on the production of effective messages.

Receiver-oriented definitions
Receiver-oriented definitions see communication as all activities in which a person (the receiver) responds to a stimulus.[7] Clearly, this view of the communication process is concerned with understanding and meaning, since the emphasis is placed on how the receiver perceives and interprets the message. In addition, this view is not limited to "intentional" behavior and thus broadens the scope of communications study.

Of course, the purpose of any definition is to be helpful. Each of the above definitions of communication will clarify the process and provide new insights for the person using it, but each definition has its limitations. Some experts say that source-oriented definitions are too narrow because they exclude nonintentional, but nevertheless message-carrying activities. Other experts argue that receiver-oriented definitions are too broad because they fail to make a distinction between communication and other kinds of behavior. Furthermore, both definitions alter a person's view of the communication process. A source-oriented view stresses certain variables—the source and the content and delivery of the message.

---

[5] Thomas R. Nielson, "On Defining Communication," *Speech Teacher*, 6 (1957), pp. 10-18.

[6] Gerald R. Miller, "On Defining Communication: Another Stab," *Journal of Communication*, 26 (1966), pp. 88-89.

[7] S.S. Stevens, "Introduction: A Definition of Communication," *Journal of the Acoustical Society of America*, XXII (November, 1950), p. 687.

A receiver-oriented view stresses different variables—the receiver and the meaning the message has for him. Both types of definitions have value, but each presents a different viewpoint of the total process.

Models of communication

The communication process is often taken for granted as a simple, daily part of our lives. But even in a preliminary study of communication, complexities begin to emerge. Communication can be defined in a number of different ways and in a number of different situations, but it is probably more helpful to represent communication in the form of a model, thereby enabling us to visualize and analyze different aspects of the process.

A model is a visual representation. Just as a map of the world is a model illustrating the continents, oceans and mountains, and helping us to conceptualize the relationships of one to the other, so a communication model can be a helpful, if symbolic, representation of the process.

One of the difficulties in creating a model of a process is that we must freeze and isolate the elements involved. For instance, a diagram of the digestive process may illustrate the various organs or elements involved in digestion, but it cannot show the process in action. A model by its nature is a static representation which arrests a process at one point. A model is also an abstraction, and simplification is inherent in abstracting. This presents another problem: in proposing a model of communication, we are probably presenting an oversimplified view of a complex process. We have seen how many elements are involved in one simple communication activity. It would be almost impossible to represent all these elements in one model.

Despite their limitations, there are many ways to utilize models in a study of communication. A model may serve as a subjective view of the process, expressing one man's unique way of viewing communication. We could also think of a model as a graphic illustration which helps us to visualize and analyze separate parts of the communication process. In fact, the very simplification which we cited as a drawback is also an asset: we use models to simplify and clarify complex systems. Models give us an observer's perspective, and with it the capacity to understand why communication problems occur and how they can be avoided.

The Aristotelian model

The Greek philosopher Aristotle was very concerned with communication. He examined and labeled several basic elements of the communication process which were later expanded into a classical model. For Aristotle, the key elements in the process were simply the speaker, the speech and the audience (see Figure 3).[8]

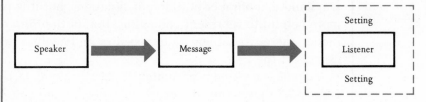

Figure 3 Artistotle's view of the communication process

Aristotle focused on rhetorical communication, or the art of public speaking, because this was a necessary skill in his day, used in the courts, the legislature and popular assemblies. Since all these forms of public speaking involved persuasion, Aristotle was interested in discovering the most effective means of persuasion in speech.

According to Aristotle, the factors which played a role in determining the persuasive effects of a speech were the contents of a speech, its arrangement, and the manner in which it was delivered. Aristotle was also aware of the role of the audience. "Persuasion is effected through the audience," he said, "when they are brought by the speech into a state of emotion."[9] Other elements which effected persuasion included the character (ethos) of the speaker and the arguments he made in the speech.

The Laswell model

In 1948, Harold Laswell, a social scientist, proposed a model of communication which analyzed the process in terms of the

[8] W. Rhys Roberts, "Rhetorica," in *The Works of Aristotle*, Vol. XI, W.D. Ross, ed. (New York: Oxford University Press, 1946), p. 14.

[9] Lane Cooper, *Rhetoric of Aristotle* (New York: Appleton-Century-Crofts, 1960), p. 9.

functions it performs in human societies.[10] Laswell isolated
and defined three definite functions. These were: 1) *surveillance*
of the environment—alerting members of a community to
dangers and opportunities in the environment; 2) *correlation*
of the different parts of society in making a response to the
environment; and 3) *transmission* of the social heritage from
one generation to another.

Laswell maintained that there were groups of specialists
who were responsible for carrying out these functions. For
example, political leaders and diplomats belong to the first
group of surveillors of the environment. Educators, journalists
and speakers help correlate or gather the responses of the
people to new information. Family members and school
educators pass on the social heritage.

Laswell recognized that not all communication is "two-way,"
with a smooth flow of information and feedback occurring
between sender and receiver. In our complex society, much
information is filtered through message controllers—editors,
censors or propagandists, who receive the information and
then pass it on to the public with some modifications or
distortions. According to Laswell, one vital function of
communication is to provide information about other world
powers, since we as a nation depend on communication as a
means of preserving our own strength. Therefore, he concludes,
it is essential for an organized society to discover and control
any factors which may interfere with efficient communication.
He suggested that a simple way to describe the communication
process is to answer the following questions:

> Who
> Says What
> In Which Channel
> To Whom
> With What Effect?

The Shannon and Weaver model

In 1949, Claude Shannon and Warren Weaver proposed one
of the first information theory models in their book *The
Mathematical Theory of Communication*.[11] Shannon was an

---

[10] Harold D. Laswell, "The Structure and Function of Communication in Society," in
The Communication of Ideas, L. Bryson, ed. (New York: Harper and Row Publishers, 1948),
pp. 37-51.

[11] Claude E. Shannon and Warren Weaver, *The Mathematical Theory of Communication*
(Urbana, Ill.: University of Illinois Press, 1949).

engineer at Bell Telephone and he was concerned with the accurate transmission of messages over the telephone. Weaver extended Shannon's concept to apply to all types of communication.

Perhaps you remember playing a game called "telephone" when you were a child. A message was passed from child to child, and the information in the message was usually quite distorted when it arrived at the last person in the chain. The Shannon and Weaver model is concerned with the same problem: accurate message transmission. It envisions a source who encodes or creates a message and transmits it through a channel to a receiver who decodes or recreates the message (see Figure 4).

A key concept introduced in the Shannon and Weaver model is *noise*, any additional and unwanted stimuli that can disrupt the accuracy of the message being transmitted. Noise can be the static interference on a phone call, or loud music at a party, or a siren outside your window. According to Shannon and Weaver, noise is always present in the channel to be picked up by the receiver along with the message. Communication experts have extended this concept to include "psychological" as well as physical noise. Psychological noise refers to the interference of a person's own thoughts and feelings which disrupt the accurate reception of a message. We have all experienced moments when our daydreams (psychological noise) have caused us to completely miss a message.

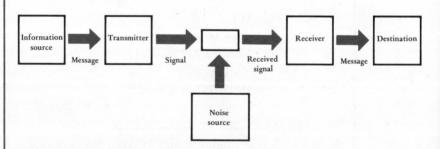

Figure 4 The Shannon and Weaver model

The Westley and MacLean model
Bruce Westley and Malcolm MacLean, communication theorists, formulated a model which covered both interpersonal and mass communication, and included feedback as an integral

part of the communication process.[12] In fact, one of the distinctions that Westley and MacLean make between interpersonal and mass communication depends primarily on the differences in feedback. In interpersonal or face-to-face communication, there is immediate feedback from the receiver. Many kinds of stimuli pass between the receiver and the source in interpersonal communication, and the source has the advantage of learning the receiver's responses almost immediately.

In mass communication, feedback is usually delayed and minimized. This is simple to understand if you picture a typical mass communication situation, like a televised presidential speech. The President may be successful in delivering his message to thousands of viewers, but he receives no immediate feedback from his listeners, since he can neither see nor hear their reactions. The feedback or reaction of the receivers to this message may be delayed for days or weeks until the general reaction of the public has been recorded. But even this is minimized feedback, since each individual's reactions are unknown to the source.

Basically there are five elements in the Westley and MacLean model: objects of orientation, a message, a source, a receiver, and feedback. The source (A) focuses on a particular object or event in his environment (X) and creates a message about it (X') which he transmits to a receiver (B). The receiver, in turn, sends feedback (f_{BA}) about the message to the source (see Figure 5).

In a mass communication situation, Westley and MacLean add another element C. C is a "gatekeeper" or opinion leader who receives messages (X') from the sources of mass media (A_s) or focuses on objects of orientation (X_3, X_4) in his environment. Using this information, the gatekeeper then creates his own message (X'') which he transmits to the receiver (B). This provides a kind of filtering system, since the receivers do not get their information directly from a source, but rather from a person who selects information from many sources. For example, if you had an interest in animal communication, you might read several books and watch a few television documentaries about the subject. During a conversation with a friend, you might mention something about an experiment to teach chimpanzees to use sign language.

---

[12] Bruce H. Westley and Malcolm S. MacLean, Jr., "A Conceptual Model for Communications Research," *Journalism Quarterly*, XXXIV (1957), pp. 31-38.

In doing this, you are filtering information. But more important, you are providing your friend with an extended environment, since you are making him focus on an object of orientation

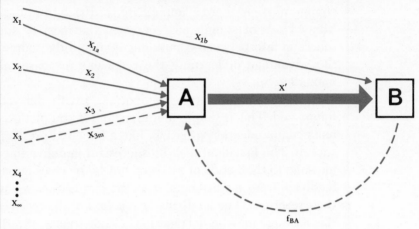

Figure 5 The Westley and MacLean model

which was not in his environment or which was previously unnoticed. In mass communication, feedback may flow in three directions: from the receiver to the gatekeeper, from the receiver to the mass media source, and from the opinion leader to the mass media source (see Figure 6).

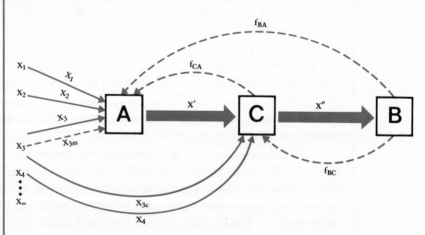

Figure 6 The Westley and MacLean model

Westley and MacLean do not confine their model to the level of the individual. In fact, they stress that the receiver may be a group or social institution. According to Westley and MacLean, any individual, group or system has a need to send and receive messages as a means of orientation to the environment.

The Westley and MacLean model encompasses several important concepts: feedback, the differences and similarities of interpersonal and mass communication, and the importance of opinion leaders as an additional element in mass communication. This model also distinguishes between purposive and nonpurposive messages. A purposive message is one which the source transmits for the express purpose of modifying the receiver's image of something in the environment. If you tell someone that a particular kind of car is poorly made, you are sending a purposive message. A nonpurposive message is one which is transmitted to a receiver directly or through a gatekeeper but with no intent on the part of the source to influence the receiver. If you overheard a professor commenting about a student to another professor, the message would be nonpurposive. In such a case, the message is actually an object of orientation in the receiver's environment.

The Berlo model

In 1960, David K. Berlo proposed a model which emphasized four major elements of the communication process: source, message, channel and receiver.[13] (The Berlo model is often referred to as the SMCR model of communication.)

As defined by Berlo, the source is the creator of the message, some person or group with a reason for engaging in communication. The message is the translation of ideas into a symbolic code, such as language or gestures; the channel is the medium through which the message is carried; and the receiver is the person who is the target of the communication (see Figure 7).

Berlo's model also specifies the need for encoders and decoders in the communication process. The encoder is responsible for expressing the source's purpose in the form of a message. In face-to-face situations, the encoding function is performed by the vocal mechanisms and muscle systems of the source which produce verbal and nonverbal messages. However, it is also possible to have another person encode a message. For example, a Presidential press secretary at a news conference functions as an encoder. In a similar way, the receiver needs a decoder to translate the messages he

---

[13] Berlo, *op. cit.*, pp. 30-38.

receives. In most instances, the decoder is the set of sensory skills of the receiver.

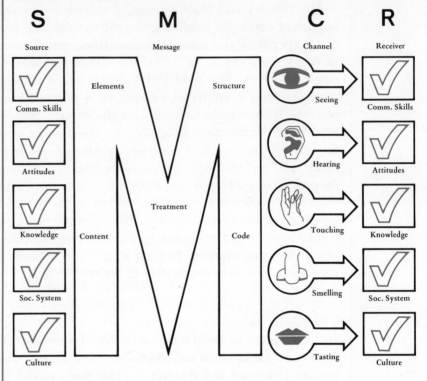

Figure 7 The Berlo model

In face-to-face, small group and public address situations, the channel is the air through which sound waves travel. In mass communication, there are many channels: television, radio, newspapers, books and magazines. Berlo's model also describes some personal factors that may have an affect upon the communication process. These elements are: the communication skills, attitudes, knowledge, social system and cultural environment of both the source and the receiver.

1. Communication is a pervasive activity which serves many important functions in society and our personal lives. The process of communication enables people to exert some control over their environment. Communication also helps to establish and maintain social relationships, thereby enabling a person to develop as an individual.

2. Communication is a process which involves constant change and interaction between the elements which comprise it. Communication also involves an on-going function; it has no easily defined beginning, middle or end.

3. All communication involves a transaction or transfer of meaning between a source and a receiver. Feedback is the reaction of a receiver to the verbal and nonverbal messages transferred in a communicative situation.

4. All communication is affective. This means that communication has an impact on either the receiver, the source, or in most cases both. Some communication experts maintain that all behavior is communicative and that it is impossible not to communicate.

5. Communication is a process which involves a shared code of verbal and nonverbal symbols. It is personal because the meanings of symbols are in the people using them.

6. Communication may be defined from either a source or a receiver perspective. Source-oriented definitions include as communication any activity in which a source deliberately transmits stimuli to evoke a response. Receiver-oriented definitions include as communication any activity in which the receiver responds to a stimulus. A source-oriented view focuses on the production of effective messages by the speaker. A receiver-oriented view focuses on the message's meaning to the receiver.

7. A model is a visual representation which helps us to conceptualize the relationship of various elements involved

in a process such as communication. Models by their nature are simplified abstractions which isolate the elements and freeze the action of a process. Although models present a distorted view of a process, they are helpful because they can clarify complex systems.

8. From Aristotle's writings it is possible to extrapolate a classical model of rhetorical communication which contains three elements: the speaker, the message and the audience. Aristotle also maintained that the construction of the message and the character of the speaker played an important part in persuading an audience.

9. According to Laswell's model, communication has three functions: surveillance of the environment, correlation of different social groups, and transmission of the social heritage. Laswell describes communication with the following questions: Who/Says What/In Which Channel/ To Whom/and With What Effect?

10. The Shannon and Weaver model is concerned with the accurate transmission of a message. This model presents a source who sends a message through a channel to a receiver. Noise is any additional stimuli in the channel which can disrupt the accurate reception of the message.

11. In the Westley and MacLean model, the source (A) creates a message (X') about an object of orientation (X) in his environment. The source then sends the message to a receiver (B) who transmits feedback (f_{BA}) about the message to the source. This model introduces a filter system in mass communication situations. A gatekeeper (C) selects information from the many sources of mass media (A_s) or from objects in his environment (X_s), creates a message, and sends it to other people (B_s).

12. Berlo's model contains four major elements: source, message, channel and receiver. This model also focuses on the encoding and decoding functions which take place during communication. It specifies five personal factors which will affect communicators: their communication skills, attitudes, knowledge, social system and cultural environment.

1. It is important for you to begin to think about your own communication behavior. Take a few minutes and write the answers to the following questions.
   a. How effective are you in communicating with other people? What are your strengths and weaknesses?
   b. Which kinds of communication situations do you have the most difficulty with? Which kinds of communication situations do you have the least difficulty with?
   c. Do you think you are generally successful in changing other people's attitudes?
   d. What specific communication abilities would you like to improve?

2. Think about a conversation which you recently had with another person. Can you identify when the interaction actually began and ended? Did you continue to think and talk about the topic of conversation after the actual interaction had ended? How does this relate to the idea of communication as a process?

3. Think about a situation in which your communication attempt was not successful—for example, one in which conflict resulted or something unexpected happened. Discuss the situation from a source-oriented view. In what ways would viewing your communication behavior from a receiver orientation have changed the course of the interaction?

4. Identify a communication event and describe it within the framework of one or more of the models of communication presented in this chapter. Can you suggest any improvements on the model?

5. Develop a model of communication that could be applied to a communication situation in which you have difficulty participating. What are the elements in this model that lead to the difficulty?

David K. Berlo, *The Process of Communication* (New York: Holt, Rinehart and Winston, 1960). This book, though a bit old, is still one of the best introductions to the communication process. The first three chapters are especially relevant to the topics covered in this chapter.

Kenneth Boulding, *The Image: Knowledge in Life and Society* (Ann Arbor: University of Michigan Press, 1956). This book attempts to formalize the importance of "image" into a new field which the author calls "eiconics." Chapters 1, 2, and 3 make fine supplementary reading.

Don Fabun, *Communications: The Transfer of Meaning* (Beverly Hills, Calif.: Glencoe Press, 1968). A very brief but excellent introduction into the nature of the communication process. The book contains many useful and delightful illustrations.

James McCroskey, *An Introduction to Rhetorical Communication*, 2nd Edition (Englewood Cliffs, N.J.: Prentice Hall, 1972). This is one of the best syntheses of classical rhetoric and contemporary communication theory. Chapter 1 traces the rhetorical tradition from early Egyptian times to the present. Chapter 2 focuses on the nature of rhetorical communication.

Thomas R. Nielsen, "On Defining Communication," *Speech Teacher*, 6 (1957), 10-18. An excellent summary and analysis of numerous "expert" definitions of the communication process. This article is particularly helpful in explaining how source- and receiver-oriented definitions affect our view of the communication process.

part 1

*The variables
in the communication process*

Source variables

Henry David Thoreau wrote, "It takes two to speak the truth,
—one to speak, and another to hear." In emphasizing the fact
that communication is a two-way relationship between the
speaker and the listener, Thoreau pointed out the transactional
nature of the relationship. No source speaks well unless his
receivers are willing to believe that he does so.

At first glance, the situation seems a dispiriting one. A speaker
can certainly work to improve the content and delivery of his
message; he can prepare a careful outline of his speech,
research the accuracy of his facts and practice the words he
will speak. But what can he do to insure that his audience is
willing to believe he can speak well? Can a source alter the way
he is perceived by receivers?

A careful study of the source variables in the communication
situation indicates that there are steps a speaker can take
(short of plastic surgery and complete personality rehabilitation)
to enhance the audience's perception of him as an effective
communicator. Certain small things help, such as arranging
to be introduced by a third party whom the receivers already
like, trust and consider competent. But while many of the
research findings suggest improved techniques such as the
incorporation within the message of a declaration of competence,
others go far beyond the merely technical. Research confirms
that the most effective source is one who is known to be
honest, who is genuinely sympathetic to the needs and desires
of his audience, who is willing to risk the threat of rejection
as he tries to reach out for a real understanding; in other words,
a good communicator is a good person.

The examination of source variables reveals the problems a
source faces going into a communication situation, problems
which may involve both technique and character. Yet at the
same time, it suggests some solutions to these problems,
setting out guidelines to achieve effective communication.

site:
ight © 1965
ul Steinberg.
The New World,
r & Row, Publishers.

Credibility as a source variable

We are all aware that some people are more effective
communicators than others. Many times the reasons for this

effectiveness are not readily apparent to the people involved in a communication situation. People who tend to persuade us, or who are naturally likeable, or who are able to enter situations and settle difficulties, are usually held in high esteem by their fellow men. When we cannot explain why these people have the impact they do, we often claim they simply possess "charisma." However, the use of a word like charisma is not very helpful to those of us who wish to obtain more understanding of human communication. Since one is hard pressed to identify those variables which make one person a charismatic leader and another person not, he is also at a loss when asked to help someone else be a more charismatic and thus more effective communicator. Therefore, we must look for specific attributes of a source, including his communication behavior, to understand the real meaning of this ambiguous term.

From antiquity to the present, scholars have recognized that people make certain decisions about a source that promote effective communication. Aristotle claimed that ethos, or the quality we call credibility, is the most potent means of persuasion. Plato, Cicero and Quintillian all wrote of the importance of source ethos or credibility but differed somewhat in their definitions of that quality. When Quintillian emphasized the importance of the "good man speaking well," he gave us little more information than is contained in the statement that "charismatic men are more effective communicators."

A considerable amount of experimental research attests to the importance of source credibility in the communication transaction. The source with high credibility is more effective in producing a variety of desired outcomes than one with low credibility. In fact, the credibility of a communicator may be the best single predictor of the course or direction of most communication transactions. Of course, no communicator possesses an inherent quality called credibility. Source credibility is something which exists "in the eye of the beholder." The receiver must confer credibility on a speaker or it does not exist. Since credibility is a perceived phenomenon, suggestions for establishing or enhancing this quality depend on many situational and personal variables.

In any communication transaction, there are personal variables that the source brings with him to the situation. These include such qualities as sex, age, ethnic origin and speech impediments. Some of these characteristics, or at least the way they are projected, may not be within the source's control. Since each receiver is an unique individual, the way he perceives the source is based on his past experience. For example, a racially prejudiced person may be incapable of perceiving former Black Panther leader Bobby Seale as highly credible. Mickey Rooney may see John Wayne as tall, whereas Willis Reed does not share this perception. In other words, two people, talking to the same person, may respond to him quite differently as a result of their prior experience and individual perceptions. Nevertheless, research has demonstrated that a speaker can, to some extent, control these factors and thereby make himself a more effective communicator. Knowledge of the way a receiver perceives a speaker's credibility can provide helpful insights into the communication process.

The dimensions of source credibility

Contemporary communication scholars have tried systematically to analyze what constitutes a "good" man, or a "credible" speaker, or a "charismatic" leader. It appears that people make decisions about at least five attributes of a source in a communication situation.[1] Earlier writers identified two of these decision points: *competence*, or the source's knowledge of the subject, and *character*, or the apparent trustworthiness of the source. Other source attributes which seem important to a receiver are *composure, sociability and extroversion.*

Each of these dimensions acts independently to influence the source's effectiveness as a communicator. For example, you can decide a person has great expertise on a particular topic but nevertheless believe he is untrustworthy. Similarly, a person can be very likeable and composed but be judged by others as having little competence on a specific subject. In any given situation, one decision may be more important than the others and therefore be a better predictor of communication effectiveness. In a social situation, you may not care whether a person is extremely knowledgeable about Elizabethan drama so long as you enjoy talking with him.

---

[1] A number of recent studies have delineated these dimensions of source credibility. See James C. McCroskey, Thomas Jensen, and Cynthia Todd, *The Generalizability of Source Credibility Scales for Public Figures,* Paper presented at the Speech Communication Association Convention, Chicago, Ill., 1972 and James C. McCroskey, Thomas Jensen and Cynthia Valencia, *Measurement of the Credibility of Peers and Spouses,* Paper presented at the Internation Communication Association Convention, Montreal, Quebec, 1973.

However, if you are injured, it may matter little if your doctor is sociable and out-going; you simply want someone who is competent to treat your broken arm.

The dimension of competence   It is common in most communication situations for a receiver to judge a source's competence on the subject being discussed. In fact, research indicates that perceptions of competence may contribute most to variance in a receiver's evaluation of a source's credibility.[2] If a speaker is not perceived to be competent or knowledgeable on a topic, it may make little difference how trustworthy, composed, sociable or extroverted he happens to be. People make competence judgments on such variables as level of education, accessibility to current or pertinent information, or direct experience with the subject under discussion. Whether or not the receivers are themselves competent to judge the source's competence seems to make little difference. In short, if the speaker is perceived as competent, he will probably be effective.

There are several things a source may do to increase his perceived competence. In public speaking situations, it is common for a speaker to be introduced to the audience by another person. If the person making the introduction refers to the speaker's title, such as doctor or professor, or even labels him as "a leading expert," this may enhance the audience's perception of the source's competence. The speaker himself may indicate his expertise on the topic by referring to previous experience with the subject or by mentioning other highly competent people with whom he is associated.

If the receivers perceive a source to be low in competence, there is little likelihood that the speaker will be effective, regardless of his actual expertise on the subject being discussed. A good example of this involves a group of students who were invited to hear a lecture on life among the Ashanti. The speaker, a white woman, was given an introduction specifically designed to ensure that she was perceived as competent; the audience was told that the source was born in Africa and raised among the Ashanti. Nevertheless, the predominantly black American audience was extremely unreceptive. The speaker was thoroughly familiar with the

---

[2] See McCroskey, Jensen, and Todd, 1972 and David K. Berlo, James B. Lemert, and Robert Mertz, "Dimensions for Evaluating the Acceptability of Message Sources," *Public Opinion Quarterly*, 33 (1969), pp. 563-576.

*Figure 1-1 In the 1972 campaign, Presidential candidate
Senator George McGovern had low credibility among many
traditional Democratic voters. In an attempt to enhance
McGovern's credibility, Senator Edward Kennedy, who
enjoyed high credibility among Democrats, introduced the
candidate at many public speaking engagements.*

African experience of the Ashanti. She could converse easily and
at length with the Ashanti people about shared cultural
experiences; in fact, the native Africans perceived her to be
"one of them" despite her skin color. But the audience of
black students had a very different perception of her competence
to speak on what they perceived to be the "black experience."
Communication was difficult because although the speaker
knew what it was like to be an Ashanti, she did not know what
it was like to be an American black, and her audience doubted
her competence to speak on the announced topic.

Clearly, the woman's skin color was not in her control, but
she could have taken steps to change the audience's perceptions.
For example, she might have been perceived as more
competent if she had directly confronted the situation and

admitted to the audience that she did not understand the black American experience but could provide information about Africa that might be of interest. Sometimes an admission of lack of competence in one area is perceived as an indication of other kinds of competence.

Many research studies have demonstrated the importance of perceived competence. In a classic study, a recording of a speech favoring national compulsory health insurance was played to several groups of subjects. When the statement was attributed to the Surgeon-General, it was very effective in persuading people of the need for compulsory insurance; however, when the same recording was attributed to a college student, it had no persuasive impact.[3] In this test, the same voice and message had drastically different effects when the source was perceived differentially on the competence dimension. A number of other studies strongly support the notion that sources perceived as highly competent will be effective, whereas those not perceived as competent will have difficulty in communicating effectively.

In most situations, a source cannot be perceived as "too competent;" an ideal source would be one who is highly competent to discuss the topic under consideration. However, the perception of competence is itself a multidimensional process involving several variables. For example, a nuclear physicist heading a research project may be so brilliant that he cannot effectively express his ideas to his subordinates. In such an instance, his research assistants may perceive him as highly competent on one dimension (mastery of subject matter) but incompetent on another (ability to express himself). Based on this example, one might caution a speaker to carefully determine those variables most important to his audience if he is to be effective.

The dimension of character   The popular rejoinder "You're a good man, Charlie Brown," is an estimate of character perceived as goodness, decency or trustworthiness. The dimension of character has a strong influence on the receiver's perception of source credibility. The term "credibility gap," popularized in the early 1960s, refers almost solely to this dimension. The government was saying one thing, and later press accounts indicated it was doing the opposite.

[3] Franklyn S. Haiman, "An Experimental Study of the Effects of Ethos in Public Speaking," *Speech Monographs*, 16 (1949), pp. 190-202.

Recent scandals in government are said to have reduced the President's credibility. When people believe a communicator to be low in character or trustworthiness, they are less likely even to listen to him, let alone to be influenced by his message. To some extent, we judge competence on the basis of objective qualifications (education, work experience and other credentials), but perceptions of character are highly personal judgments about the nature of a source.

In a recent Gallup poll, CBS newscaster Walter Cronkite was found to be the most trusted man in the United States. One can only speculate as to the reasons for these findings. People obviously feel that he is an honest reporter who does not bias the news with his own feelings and cannot be compromised. Therefore, if Cronkite said one thing and the government said another, the position advocated by Cronkite would probably be believed by the majority of people who heard both messages. Another former network newscaster, Chet Huntley, created some controversy when he appeared in a commercial for an airline. The decision makers at the airline probably did not believe Huntley would be seen as competent to discuss the construction of airplanes; however, they were betting that the American people believed him to be of high character and would therefore be persuaded by the commercials. Other newscasters criticized this arrangement, claiming that Huntley's lack of objectivity on the airline would damage the perceived objectivity of all newsmen.

The question of how one establishes and maintains perceptions of high character is a difficult one. Obviously any past experience that questions a person's integrity reduces perceived character. People who change positions over time can be seen as less trustworthy, even if the change itself is a good one. It is doubtful that an ideal source would be anything other than high in character. The best advice to ensure perceptions of high character is to be consistently honest. To the extent a person is perceived to be one of high character, he will be able to facilitate more effective communication. It is certainly a goal worth seeking.

The dimension of composure   A person who is composed, especially under conditions of considerable stress, is perceived to be more credible than a person who is not composed. Research indicates that a speaker who is nervous or produces a number of nonfluencies (stammering, "uhs" and "ers") is less credible and less able to persuade others.[4] Many speech students are immediately perceived as more credible in the early part of the course, because they can keep composed during the stress-producing first speeches. Many people we call "good public speakers" are not more competent or of higher character, but more composed.

To increase his perceived composure, the beginning public speaker can practice his delivery to reduce nonfluencies and apparent nervousness. Fidgeting, shuffling of papers and other distracting behavior often reduce a speaker's perceived composure. In American culture, extreme displays of emotion are also perceived as lack of poise. Many political commentators attribute Senator Muskie's defeat in the Presidential primaries of 1972 to a moment when he lost his composure and publicly cried because of newspaper attacks on his wife. However, it is very difficult to predict the effects specific evidence of lack of composure will have. In two different instances, Walter Cronkite lost his composure. During the 1968 Democratic Convention, he became visibly angry when a floor reporter was accosted. When the first man landed on the moon, he was clearly elated and used emotional language unusual for him. Certainly, the Gallup poll indicates that Cronkite did not suffer any loss of credibility because of his behavior on these occasions. However, few of us enjoy the status that Walter Cronkite has in the eyes of the American public. Therefore, the best advice, according to the research available, is for a speaker to retain his composure whenever possible, since evidence of lack of composure may reduce his effectiveness as a communicator.

The dimension of sociability   The source that projects likeableness to his receivers is regarded as sociable. People who like each other tend to spend more time communicating with each other and are influenced by each other. Research indicates that our interpersonal communication contacts are very influential in shaping and changing our attitudes on a variety of issues. Peers influence our political behavior, help determine the products we consume, and shape our thinking in numerous ways. The recent trends in advertising try to present advocates of consumer products as likeable

---

[4] Gerald R. Miller and Murray A. Hewgill, "The Effects of Variations in Nonfluency on Audience Ratings of Source Credibility," *Quarterly Journal of Speech*, 50 (1964), pp. 36-44.

people; much of the "image advertising" in politics is also designed to do just this. We tend to like people who give us the feeling that they like and respect us and avoid those who do not. Therefore, we are more likely to attend to and be influenced by those whom we perceive as sociable.

There is more to sociability than just interpersonal liking. Although we may not have a friendship with or a deep liking for a person, if he is cooperative and friendly in task situations, he will be perceived as more sociable. The person who goes about his work in a cheerful, friendly manner is likely to be a preferred co-worker. All of these things combine to make a person appear to be more approachable and communicative. In all likelihood, those we consider unsociable will not be a part of our communication activities and will have little influence on us.

The dimension of extroversion The outgoing personality who engages readily and unselfconsciously in communication situations is considered an extrovert. The person who is talkative and not timid in his communication activities is sometimes said to be a dynamic speaker; he may be a very effective communicator. However, a person who is too extroverted may talk too much and take over conversations. We have all been in situations in which very dynamic, extroverted people so dominated the communication that we felt like an unnecessary part of the conversation. Although the optimum amount of source extroversion varies from receiver to receiver, people generally prefer to communicate with those who possess this attribute in moderation.[5]

Jack Parr, for example, is often criticized for being so extroverted and talkative that his guests are rarely allowed to say anything. These critics probably prefer to watch another talk show host—Dick Cavett or Johnny Carson—who dominates less and who allows his guests to carry more of the conversation. However, Parr's show has a large audience whose members obviously enjoy his communication behavior. In most social situations, there is a fine line between being "the life of the party" and "a smashing bore." Figure 1-2 may help to clarify the relationship between extroversion and effective communication.

---

[5] For an excellent study providing empirical support for this model see Judee K. Heston, *Ideal Source Credibility: A Re-examination of the Semantic Differential*, Paper presented at the Internation Communication Association Convention, Montreal, Quebec, 1973.

As extroversion increases, people enjoy talking with and listening to a dynamic person. An extroverted person holds their attention and is generally interesting. However, at some point, and this point varies with people and situations, increased extroversion annoys people and makes them either dislike the person or withdraw from the situation.

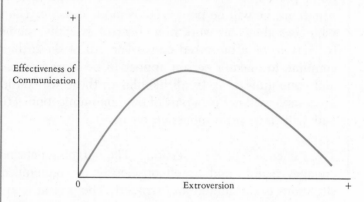

Figure 1-2 *Relationship of extroversion and communicating effectiveness.*

The dynamics of source credibility

Perceptions of a source's credibility are subject to change. Often a source comes to the communication situation with some degree of credibility already established. The degree of credibility perceived in the source prior to any specific communication event is called *initial credibility*. When we say of a speaker that "His reputation preceded him," we are commenting on his initial credibility. For example, a world-famous Arctic explorer talking before a group of professional geographers could expect to have a high degree of initial credibility with his audience. The speaker with a high degree of initial credibility is likely to use a very different communication strategy than a person who is seeking to establish or enhance his credibility.

During any communication event, the source's credibility may be reevaluated and either heightened or lowered in the receiver's mind. This assessment or modification of initial credibility is called *transactional credibility*. People continually assess a speaker and make evaluative changes during a communication transaction, because they react to many kinds of verbal and nonverbal behavior. For example, if the Arctic explorer told his audience of geographers that he had a poor sense of direction and had to rely on a hired guide, the audience members would probably reduce their initial perceptions of his credibility. A source may also improve his credibility during a transaction by not behaving as expected. Civil behavior on the part of a very militant person may be so unexpected that it catches his audience by surprise and makes him appear to be very "reasonable" or credible and therefore persuasive. What a speaker says and does is continually being processed and evaluated by the people with whom he is communicating. If a source is aware of the criteria by which he is being judged, he can make better decisions about what he must do to ensure continued perceptions of high credibility.

Terminal credibility is the receiver's perception of a source at the completion of a communication event. For example, if the militant person continued to behave in a polite manner throughout his speech, the audience would probably have a higher evaluation of him when he finished than when he began. All of us have, at one time or another, entered a conversation with low regard for someone and ended the communication with a completely altered perception. Terminal credibility is important because it will influence a person's initial credibility if he should communicate again with the same receiver.

People's perceptions of others change between communication events. A receiver might change his attitude or values and therefore be less receptive to a given source the next time they communicate. It is also possible that external variables will cause a receiver to change his evaluation of a source between communication events. We learn about people by receiving new and different information from other sources; this information may, in turn, alter our perceptions. Sometimes this change is positive and allows us to make more valid judgments, but sometimes we allow rumor and innuendo to alter our perceptions. Therefore, it is important to evaluate the sources of information about other people as well as the people with whom we communicate.

Other things may change a receiver's perception of a source's credibility. A person may have high terminal credibility in a previous encounter because the topic of conversation was one which he was competent to discuss. In the next communication transaction, this same source may discuss a subject about which he has little knowledge. This may affect the receiver's perception of his competence in a negative way. However, a source who had high terminal credibility at an earlier time on a completely different topic may be held in high esteem on unrelated topics. This "halo effect" operates in a variety of situations. For example, a student who writes a good first examination paper may have an easier time in the rest of the course because of the early establishment of credibility. Clearly, credibility is ever-changing between and within communication events, topics and people. But even though this variable is subject to change, it deserves serious attention from those wishing to be effective communicators.

Figure 1-3 Sometimes a source's message is transmitted through another person called a sender. Ron Ziegler, the White House Press Secretary, acted as a sender when he held this news conference in behalf of President Nixon.

Homophily–heterophily in communication

Do opposites attract or does like attract like? This age-old question is related to the communication concepts of homophily and heterophily. *Homophily* refers to the degree to which interacting individuals are similar in certain attributes. These attributes may include demographic characteristics such as age, education and socioeconomic status, or they may include attitudes, beliefs and values. If another person were completely identical to you (which is, of course, an impossibility), he would be completely homophilous with you. Some twins come close to meeting this definition. At the opposite end of the similarity continuum is *heterophily*, or dissimilarity. The degree to which someone differs from us in various attributes is the degree of heterophily between us.

Because homophily–heterophily involves a variety of attributes, we can be both homophilous and heterophilous with another person at the same time. An electrician and a physician are heterophilous along the dimension of occupation, but homophilous on political attitudes if they both vote Republican and oppose higher taxes. Two college students may be highly homophilous in terms of age, race, education, status and background but heterophilous in beliefs, if one is convinced that marijuana is physically harmful and the other believes it is completely safe. Their heterophily may only involve one belief or it may involve several; the homophily–heterophily relationship of any two people is highly complex. Knowing their level of similarity on one attribute does not make it possible to predict their similarity on another. We cannot conclude that all persons of the same racial background will behave the same way, that all conservatives support wars, or that all wealthy doctors play golf. By generalizing on the basis of a few known similarities or dissimilarities, we make false assumptions that lead to ineffective communication.

It is important to recognize that the homophilous or heterophilous relationship between a source and a receiver is just that—a relationship. Homophily is not something inherent in a source or a receiver himself. It can only be measured by the relationship of the two people involved. Thus, a source can be highly heterophilous with one receiver and highly homophilous with another at the same time. The perceptive source recognizes his degrees of likeness and difference on several dimensions with *each* of his receivers.

The measurement of homophily–heterophily

If a source is to identify his homophily or heterophily relationships with his receivers, he must in some way measure the similarity or dissimilarity between the two of them. There are two ways of measuring homophily–heterophily: one is objective and other is subjective. An objective measure is the amount of similarity or dissimilarity that is apparent to an impartial observer. The same IQ score or the same yearly income would be two objective measures of homophily. Subjective measures, on the other hand, are those based on the perceptions of the interactants. In any communication transaction, both source and receiver act in light of their perceptions of each other rather than some objective indicator of their heterophily level. If a source believes that he has much higher status than his receiver, no amount of objective measures and observations revealing equality will make the communication relationship homophilous.

This is not to suggest that subjective and objective measures are totally unrelated. In fact, subjective and objective homophily are positively correlated; the level of perceived (subjective) similarity is higher than the actual (objective) similarity.[6] In other words, individuals tend to think they are more similar than they actually are. The degree of perceived homophily between two persons is influenced by the frequency of their interaction and the degree of their personal attraction.[7] The more often they interact and the more they are attracted to each other, the more they will perceive similarities.

The relationship of homophily–heterophily to communication

The homophily–heterophily relationship between the source and receiver will affect their communication transactions in two important ways: it determines who will communicate with whom, and how successful that communication will be. When a person has a choice of whom he will communicate with, he will tend to choose someone like himself.[8] People of the same status who live close to each other or who work together will interact more.[9] Iowa farmers talk about

---

[6] I. E. Bender and A. H. Hastorf, "The Perception of Persons: Forecasting Another Person's Responses on Three Personality Scales," *Journal of Abnormal and Social Psychology*, 45 (1950), pp. 556-661.

[7] Theodore M. Newcomb, "The Prediction of Interpersonal Attraction," *American Psychologist*, 11 (1956), pp. 575-586 and Milton Rokeach, *Beliefs, Attitudes and Values: A Theory of Organization and Change* (San Francisco: Jossey-Bass, 1968), p. 63.

[8] Everett M. Rogers and Dilip K. Bhowmik, "Homophily-Heterophily: Relational Concepts for Communication Research," in Larry L. Barker and Robert J. Kibler, eds., *Speech Communication Behavior* (Englewood Cliffs, N.J.: Prentice-Hall, 1971), p. 212.

[9] Barry E. Collins and Harold Guetzkow, *A Social Psychology of Group Processes for Decision Making* (New York: John Wiley and Sons, 1964), p. 178.

agricultural innovation to persons who share similar interests and attitudes,[10] while ghetto residents discuss family planning with persons of the same age, family size and status.[11] This tendency for voluntary communications patterns to be homophilous makes sense. People who are similar share common interests that provide the subjects for communication.

As might be expected, homophily leads to more effective communication.[12] The effectiveness, of course, depends on the degree of homophily. Total homophily produces a static state; people who are in complete agreement have nothing to talk about. Conversely, people who are highly heterophilous may lack the common experiences or vocabulary necessary for understanding and effective communication. The Hindu and the American will have difficulty discussing the nutritive value of beef, because of their different attitudes toward cows. The industrial executive may be unable to discuss company business with a local plant worker due to a lack of a common vocabulary, background or perspective. The best degree of similarity is therefore what has been labelled "optimal heterophily."[13] Optimal heterophily is slight dissimilarity. If two people are homophilous on several attributes but optimally heterophilous on the subject of discussion, they will be more likely to communicate effectively. They will have the common ground for understanding with enough difference to produce a dynamic, beneficial interaction. Figure 1-4 illustrates the different possible combinations of homophily.

Another consideration related to optimal heterophily is the relevance of the homophilous or heterophilous attributes. Homophily or optimal heterophily need only exist on those attributes that are relevant to the issue of concern. A receiver's age may be a very important characteristic for the source discussing political views, but a dissimilarity in age is unlikely to affect a discussion of the best types of fishing lures. To insure effective communication, a source should identify

---

[10] Rex H. Warland, *Personal Influence: The Degree of Similarity of Those Who Interact*, Unpublished masters thesis, Iowa State University, 1970.

[11] James Palmore, "The Chicago Snowball: A Study of the Flow and Diffusion of Family Planning Information," in Donald J. Bogue, ed., *Sociological Contributions to Family Planning Research* (Chicago: University of Chicago Community and Family Study Center, 1972).

[12] Everett M. Rogers and F. Floyd Shoemaker, *Communication of Innovations: A Cross-Cultural Approach* (New York: Free Press, 1971), p. 14.

[13] *Ibid.*, p. 15.

the relevant attributes and emphasize similarities on these dimensions. This is not a simple task, since what is relevant to one person may be irrelevant to another.

The credibility of a source is also related to optimal heterophily. The homophily relationship affects a source's credibility. A person who is heterophilous may be perceived as having more competence, whereas the person who is homophilous may be more credible on other dimensions such as composure and sociability. Under some circumstances, a heterophilous relationship between the source and receiver may be acceptable. For instance, heterophilous sources are often consulted for information because of their competence. However, optimal heterophily is probably preferable when it comes to decision–making: we are more likely to trust and be influenced by those who are homophilous on the other dimensions of credibility.

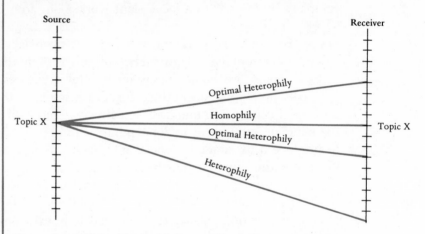

Figure 1-4 Model of homophily-heterophily between source and receiver.

Homophily and communication seem to work in a synergistic fashion: homophily leads to more effective communication, and effective communication leads to increased homophily.[14] This is reasonable, since individuals who are homophilous communicate more with each other and are better able to communicate. Their efforts to influence each other are more successful, leading to more similarities in attitudes, beliefs and values. Homophilous pairs are also more attracted to each other, increasing the success of their communication. The natural end result of this successful homophilous

---

[14] *Ibid.,* p. 211.

Figure 1-5 Homophilous people tend to be attracted to each other and are, therefore, likely to communicate more frequently and more effectively than heterophilous people. The homophilous attributes of dress and age probably indicate that these two people share similar views on a number of subjects.

communication is increased similarities in behavior, knowledge, beliefs and attitudes.[15]

It appears that if people begin with a homophilous (or optimally heterophilous) relationship, communication has a high probability of success. But what about the situations in which the initial relationship is heterophilous? Heterophilous communication cannot be avoided. In fact, many of our daily communication activities can be classified as heterophilous: teacher to student, parent to child, employer to employee. The problem of heterophilous relationships has long confronted agencies, such as the Peace Corps, that are attempting to bring about social change. How does a clearly heterophilous source convince a Peruvian peasant to adopt water boiling techniques or Pakistanis to adopt birth control methods? How do you gain acceptance of your grading proposals by a faculty committee or persuade your employer to give you a raise?

[15] Rogers and Bhowmik, *op. cit.*, p. 223.

Compensations for heterophily

There are several ways of compensating for or overcoming heterophily. One of the most effective is frequent interaction, which can increase attraction and homophily. For example, students living on the same dormitory floor can overcome initial dissimilarities through frequent conversation. However, if the initial dissimilarities are too severe, communication attempts may not only be unrewarding but may discourage future communication. The Indonesian visitor who condemns Americans for the wastefulness and excessive use of pollution-causing disposable paper products will probably be too heterophilous with the owner of a paper products company for effective communication to take place.

Another way to compensate for heterophily is for a source to develop empathy, or the ability to project himself into another person's role—in this case, the role of the receiver. If a source has more empathy than a receiver, communication will be more effective than if he has less empathy than the receiver.[16] This is especially true in a persuasive communication transaction. A receiver who has more empathy than a source is likely to see the speaker's persuasive intent and react to it in a negative way. Developing empathy is a difficult task in a heterophilous relationship, since the existence of heterophily suggests that each interactant has had little experience with the other's role. If a person can actually place himself in some of the same circumstances as the other, he may better develop empathy. This is why Peace Corps volunteers undergo extensive training in the customs and language of the country in which they are to live. To be effective communicators in such a situation, they must live like the natives.

A source may compensate for heterophily in a communication situation by paying close attention to the feedback of his receivers.[17] Of course, feedback may be necessary just to indicate to the source that heterophily does exist; people tend to assume that others are homophilous with them until it is proven otherwise. When dissimilarities do exist, these need to be recognized so that misunderstandings do not develop. Thus, feedback provides the source with the necessary information about his receivers. By attending closely to feedback, the source can better understand the receiver's

---

[16] *Ibid.*, p. 221.

[17] *Ibid.*, p. 222.

language patterns, norms, beliefs and behavior, and can develop more empathy. The social worker in the ghetto or on the Indian reservation must be especially attuned to the unique vocabulary and habits of his clientele, if he is to communicate with them in any helpful way.

Homophily, then, is an important consideration for a source. The degree of his homophily with others will affect his choice of receivers, the effectiveness of his communication and his receivers' perception of his credibility. To facilitate his communication, a source should emphasize relevant similarities with homophilous receivers, work to achieve empathy with heterophilous receivers and pay close attention to all receivers' feedback. Frequent interaction and interpersonal attraction will also contribute to the source's success.

Power as a source variable

Although power is often ignored in discussions of interpersonal relationships, it does affect many of our daily communication activities. The fact that teachers can assign passing or failing grades, that parents can give or withhold allowance money, or that employers can promote or dismiss workers, will influence the nature of the communication that takes place between each group of interactants. Power, like credibility and homophily, is a perceived phenomenon; it exists in a source to the extent that a receiver perceives it to be there. Researchers have determined that a receiver makes three decisions about the power of a source in a communication situation.[18] These decision points are known as the dimensions of power.

The dimensions of power
The first dimension of power is *perceived control*, or the receiver's decision as to whether or not the source can apply positive sanctions (rewards) or negative sanctions (punishments) if he does not comply with the source's request. For example, if a stranger in street clothes tells you and your friends not to stand on the corner talking, you will probably ignore the

---

[18] William T. McGuire, "The Nature of Attitudes and Attitude Change," in Gardner Lindsey and Elliot Aronson, eds., *The Handbook of Social Psychology*, 2nd edition, Vol. 3, (Reading: Addison-Wesley, 1969), pp. 194-196.

request unless he pulls out a police badge and accuses you of loitering. Conversely, if a receiver perceives a source to have power (even if he does not), the receiver is likely to comply with the source's request. Thus, if you and your friends thought the stranger to be a plain clothes detective, you would probably comply with his request to "move along" without challenging him.

The second dimension of power is *perceived concern*, or the receiver's decision as to whether or not the source really cares if the receiver complies with the request. For instance, suppose a mother tells her untidy eight-year-old son to clean up his room "for me" or "like a good boy." If the son knows from past experience that his mother does not really care whether or not he performs this task, and that she will not say or do anything if he does not comply, then there is little likelihood that the boy will clean his room.

The third dimension of source power is *perceived scrutiny*. The receiver must decide if the source has the ability to scrutinize whether or not he has complied with the source's request. Suppose, for instance, an English professor assigns a novel, stating that the students will not be tested on the content of the book but that they will discuss it at the next class session. A student who intends to be at that class meeting is likely to comply, because to him the source has the ability to detect whether or not he actually read the work in question. However, if the student decides to cut the next class meeting, he may not read the novel, since there is no other way for the professor to know whether he did, in fact, complete the assignment.

The components and types of power
A source brings with him to a communication situation certain personal resources which may be perceived as power elements by the receiver. Among these resources of power are such personal qualities as wealth, prestige, skill, information and physical strength. Thus, if the mayor of a city asked a resident to head an anti-litter campaign, the citizen will probably accept the mayor's offer because he perceives the official to have power by virtue of his prestige and position. A complete list of the resources of power available to a source in a communication situation cannot be constructed, since any particular quality may be perceived (or not

perceived) as a power element by the receiver. Thus, a person who earns $10,000 a year may be so "impressed" by a president of a corporation who earns $100,000 a year that he may follow the president's advice to invest his savings in a particular stock. However, the illusive billionaire Howard Hughes is not likely to be very impressed by the same man and, therefore, will not follow the advice. The resources of power available to a source are relative to the receiver's perception in a particular communication situation.

In any communication interaction, a receiver has certain unique physical, psychological and social needs. The source's potential for meeting a receiver's needs provides the motive bases for power in a communication situation. Thus, the citizen who agrees to head an anti-litter campaign may be satisfying his need to be a community leader. The worker who agrees to invest his savings may be satisfying his need to be associated with "higher-ups" or to make a "fast buck." Clearly, the resources of power are contingent upon the motives bases of power in a particular receiver or group of receivers. Indeed, these two components (the resources and the motive bases of power) may combine to create five distinct types of power in a communication situation.[19]

Reward power   The ability of a source to provide positive sanctions if the receiver complies with the source's request is called reward power.[20] The actual sanctions administered by the source may take the form of concrete rewards, such as money and other physical objects, or they may be intangible rewards, such as praise and affection. An employer who gives his salesmen bonuses based on their performance is exercising reward power. Of course, the actual reward offered must be perceived by the receiver as worthwhile or it will have little impact on him. To one salesman, a week's vacation in the Bahamas may not be worth the extra effort needed to secure the bonus. To another salesman, simply being "Number One" may be a sufficient reward for working the extra hours necessary to top the other members of the sales force. Thus, to a great extent, the exercise of reward power is dependent on the source's ability to accurately perceive the needs of the receiver.

---

[19] John R. P. French, Jr. and Betram Raven, "The Bases of Social Power," in D. Cartwright and A. Zander, eds., *Group Dynamics* (New York: Harper and Row, 1968), pp. 259-268.

[20] *Ibid.*, p. 263.

In addition to perceiving the reward as worthwhile, the receiver must see the potential reward as being within the source's power to bestow. For example, a person seeking public office who offers another person a position in his administration in return for campaign work must be perceived by the receiver as having a chance to fulfill the promise. If the receiver thinks there is no possibility that the candidate will win (and if winning is the only base of power the source might have), it is unlikely that he will comply with the candidate's request to work in his campaign. In other words, an empty promise is not likely to influence a receiver if he perceives it as such.

As one would expect, the ability of the source to induce compliance increases as the magnitude of the reward increases. The sales manager who offers the position of assistant manager as a reward to the best salesman is likely to have more power than one who offers a week's salary as a reward. (This is dependent on each salesman's perception of the reward as worthwhile and within the sales manager's power to bestow.) The successful use of reward power may further increase the source's power, since the receiver is likely to attach more significance to promises of future rewards. Therefore, if the sales manager does, in fact, promote his best salesman to the position of assistant manager, other salesmen are likely to perceive future promises of rewards as highly probable. In other words, the manager's credibility along the character dimension will be enhanced, making him more effective. Conversely, if the sales manager fails to live up to his promise, his credibility will probably be diminished, and his ability to exercise reward power over his sales force is likely to be decreased.

Coercive power Coercive power refers to the ability of a source to administer negative sanctions (punishment) if the receiver does not comply with the source's request.[21] For example, American prisoners of war in North Vietnam were forced to make "confessions" and "repudiations" through the threat of torture and even death. From this perspective, coercive power may be seen as a negative form of reward power. However, coercive power may also involve the threat to withhold reward, as in the case of a manager who threatens

---

[21] *Ibid.*

to withhold the raise of a salesman who does not maintain
a minimal level of performance.

The fact that the source in many communication situations
may exert either reward or coercive power leads to an
inevitable question: Which is more effective? Studies have
shown that positive and negative sanctions are equally
effective in inducing overt compliance to the source's request.[22]
It is important to note, however, that the use of either kind
of power may have profound impact on other variables in
the communication interaction. For example, the use of reward
power is likely to increase the attraction of a receiver to a
source, whereas the use of coercive power tends to decrease
this attraction. Thus the manager who administers only
negative sanctions to the members of his staff will probably
be disliked and may very well find it difficult to retain his
employees. Since the use of negative sanctions requires more
surveillance or scrutiny by an administrator, the manager
who employs coercive power may find that he must devote most
of his time to "catching" his workers. Needless to say, this
can have a detrimental effect on morale, and may affect
the manager's ability to perform other functions that support
his role relationship with subordinates.

Referent power   If the source in a communication situation
makes an appeal to a receiver to "do this for me," the source
is exercising referent power. In such an instance, the source is
appealing to the receiver's wish to please him or to be like
him. At the basis of referent power is the feeling of oneness
or identification that the receiver perceives in his relationship
to the source.[23] For referent power to exist, the receiver
must want to be like the source. Most people have, at one
time or another, imitated the behavior or "parroted" the
beliefs or attitudes of someone whom they found attractive.
Most parents can attest to the existence of referent power.
For example, when the leader of a group of teenagers
adopts a new style of clothing, the other members of the
group are likely to conform.

Referent power differs from reward power and coercive
power in the motive for compliance. For example, a musician
in an orchestra may "play his heart out" to please his conductor

---

[22] McGuire, *op. cit.*, p. 194.

[23] French and Raven, *op. cit.*, p. 266.

and get a raise in pay. The conductor in such a situation is exercising reward power over the musician. Then too, the musician may play well after the conductor has noted that his technique is rusty and needs improvement if he is to keep his job in the orchestra. In this situation, the conductor is exercising coercive power. However, if the musician plays his best because he wants the orchestra leader to like him, then the conductor is exercising referent power.

The use of referent power in a highly structured organization such as a corporation may cause long-term problems. The manager who is well-liked by his subordinates may be able to get them to perform well by asking them "to do this for me." However, the manager's success may result in his promotion to a different position. In such a case, the new administrator may find his subordinates difficult to manage, since he does not have referent power over them.

Expert power   The concept of expert power is closely related to the competence dimension of source credibility discussed earlier in this chapter. A person in a communication situation may be accorded power because the receiver perceives him as having superior knowledge or expertise on a particular subject. For example, a patient is likely to accept a doctor's diagnosis and follow his instructions, even though the patient does not understand the medical reasoning behind them. Thus, expert power may bring about compliance without affecting a receiver's understanding, attitudes or beliefs.

A receiver tends to perceive a source's expertise in relation to his own knowledge of the subject being discussed.[24] For example, a person who perceives himself as the best player in his golf club is more likely to accept advice from Arnold Palmer than from his caddy—even though both say exactly the same thing, "Keep your head down!" The power accorded an expert source varies from topic to topic. Although millions of parents may consider Dr. Benjamin Spock an expert on baby care, he is not considered an expert on politics and is therefore likely to have little influence on people's choice of a Presidential candidate. In fact, some research has shown that a source's ability to exert expert power may be diminished by a source's attempt to influence receivers on a topic outside his area of expertise. Some people may reject

---

[24] *Ibid.*, p. 267.

Spock's recommendations on child-rearing because of his political affiliations.

Like referent power, expert power is invested in an individual. This may cause problems within an organization that relies heavily on an expert's judgment. For example, the staff of the engineering department of an airplane manufacturer may rely on the expertise of a single person to solve all its technical problems. The rest of the staff accepts his orders without questioning them, in deference to his expert power. If he should leave, they would be unable to carry on without him, since they were not in the habit of asking about the expert's reasons for giving certain orders.

Legitimate power Legitimate power stems from the internalized values of the receiver that affirm that the source has a "right" to influence him.[25] When an irate parent tells his recalcitrant child to come inside "because I said so," he is exercising legitimate power. The child is likely to comply because values that have been reinforced for many years tell him that his mother or father has the right to command him to do this. Similarly, if a person is a practicing Roman Catholic or a Jew, he will feel "obliged" to comply with the advice of his priest or rabbi on religious matters, because this person has legitimate power over him.

Persons holding certain positions within highly structured organizations or social institutions may be accorded the right to prescribe other people's behavior. Thus, a judge has the right to place a prisoner on probation; a teacher has the right to assign homework; and a supervisor has the right to request an employee to perform certain tasks. In such instances, the receiver—the prisoner, student, or worker—is obliged to comply with the source not by virtue of the source's personality but by virtue of the office he holds.

To some extent, the use of legitimate power may direct the nature and flow of communication between people. Thus, in the military, each person may prescribe certain behavior for his subordinates, but no subordinate may prescribe the behavior of a superior. Likewise, the statement "The Cabots speak only to the Lowells and the Lowells speak only to God" defines the communication lines within a particular social structure—that of upper class Bostonians.

---

[25] *Ibid.*, p. 265.

The range of legitimate power that a source can exert over a receiver varies from situation to situation. When legitimate power is based on mutually shared cultural values, the source's influence is usually broad.[26] Thus, for many years, a husband was able to prescribe his wife's behavior in practically every area of her life. He could tell her whom to talk to, where she could and could not go, what she should wear. This was possible because both shared the cultural belief that the wife was subordinate to the husband. Parents have broad legitimate power over their children, since children are still perceived as extensions of their parents. In most instances, however, legitimate power is rather narrowly defined by the context of the communication situation. A supervisor has the right to tell his employees what work tasks to perform, but he does not have the right to tell them which candidates to vote for in an election. In fact, if a source attempts to exert influence in an area in which he does not have legitimate power, he may decrease his ability to influence in all areas, including those in which he has the right to influence.

Legitimate power may involve the exercise of other types of power. Thus, a judge may be perceived as having legitimate power to exercise coercive power over a prisoner. An employer may be perceived as having the right to exercise reward power over his employers. Of course, a receiver may also perceive a source's power to be illegitimate. Thus, a student in a required course may resent a professor's attempt to use referent power since the student feels he was "forced" to take the course. However, a student may perceive the professor's attempt to use referent power in an elective course as acceptable.

---

[26] *Ibid.*

1. An important variable in any communication situation is source credibility; a source with a high credibility is more effective than one with low credibility.

2. There are five decisions which a receiver makes about a source; these are known as the dimensions of credibility. These decision-points are: competence, or the source's knowledge of the subject; character, or the apparent trustworthiness of the source; composure, especially in regard to smoothness of delivery; sociability, or the degree to which the source seems likeable and friendly; extroversion, or an outgoing personality. Each of these dimensions acts independently to influence the source's effectiveness as a communicator.

3. Source credibility, which exists only as it is attributed by receivers, may change over time. At the beginning of the communication transaction, the receiver assesses the source's initial credibility. During the transaction, a receiver may modify his initial impression; this is known as transactional credibility. After the transaction is completed, the receiver is left with a final perception of the source's credibility called terminal credibility.

4. Another variable in the communication situation is homophily, or the degree of similarity betwen the source and the receiver. Heterophily refers to the degree of dissimilarity between the interactants. The best degree of similarity for effective communication is optimal heterophily, or slight dissimilarity; optimal heterophily also enhances a source's credibility. Frequent communication, the development of empathy, and close attention to feedback will all help to overcome problems of heterophily.

5. A third important source variable is power. The dimensions of power in a communication situation include: perceived control, or the receiver's decision as to whether or not the source can apply sanctions; perceived concern, or the receiver's decision as to whether the source really

cares if the receiver complies with the request; and perceived scrutiny, or the receiver's decision whether the source has the ability to determine if the request has been complied with.

6. There are five types of power which may operate in a communication situation. Reward power is the ability of the source to apply positive sanctions. Coercive power is the ability to apply negative sanctions. Referent power is the ability to appeal to a receiver's wish to please or be like the source. Expert power is accorded to the source when the receiver perceives him to have superior knowledge or expertise. Legitimate power stems from the internalized values of the receiver that affirm the source's right to exert influence in the communication situation.

1. Think of someone whom you consider to be a highly credible source. Make a list of all the words that you would use to describe this person. Do you seem to judge this person on the bases of the dimensions of credibility suggested in this chapter? Repeat this exercise for someone whom you do not consider to be highly credible.

2. Write an anecdotal description of a situation in which each dimension of credibility would be more important than all the others.

3. Identify your three closest friends and describe the ways in which they are homophilous or heterophilous.

4. How might a professor use the concepts of homophily or heterophily to structure a class situation?

5. Write an anecdotal description of an example of each type of power discussed in this chapter.

6. Imagine that you are planning a political campaign for a candidate running for local office. How would you make use of the principles of credibility, homophily–heterophily, and power to get your candidate elected?

Kenneth Anderson and Theodore Clevenger, Jr., "A Summary of Experimental Research in Ethos," *Speech Monographs, 30* (1963), pp. 59-78. Although it is somewhat old, this article is still one of the best summaries of research findings on the subject of source credibility.

John R. P. French and Bertram Raven, "The Bases of Social Power," in D. Cartwright and A. Zander, eds., *Group Dynamics* (New York: Harper and Row, 1968), pp. 259-268. This is an excellent, though highly technical, discussion of the five types of power which may operate in a communication situation.

James C. McCroskey, "Ethos: A Dominant Factor in Persuasive Communication," in *An Introduction to Rhetorical Communication*, 2nd Edition (Englewood Cliffs, N.J.: Prentice-Hall, 1972), pp. 63-81. This chapter presents an excellent discussion of the traditional concept of ethos and the contemporary concept of source credibility and their effects on communication.

James C. McCroskey, "Scales for the Measurement of Ethos, *Speech Monographs, 33* (1966), pp. 65-72. In this article, one of the leading researchers attempts to establish guidelines for the measurement of the different dimensions of source credibility.

Everett M. Rogers and Dilip K. Bhowmik, "Homophily-Heterophily: Rational Concepts for Communication Research," in Larry Barker and Robert Kibler, eds., *Speech Communication Behavior* (Englewood Cliffs, N.J.: Prentice-Hall, 1971), pp. 206-225. The authors present a detailed discussion of the principles of homophily and heterophily and their application to communication theory and future research. This is difficult but worthwhile reading.

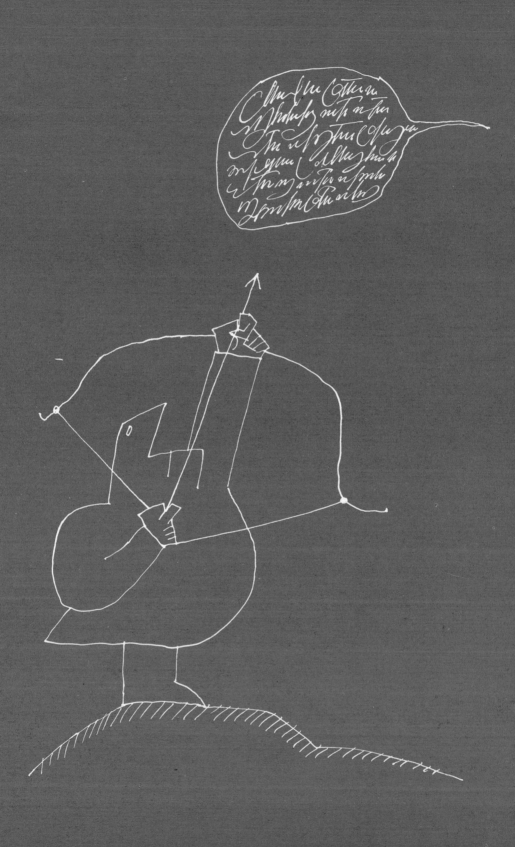

Receiver variables

The receiver is often thought of as the passive person in the communication process. To some extent, communication research tends to reinforce this notion, with its focus on the speaker and the best ways to construct a message. However, theory and common sense tell us that the receiver is just as important as the source in a communication situation. There would be no transfer of meaning if there was no one to receive the message. Although no thoughtful person is willing to contest the idea that receiving or decoding a message is a different process than constructing or transmitting it, most people overlook the fact that both activities are precisely that—active!

Nowhere is the dynamic nature of communication more evident than in a face-to-face situation. During the course of a conversation, the two participants frequently exchange communication roles. One may initiate the conversation, acting as the original source or sender of the message, but when he responds to his friend's comments, he becomes the receiver. A similar exchange occurs in small group situations, when several people participate in a conversation, both sending messages and responding to them simultaneously or in rapid succession.

In this chapter the receiver comes under focus as an important variable in the communication process. As responder to the source and his message, the receiver exerts definite control over the communication situation. The receiver makes the initial decision of whether or not he will interact with a source. When the receiver does enter a communication situation, his presence is influential. The receiver can decide how much of his attention he will give to the source and his message. In an unconscious way, the receiver may also control what he "hears" in a message. Even the verbal response of the receiver may affect the nature of the transaction. Most people have experienced moments when they have "snapped" at another person's remarks and the person responded by changing the topic of conversation.

While highlighting the receiver's ability to control the transaction, this example also points up the accommodation that takes place between the source and receiver in a communication interaction. Just as the receiver adjusts to the source, the source must also adjust his message to the receiver. Each receiver is unique in terms of his age, sex, personality, intelligence, skills and experiences—characteristics that he brings to the communication situation which will have an impact upon the source and his message. The accommodation of the source to these receiver characteristics helps to develop a feeling of trust and mutual sharing between the interactants which, in turn, may help make the communication more effective.

Demographic analysis of an audience

When a communicator is aware of the characteristics of his audience, and understands how these characteristics may affect its reception of a message, he is better able to structure that message and alter his delivery to the particular needs of the audience members. The audience may consist of just one or a few receivers in face-to-face and small group situations, or the audience can number in the thousands or even millions in a mass communication experience. Because of the vast number of receivers who respond in a mass communication or large group situation, the audience in such instances can best be analyzed according to demographic characteristics. These are vital statistics such as age, sex, race, and social and economic background.

Age

The familiar expression, "You can't teach an old dog new tricks," sums up, to some extent, our knowledge of the impact of age on the persuasibility of the receiver. Indeed, communication research on the subject is almost nonexistent. Two early studies do seem to confirm the idea that as age increases a person's susceptibility to persuasion decreases.[1] Psychological research on the relationship between age and suggestibility to hypnosis provides some tangential support for this hypothesis.[2]

One can only speculate as to the reasons for this seemingly inverse relationship between age and persuasibility. From casual observation, it does seem evident that, in general, young

[1] Clare Marple, "The Comparative Susceptibility of Three Age Levels to the Suggestion of Group versus Expert Opinion," *Journal of Social Psychology*, 4 (1933), pp. 176-186 and I. L. Janis and D. Rife, "Persuasibility and Emotional Disorder," in Carl I. Howland and Irving L. Janis, eds., *Personality and Persuasibility*, (New Haven: Yale University Press, 1959), pp. 121-137.

[2] William J. McGuire, "The Nature of Attitudes and Attitude Change," in Gardiner Lindsey and Elliot Aronson, eds., *The Handbook of Social Psychology*, 2nd edition, Vol 3 (Reading: Addison-Westley, 1969), pp. 248-249.

people are more idealistic, optimistic and liberal in their views than older people. Older adults tend to be more pragmatic and cautious, perhaps as a result of having experienced more discouragements and rejections in life. Certainly, the middle-aged and elderly have a greater stake in our society, since they earn more money and own more property and possessions than young people. The fact that they have more to lose may explain their reluctance to accept change.

Regardless of the exact relationship between age and persuasibility and the reasons for this relationship, it is clear that the age of an audience is a demographic characteristic which the source should assess. Obviously, different age groups will show an interest in different subject matter. A group of high school students may be vitally interested in a panel discussion on the merits of a liberal arts versus a business education, but the subject is likely to have little appeal to forty-five-year old executives. Politicians have often considered the age of their audience when deciding which campaign issue to talk about. A smart politician is likely to campaign for better housing and medical care for the elderly when addressing a group of senior citizens, whereas he may switch his topic to federal assistance for education when speaking on a college campus.

Sex

Sex is a variable that involves both biological and social factors. Some scientists argue that women are psychologically different from men because of differences in their biological characteristics —especially their ability to bear children. Regardless of the validity of this theory, people often attribute certain qualities to women based on sexual stereotypes: softness or femininity, maternal instincts, emotionality and greater persuasibility. Many communication researchers have tested the hypothesis that women are easier to persuade than men. In one study, a group of college students at the University of Washington listened to a short persuasive speech opposing further expansion of federal government power in health and education. They were then tested for the degree of attitude change caused by the speeches. The results showed that the female students were more persuaded by the speech than male students. In addition, the women transferred the effects of the persuasive appeal to general and nonrelevant items more than men did. Specifically, the female subjects showed more attitude change on statements such as "Government power has already been expanded too far," and "Government price control would result in unfair discrimination."[3]

A considerable number of other experiments support the claim that women are generally more persuasible than men. However, when other variables are introduced, the results are not as clearcut. One study with college students focused on the relationship between frustration, sex and persuasibility. The subjects in the "frustrated" group were told that they were inferior students; those in the "ego-satisfied" group were told that they were superior students. The subjects were then tested to determine the degree of attitude change toward the topics of the persuasive messages. The results show that frustrated females change attitudes more than frustrated males. However, in the "ego-satisfied" group, no significant differences appeared between male and female subjects.[4] In another experiment, there was no difference in persuasibility between male and female receivers when the speaker was a woman.[5]

Analysis of the sex variable is particularly complex because of the role of social conditioning in the formation of male and female attitudes. From an early age, girls are taught that agreeableness and yielding are desirable behaviors for women in our society, whereas males are reinforced for aggressive behavior. Research has shown that there is no difference in persuasibility between preadolescent boys and girls. Other research has shown that aggressive people tend to be more resistent to persuasion than submissive people. These findings tangentially support the notion that differences in persuasibility may be caused by social factors. If this line of reasoning is correct, we might expect the women's liberation movement and new child-rearing patterns to have a tremendous impact on the difference in persuasibility between men and women.

Still another explanation for greater persuasibility among women is that they may be more verbal than men. Girls usually learn to talk and read earlier than boys. Some experts contend that women are better message receivers than men; they attend to and comprehend the spoken and written word more

---

[3] Thomas M. Scheidel, "Sex and Persuasibility," *Speech Monographs, 30* (1963), pp. 353-358.

[4] Carl W. Carmichael, "Frustration, Sex and Persuasibility," *Western Speech, 34,* No. 4 (1970), pp. 300-307.

[5] Franklin H. Knower, "Experimental Studies of Change in Attitudes: 1. A Study of the Effect of Oral Argument on Changes of Attitude," *Journal of Social Psychology, 6* (1935), pp. 315-344.

carefully.[6] This may also explain the greater attitude change observed in women after listening to a persuasive appeal.

Social and economic background

Studies in the field of communication have indicated that the social and economic background of the audience will have a significant impact upon their responses to a speaker and his message.[7] A poor person and a wealthy person are likely to be so heterophilous on such a wide range of attributes that effective communication may be hampered. Each interactant in such a situation comes from a different culture, each has had different experiences, each holds different attitudes, values and goals. In short, the lack of a common frame of reference may make communication between the two extremely difficult.

The communication problems which arise when people of different social and economic backgrounds interact become evident upon a consideration of a hypothetical, though not unrealistic, communication situation. Suppose a well-meaning (and well-dressed) social worker comes to a ghetto neighborhood once a week to talk to teenagers about career guidance. The social worker is white, well-educated, and from an upper middle-class neighborhood. The teenagers are Puerto Rican, high school dropouts or indifferent students, and live in a rundown neighborhood. Before the social worker even opens his mouth, he is at a disadvantage. First, he is probably unfamiliar with the verbal and nonverbal dialect and customs of the group; to them, he is an outsider. Secondly, his values are not the same as theirs. He was raised in a culture that favored education and rewarded good marks in school. The teenagers grew up in a culture which reinforced the importance of living for the moment—after all, who knows what tomorrow may bring, especially to the poor. The teenagers are also likely to be hostile and mistrusting of the social worker, for to them it may seem as if everything was handed to him.

Clearly, the differences in the social and economic backgrounds of the social worker and the teenagers will cause communication problems. Conversely, if the communicator and receivers are

---

[6] McQuire, *op. cit.*, p. 251.

[7] For an especially good discussion of this problem see Jack Daniels, "The Poor: Aliens in an Affluent Society: Cross-Cultural Communications," *Today's Speech*, *18*, No. 1 (1970), pp. 15-21.

homophilous in their social and economic backgrounds, if they share common life experiences, more communication is likely to occur and the communication attempts will probably be more successful. This is one reason that many programs in poor neighborhoods have found greater success using community members as leaders.

Racial and ethnic factors

It would seem logical that communication between interactants of the same race or ethnic group would be more effective than communication between people of different races or ethnic groups. Prejudice and hostility between the different groups may account for some of the communication problems. In addition, members of different races and ethnic groups are often from different social and economic background. Cultural differences are an inherent part of racial and ethnic differences.

Once again the principles of homophily and heterophily come into play. A person is more attracted to someone who is like himself than to someone who is different. People perceive blacks to be different from whites, Puerto Ricans to be different from Wasps, Chicanos to be different from Italians. The fact that members of different racial and ethnic groups are less likely to interact facilitates misunderstanding and the maintenance of stereotypes. A Jewish teacher in a public school in New York City was once observed scolding a young Puerto Rican boy. "Look at me when I talk to you," the angry woman shouted. The boy lowered his head even more; his eyes stared at the ground. "Did you hear me?" said the teacher. "Look at me!" The boy shook his head to acknowledge that he had indeed heard the teacher's words, but his head remained down. "You're absolutely impossible," the teacher said in exasperation. Unfortunately, the teacher did not realize that in his culture it would have been a sign of disrespect for the boy to look at her while she was scolding him. He was already in trouble and was instinctively trying to avoid more. His exasperation was probably as great as the teacher's when he was dragged off to the principal's office.

Intelligence

Many of the studies which have attempted to determine the relationship between intelligence and persuasibility have

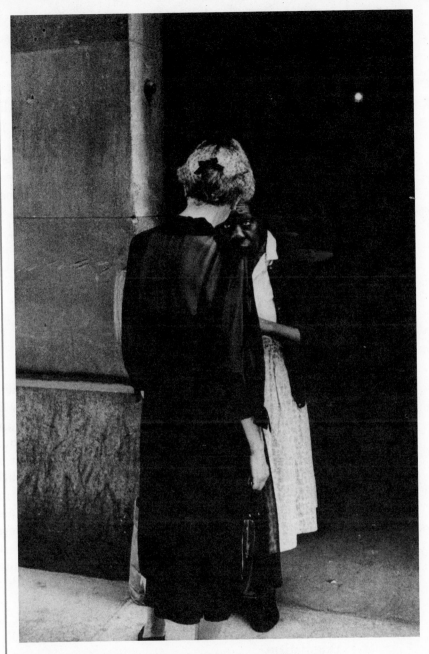

Figure 2-1 *Differences in race and social and economic background often cause communication problems between people.*

been beset by measurement problems. In one early study, unsupported propaganda statements effected less attitude change in people with high intelligence than people with low intelligence.[8] In another study conducted among army recruits, it was found that educated subjects were more persuasible than subjects with little education when the speech was a logical one.[9] However, one must question the validity of using formal education as a measurement of intelligence. In general, there seems to be no evidence to support the hypothesis that intelligence and persuasibility are related in either a positive or negative way.

Members of a well-educated audience may possess many advantages as receivers: they are usually knowledgeable on a wide range of topics, their vocabulary is good, and their message comprehension is also likely to be good. Since well-educated people tend to be knowledgeable, they also tend to be critical of unsupported messages. However one cannot assume that there is any relationship between a person's critical ability and his persuasibility.

Personality analysis of a receiver

Demographic analysis of an audience may be useful to a source in some situations, but it is also beneficial to view the receiver as an individual who possesses an unique personality that will affect his response to a message. Being outgoing, shy, hostile or anxious are characteristics of one's personality that remain fairly stable from situation to situation. Therefore, it seemed logical to a number of communication theorists that one should be able to predict a person's response to a message based on a particular personality trait. Indeed, a considerable amount of time and effort has been devoted to determining the relationships between certain personality traits and persuasibility. The findings may be of use to a source since they provide some insights into the nature of the decoding process.

Dogmatism
Dogmatism has been defined as a relatively closed system of

[8] H. J. Wegrocki, "The Effect of Prestige Suggestibility on Emotional Attitude," *Journal of Social Psychology*, 5 (1934), pp. 384-394.

[9] C. I. Hovland, A. A. Lumsdaine, and F. D. Sheffield, "The Effects of Presenting 'One-Side' versus 'Both Sides' in Changing Opinions on a Controversial Subject," in *Experiments in Mass Communication*, Volume 3 of *Social Psychology in World War II* (Princeton, N.J.: Princeton University Press, 1949), pp. 201-227.

beliefs or disbeliefs about reality.[10] A dogmatic person is authoritative, self-opinionated and closed-minded. He is unbending in his beliefs and slow to accept new ideas or concepts. Because he believes he is always right, the dogmatic individual has low tolerance for others he perceives as wrong—that is, those who do not agree with him. The television character, Archie Bunker, is a perfect example of a dogmatic person. Archie is steadfast in his beliefs; he "knows" he is right and therefore anyone who has a diverse opinion is wrong. For instance, if Archie's son-in-law, Michael, tries to persuade Archie to believe that President Nixon was wrong to impound funds appropriated by Congress for day care centers, Archie is likely to argue that this cutback must have been necessary because the President is always right. Of course, dogmatism is not a personality trait limited to political conservatives. Michael himself is equally as dogmatic as Archie and would probably automatically disapprove of any conservative political action.

Dogmatic people are definitely not free thinkers; they are likely to place great emphasis on authority figures. In fact, research indicates that dogmatic people may be more persuasible than open-minded people when they consider the source of the message to be authoritative.[11] Thus, Archie probably changed his attitudes about those "Commies" after President Nixon's trips to Russia and China. Dogmatic people also tend to have difficulty discriminating between the content of a message and its source.[12] A highly dogmatic receiver who is extremely patriotic is likely to perceive a patriotic speech by a person he knows to be an anti-war leader as anti-American because of his difficulty in separating the message from the source.

Self-esteem

Every individual has a personal concept of self, formed partially from his own perceptions, and partially from the feedback he receives from others in social situations. At the basis of a person's concept of self-esteem is the evaluation he makes of himself

---

[10] Milton Rokeach, "The Nature and Meaning of Dogmatism," *Psychological Review*, 61, No. 3 (1954), p. 195.

[11] Martin Hunt and Gerald Miller, *Open- and Closed-Mindedness, Belief-Discrepant Communication Behavior, and Tolerance for Dissonance*, Paper presented at Speech Association of America Convention, New York, December 1965.

[12] Ralph Vacchiano, Paul Strauss, and Leonard Hockman, "The Open and Closed Mind: A Review of Dogmatism," *Psychological Bulletin*, 71, No. 4 (1969), p. 261.

in relation to other people. If a person has low self-esteem, he generally considers himself an inferior person. An individual with high self-esteem has confidence in himself, because he feels he is at least equal or superior to other people.

Self-esteem is a personality variable that will greatly affect the way a person receives and reacts to a message. Individuals with low self-esteem are generally easier to persuade than those with high self-esteem.[13] Low self-esteem persons are conformists by nature; they have little confidence in their own opinions and so are easily persuaded by someone else's ideas. Individuals with high self-esteem have greater confidence in their opinions and find it easier to challenge the ideas of others. This makes them less susceptible to persuasion.

Relationships between self-esteem and persuasibility may also be discussed in terms of defensive behavior. One experimenter found that persons high in self-esteem use avoidance mechanisms which lead them to reject threatening persuasive appeals.[14] In the study, a group of Yale students with high self-esteem rejected a persuasive communication which presented very negative statements about army life, because the topic was threatening to their concept of self and their life style. Students with high self-esteem were influenced more by an optimistic message which enhanced their self-image by presenting favorable attitudes about army life. On the other hand, subjects with low self-esteem used defense mechanisms which led them to reject the optimistic appeal and accept the threatening one. Based on these findings, it would seem likely that a student with low self-esteem would reject a professor's optimistic statement that the student will be able to pass the next examination if he studies. Conversely a student with high self-esteem is likely to reject the same professor's pessimistic statement that the student will probably fail the examination.

In several experiments, the self-esteem of subjects has been manipulated to determine the effects which changes in this variable have on a person's resistance to persuasion. Studies have shown that increasing a person's self-esteem before he listens to a persuasive appeal makes him less persuasible.[15] This seems

---

[13] Irving L. Janis and Peter B. Field, "A Behavioral Assessment of Persuasibility," in Hovland and Janis, *op. cit.*, pp. 29-54.

[14] Howard Leventhal and Sidney I. Perloe, "A Relationship Between Self-Esteem and Persuasibility," *Journal of Abnormal and Social Psychology*, 64, No. 5 (1962), pp. 385-388.

[15] For a complete discussion see Gerald R. Miller and Michael Burgoon, *New Techniques of Persuasion* (New York: Harper and Row, 1973), pp. 21-23.

to be true even if the success experience prior to the persuasive appeal had nothing to do with the content of the message. These findings seem logical and consistent with others, since providing a person with a success experience is likely to increase his confidence, thereby making him less vulnerable to the persuasive attempts of others. However, these results seem applicable only when the persuasive message is a simple one. When the message is complex, it is difficult to make predictions about the persuasibility of receivers. There is no discernable pattern that distinguishes receivers with high self-esteem from those with low self-esteem.

Aggressiveness and hostility

Closely related to a person's self-esteem is the personality trait called aggressiveness. An aggressive person tends to be outgoing, self-assertive, forceful in his interactions with others and generally very confident in his own abilities. Logically, aggressive people also tend to have high self-esteem. This led some communication theorists to speculate that aggressive people are probably less persuasible than unaggressive people. Several experiments have confirmed this hypothesis.[16]

When an aggressive person is frustrated, he is likely to become hostile. A hostile receiver is one who is antagonistic and unfriendly toward the source. The relation between aggression, frustration and hostility lead some communication researchers to suggest that raising a receiver's level of hostility by abusive treatment prior to a persuasive appeal will make the receiver less persuasible. The results of several experiments demonstrate that the relationship between the receiver's hostility level and his persuasibility is not quite that simple. A receiver who has been annoyed prior to hearing a persuasive appeal is more receptive to appeals that call for harsh actions and less receptive to appeals that call for neutral or good actions. In other words, the content of the message seems to affect the persuasibility of a hostile receiver. Thus, a student protestor who has just been jostled by police in a campus demonstration is likely to be more persuaded by an appeal to forcibly occupy the administration office than by one which suggests that he and the other demonstrators go home.

---

[16] See R. P. Abelson and G. S. Lesser, "The Developmental Theory of Persuasibility," and I. L. Janis and D. Rife, "Persuasibility and Emotional Disorder" in Hovland and Janis, *op. cit.*, pp. 121-166.

Anxiety

Anxiety is a state of worriedness, tension and apprehension about the unknown. Early studies which focused on the question of whether or not anxiety affected the receiver's persuasibility resulted in confusing and contradictory findings. One study showed receivers with high anxiety to be more persuasible than receivers with low anxiety.[17] Another study found the opposite to be true.[18] As in the case of hostility, anxiety and persuasibility seem related to the content of the persuasive appeal.[19]

When receivers with chronically high anxiety are exposed to an anxiety producing message, they tend to become less persuasible.[20] This behavior is probably defensive. The highly anxious person seems to have a threshold of anxiety beyond which he blocks out messages he is unable to cope with. Thus, a smoker who is very anxious about his health is likely to reject a strong fear appeal that attempts to persuade him to stop smoking. On the other hand, when receivers with low anxiety are exposed to anxiety producing messages, they tend to become more persuasible. In such cases, the message stimulates the receiver, causing him to pay more attention to its content and thereby enhancing the possibility of attitude change. If a receiver with low anxiety hears the same strong fear appeal to stop smoking, he will probably be persuaded by it.

Prior attitudes

Every receiver brings to the communication situation a set of prior attitudes, or preconceived notions, that are the result of past learning experiences. Suppose a white Southerner was raised on the theory that blacks are intellectually inferior to whites. If he hears a speech given by Julian Bond, a black Congressman from Georgia, his prior attitudes about blacks will probably interfere with accurate message perception. No matter how intelligently Representative Bond speaks, the listener may still see the speech as further evidence of black inferiority because of his prior attitudes.

Research in the fields of psychology and communication

---

[17] J. Nunnally and H. Bobren, "Variables Influencing the Willingness to Receive Communications on Mental Health," *Journal of Personality*, 27 (1959), pp. 38-46.

[18] Irving L. Janis and S. Feshbach, "Effects of Fear-Arousing Communications," *Journal of Abnormal and Social Psychology*, 1 (1965), pp. 17-27.

[19] Miller and Burgoon, *op. cit.*, pp. 24-27.

[20] Miller and Burgoon, *op. cit.*, pp. 23-24.

clearly demonstrates that people who have strong attitudes and beliefs on a particular topic behave in ways that reinforce their opinions.[21] They may do this by seeking out messages that confirm their beliefs and avoiding messages that challenge their opinions; they may misperceive messages which are discrepant, or different from their own views; or they may disparage the source of the message or the message itself. In other words, people with strong prior attitudes on a topic are difficult to persuade, and the more extreme their attitudes, the less persuasible they become.

The extent to which a receiver is involved in or committed to his prior opinions will influence his persuasibility. In one study, a group of boys and girls were exposed to two messages.[22] One message argued for stricter school rules for boys, the other argued for more school control over the type of clothing girls could wear. The boys in the experiment disparaged the relevant message (stricter school rules for boys) and the speaker more than the girls did; the girls disparaged the message they were involved in more than the boys did. Similarly, people who have made a public commitment to a position are more difficult to persuade than those who have not made such a commitment.[23] Thus the wise communicator avoids pushing his receivers into a situation in which they feel compelled to take a strong stand on the issue under debate.

Directly related to the prior attitudes of a receiver is the degree of attitude similarity between him and the source. A receiver will favor a source he sees as having similar attitudes to his own. He will view that source as more intelligent, better informed and better adjusted than one with dissimilar attitudes.[24] Simply speaking, we like people who have similar views to our own and are generally more responsive to a message from a source we perceive as similar to ourselves. This is often the case among friends, and may help to explain why people find it easier to communicate with their friends than with strangers.

---

[21] J. M. Levine and G. Murphy, "The Learning and Forgetting of Controversial Material," *Journal of Abnormal and Social Psychology, 34* (1943), pp. 507-517.

[22] A. H. Eagly and M. Manus, "Evaluation of Message and Communicator as a Function of Involvement," *Journal of Personality and Social Psychology, 3* (1966), pp. 483-485.

[23] H. B. Gerard, "Conformity and Commitment to the Group," *Journal of Abnormal and Social Psychology, 68* (1964), pp. 209-211.

[24] Don Byrne, "Interpersonal Attraction and Attitude Similarity," *Journal of Abnormal and Social Psychology, 62*, No. 3 (1961), pp. 713-715.

In order to understand the way trust influences the effectiveness of communication and thus to become aware of dysfunctions created by a lack of trust, it is first necessary to understand the dynamics of a trusting relationship. There are three variables which are operative in any such relationship: the person's concept of himself; his perception of the other person's behavior; and the resultant effect of his own demonstration of trust on the total communication process.[25]

The first variable undoubtedly affects the degree of openness and spontaneity in personal relationships. For example, if John's concept of himself is secure—that is, if he has confidence in his ability to express his ideas without feeling threatened by the ideas and attitudes of others—he is more likely to risk disclosures which may leave him potentially vulnerable to rejection or disparagement by the person with whom he is communicating. In other words, if John's identity is not based on his "reflection in the eyes of others," but instead derives from a deep trust in his own worth, he will probably be more open about what he says, whether or not he initially trusts in the candidness and acceptance of others.

However, John cannot help being affected to some degree by his perception of the other person's behavior. Though his original intention may have been to trust the other person, he will modify his disclosures if he believes that the receiver of the communication is deliberately distorting his meaning, that he is trying to use his disclosures to ridicule him, or that he is not behaving with mutual honesty and openness. On the other hand, if the receiver behaves with genuine warmth and receptiveness and responds appropriately to John's message, John's trust will be reinforced.

In the latter case, John will probably invest increasingly greater efforts into communicating his message accurately and into trying to perceive the message of the other person. The net effect of John's demonstration of trust on the communication process will be the growth of mutual confidence and respect and a lessening of defensiveness and suspicion. In such an atmosphere, misunderstandings are less likely to occur and, if they do, more effort will be given to clarifying the situation than

[25] For an excellent discussion of interpersonal trust see Jack Gibb, "Defensive Communication," *Journal of Communication*, 11 (1964), pp. 141-148 and K. Giffin, "Interpersonal Trust in Small Group Communication," *Quarterly Journal of Speech*, 53 (1967), pp. 224-234.

to proving the other person is wrong or to parrying threats to one's own ideas implied by the misunderstanding.

For example, let us say that John and Phil have established a sense of mutual trust in their discussion about a work project. If, at this point, Phil says that John's latest report contained certain errors, John is more likely to perceive Phil's comment as an attempt at an objective evaluation than as a personal attack. Therefore, instead of blindly defending his report and withdrawing himself from any further efforts to communicate with Phil, John will probably seek out an explanation of his alleged errors and then try to give an accurate and logical presentation of his own views on the matter. Continuance of open and honest communication between John and Phil is thus facilitated by the foundation of mutual trust; there is greater motivation to surmount obstacles to communication than to defensively withdraw from further mutual disclosures.

This brief examination of the favorable effects of a trusting relationship suggests certain factors that can negate or seriously impair the effectiveness of communication. One of these factors

Figure 2-2 Frequent interaction, mutual trust and empathy can overcome communication problems caused by differences in race and ethnic background.

is an inaccurate or fragile self-concept. If a person seriously doubts his own worth—if he has little trust in the value of his own ideas or his ability to present them—he may enter a communication situation with feelings of apprehension and distrust. He expects to be contradicted or threatened and thus behaves defensively before he is even given cause to. Because of his lack of self-trust, he is likely to curb his own disclosures and thus distort the intended meaning of his message. And because of his suspiciousness toward the intentions of others, he is likely to perceive meanings that were never intended. In any event, he would not be able to treat actual hostility with any degree of objectivity.

The behavior of others can reinforce these initial feelings of distrust and increase the likelihood for conflict and defensive behavior. An obvious attempt to control the listener's emotions or to bend his thinking in a certain direction; an attempt to vindicate one's own position rather than to achieve an understanding of the other person's message; an attitude of superiority regarding one's own ideas and the concommitant attitude of ridicule toward the ideas of others—all these forms of behavior can create suspicion, decrease the receptivity of the listener, and prevent the growth of mutual trust and tolerance.

The cycle of mistrust is very difficult to break once defensive behavior has become the dominant element in the communication pattern. Neither party receives enough support or acceptance for his message to warrant openness and understanding. At this point, one of the few ways to salvage the situation is by introducing the ideas of a disinterested third party. By expressing an empathy with both positions, by attempting to describe the problems that have developed rather than imposing his own ideas or attitudes, and by introducing new information that may resolve the misunderstandings, a third person can create an atmosphere of trust within which the original communication can be effectively reevaluated and discussed.

The receiver's listening ability

The essential receiver skill in any communication situation is listening. Listening is a combination of hearing, comprehension and retention. Hearing is the physical ability to receive sounds; comprehension is the ability to interpret and understand the spoken message; retention is the ability to remember what has been heard.

Only recently has listening been recognized as a skill which can be taught. Listening ability is especially critical to college students, who depend on good listening skills in lectures and discussion classes. Yet studies at the University of Minnesota have shown that students often recall better than they understand. To discover the reasons that listening comprehension among students is poor, experimenters hypothesized that if students anticipated what they were looking for in a speech, their comprehension and retention of the material would be increased. During the experiment, two groups of freshmen listened to the same speech and were then questioned on its content. In one group, however, the material was prefaced by anticipatory or "goal-setting" comments, that directed the students to look for certain items in the material. The results confirmed the hypothesis that anticipation is an important part of effective listening.[26]

Experiments such as these point up the need for specific training in listening. They are helpful in isolating variables that contribute to good listening skills. For many years, educators believed that improving reading ability automatically improved listening ability. Today we know there is no direct relation between reading and listening skills.

Because of a lack of training in listening, most people have developed bad listening habits. These include avoiding difficult listening, dismissing a subject as uninteresting and faking attention. Everyone enjoys listening to a clever, entertaining speaker discussing an interesting topic, but what happens when the speaker is humorless, the topic boring, and the vocabulary difficult? In such a situation, the receiver is likely to turn off his listening powers and begin to daydream. This is a fine escape mechanism, but not very helpful in increasing a person's knowledge or improving his listening skills. Faking attention can be a very embarrassing practice. Practically every student has been startled into reality by a direct question from a teacher whom he thought he was fooling.

Listening is a difficult task requiring attention, energy and skill. A good listener must adjust to the peculiarities of the speaker and to the physical surroundings in which the communication transaction is taking place. It is easy for a

---

[26] Charles T. Brown, "Studies in Listening Comprehension," *Speech Monographs, 126* (1959), pp. 288-294.

person to focus his attention on a speaker's good looks, or a nearby conversation, or the uncomfortable temperature of the room. But all these distractions interfere with good listening and effective communication. The rewards of improved listening skills are many and varied. A good listener is not only a better student, but will probably be a better businessman, a more informed voter, and a generally well-liked individual.

Feedback: The receiver's response

Rarely when in sound mind do we find ourselves conversing with a chair or a coffee table. The reason seems obvious: these are inanimate objects. Yet a computer is an inanimate object, and we can engage in a kind of communication with it. The fundamental difference between a chair and a computer is that the latter can respond to us. This response of a receiver to the source's message is called *feedback,* and it is a vital part of the communication process.

Human feedback differs greatly from the feedback provided by a machine. A machine such as a computer is coded to answer certain questions in a specific manner, providing such information as "correct," "incorrect," or "insufficient input." When a human receiver provides feedback for a source, he engages in a complex series of verbal and nonverbal behavior. He may smile, frown, sigh, yawn, wiggle, nod his head in agreement or disagreement, and make a variety of verbal answers. These cues let the source know whether his message is being accurately received; they are one of the most powerful means of control the receiver has.

Feedback enables the source to correct and adjust his message to fit the needs of the receiver. Suppose a college professor is demonstrating a difficult principle to his class. Midway through his lecture he notices a negative response from his students. Some yawn, others look confused, and several classmates are whispering and comparing notes. From the feedback he is receiving, the professor concludes that his message is not getting through to the students. So he changes his words and gestures in an attempt to improve his message. The receivers in this situation have exercised control over the source through feedback; consequently the feedback was useful to the source by providing information that helped him accomplish his objectives.

The significance of feedback in the communication process cannot be exaggerated. Feedback is the link between source and receiver that gives communication its transactional nature; just as the receiver provides feedback for the source, the source responds and emits cues back to the receiver. The speaker adjusts to the receiver, but the receiver also adjusts to the speaker in a simultaneous process. All the persons involved in a communication send messages and emit feedback, so that they are linked together in a dynamic transaction.

The greatest advantage of face-to-face or small group communication lies in the amount and type of feedback provided. Face-to-face communication provides a continuous flow of immediate feedback. The source can easily see and hear the responses of the receiver, which help him evaluate the effectiveness of his message. If the feedback indicates that the message is not coming through, the communicator has the opportunity of immediately changing his tactics.

In mass communication situations, however, feedback is often delayed because of the separation of source and receiver. Consider the writer, TV performer or political candidate who records a speech for radio. Each is a source with a message to get across to the public, and each is concerned about the way that message will be received. Yet these sources can neither see nor hear the reactions of their listeners; they may not even be sure that they actually have an audience. Any feedback they may receive is delayed, so they do not have the opportunity to adjust and retransmit their message immediately to the audience.

When feedback is delayed, the receiver's ability to respond to a message, and to create an impact through his responses, is minimized. He may write a letter to the source or even call the TV or radio station, but he will never be sure that his message is noted by the source. Nor can the source rely on the few random samples of feedback he receives as being indicative of the reaction of the entire audience.

The effects of feedback on learning situations were tested in a classic study by two communication experimenters, Harold Leavitt and Ronald Mueller.[27] In the experiment, specific material was communicated to four groups of students under different feedback conditions. In the *zero feedback* condition, the teacher sat behind a blackboard and allowed no questions

---

[27] Harold J. Leavitt and Ronald A. Mueller, "Some Effects of Feedback on Communication," *Human Relations*, 4 (1951), pp. 401-410.

*Figure 2-3 In a mass communication situation, whatever
feedback may exist between the source and the receiver is
delayed. Here, two reporters watch President Nixon deliver
a speech about the Watergate scandal.*

from the students. In the *visual audience* condition, the students
could see the teacher, but no verbal feedback was allowed.
In the *yes–no* condition, the students were allowed to respond
with only "yes" or "no." Finally, in *free feedback*, the students
were permitted to ask questions and make comments as often
as they wished. The results confirmed the beneficial effects of
feedback in learning situations. Scores indicating how well
students learned the material increased steadily from zero to
free feedback conditions.

Not all feedback is perceived as good or helpful to the source.
Every receiver has the ability to emit positive or negative
feedback, and we have all consciously used this power to exert
control over a source. If a man approaches a woman at a party
and begins talking to her, the woman may emit positive feedback
by smiling, using direct eye contact, and participating in the
conversation. Negative feedback might consist of yawning in
the man's face, glancing around the room, and answering only
direct questions in monosyllables. Positive feedback is
encouraging and rewarding to the source. If a source receives
positive feedback, he is likely to repeat the actions which
produced the feedback. Negative feedback is unpleasant or

punishing to the source, and will probably cause him to change his tactics.

Studies have shown that positive and negative feedback may have a tremendous impact on the delivery of a speaker.[28] Negative feedback tends to make a speaker less fluent than positive feedback. The communicator's rate of speaking has been found to increase with positive feedback and decrease with negative feedback. In one study, negative feedback produced a significant increase in the loudness of the speaker's voice, but positive feedback had no effect on volume. Negative feedback causes speakers to shorten their presentation, whereas positive feedback causes speakers to perceive their presentations as longer than they actually are. Negative feedback generally inhibits the delivery of a speaker.

Feedback may even affect the source's attitude toward the subject he is discussing.[29] It has been demonstrated that if a person receives positive feedback when defending a belief that is discrepant from his own, he is likely to change his attitude about the topic. For example, suppose a student in a social problems course is required to make a speech on the legalization of marijuana. The student knows that the professor is against its legalization and so the student decides to argue this position, even though he believes marijuana should be legalized. If the student receives praise from his classmates and a good grade from his professor, the student is likely to change his own attitude and favor the position that marijuana should not be legalized. However, if a speaker receives negative feedback when arguing a position in which he does not believe, he probably will not change his opinion. When a speaker argues from a position which is consistent with his own beliefs, both very positive and very negative feedback will strengthen his attitude.

The way a person perceives the feedback he receives depends on his personality, feelings and experiences. For example, a person may hear only what he wants to hear. Selective attention is the ability to attend closely to messages that are consistent with one's attitudes, while attending less closely or ignoring messages that are inconsistent. A dogmatic person often uses selective attention to avoid coping with conflicting ideas. A parent may attend a lecture on the pros and cons of legalizing marijuana, and "hear" only the cons because he wants these ideas reinforced.

---

[28] James C. Gardiner, "A Synthesis of Experimental Studies of Speech Communication Feedback," *Journal of Communication*, 21 (March 1971), pp. 17-20.

[29] *Ibid.*, pp. 20-24.

Another problem exists when a person tries to interpret nonverbal cues, which may not be consistent with another person's true inner feelings. A frown may not mean displeasure but concentration; a smile can be sarcastic and not a sign of approval. Interpreting a receiver's responses to a message is a difficult and complex task, and one which unfortunately carries a high margin of error.

Man is dependent on communication for his very survival, and feedback is the essence of the communication process. Without feedback, we could never exchange ideas, test new theories, or even learn about each other. Our dependence on feedback is moist poignantly illustrated when a former prisoner-of-war speaks of his years in isolation as the cruelest experience of all. Feedback also plays a vital role in our development, since our concept of self is formed and constantly challenged by our perception of the way others see us. Vital personal needs are also met by feedback. Each of us has the need to feel significant, worthwhile and loved, and these needs can be met by positive, supportive feedback.

1. The receiver is often the forgotten person in the communication process, although without him there would be no transfer of meaning. To some extent, the receiver exerts control over the source, and both the source and the receiver must accommodate each other in the communication transaction.

2. A source may analyze his audience according to five demographic variables: age, sex, social and economic background, racial and ethnic factors, and intelligence. There is some evidence that old people are more difficult to persuade than young people. Women are generally more persuasible than men although this may be the result of social rather than biological factors. Social, economic, racial and ethnic differences between the source and the receiver are likely to make communication between the two difficult.

3. An individual's personality traits remain fairly stable and may therefore affect the way a receiver responds to a message. When dogmatic people are confronted with a persuasive appeal from a source whom they consider to be authoritative, they are generally more persuasible than open–minded people. People with high self-esteem tend to be more persuaded by a simple appeal than people with low self-esteem. Aggressive people are generally less persuasible than unaggressive people. A hostile receiver will tend to be more receptive to a message which makes a harsh appeal than one which makes a benign or neutral appeal. The anxiety level of a receiver seems to interact with the content of a message, thereby affecting the receiver's persuasibility. Receivers with high anxiety tend to be less persuaded by anxiety producing messages, whereas receivers with low anxiety tend to be more persuaded by anxiety producing messages. The prior attitudes of a receiver will also affect his reaction to a message. Receivers with strong prior atttitudes on a topic are less persuasible than receivers with neutral attitudes. A high degree of involvement in or commitment to an idea will make a receiver less receptive to a message which argues counter to the receiver's prior attitudes.

4. Listening involves three skills: hearing, comprehension and retention. Most people have developed poor listening habits which include avoiding difficult listening situations, dismissing the speaker or topic as uninteresting, and faking attention. The source may effectively increase the audience's reception of his message by prefacing his speech with goal-setting statements.

5. Three factors seem to operate in the development of trust in an interpersonal communication situation: the person's concept of himself, his perception of the other person, and the effect of his own demonstration of trust on the situation. The development of mutual trust is likely to reduce the possibility of defensive behavior and thereby increase the effectiveness of the communication between the interactants.

6. Feedback is the response of a receiver to the message of a source. Feedback serves as the link between the interactants, giving the communication situation its transactional nature. Feedback enables a speaker to adjust his message to the needs of the receiver; it may also affect the source's delivery and attitudes toward the topic being discussed. In face-to-face and small group situations, there is generally a great deal of feedback, whereas in public speaking and mass communication situations when feedback exists it is usually minimal and delayed. The greater the amount of feedback the more effective the communication is likely to be.

1. Select a public figure who in your opinion possesses one of the personality variables discussed in this chapter. What aspects of this person's communication behavior lead you to believe he possessed this personality trait? Discuss your observations in class and compare them with your classmates.

2. In what ways might you change your communication behavior when interacting with a person who is high or low in dogmatism? Repeat this exercise for someone who is high or low in self-esteem.

3. As a class, select two people who have opposing views on some important issue. Have Person 1 express his opinion on the topic. Person 2 should then repeat the message of Person 1 to the satisfaction of Person 1. Repeat this procedure, but this time have Person 2 express his opinion and Person 1 repeat it to the satisfaction of Person 2. What happened in this situation? What differences in behavior did you observe when the receiver knew he was going to be a source of communication? What receiver skills were demonstrated in this exercise?

4. To test the effects of different types of feedback, complete the following exercise. Divide the class into three groups and then select one student to be the subject of the experiment without telling him this. Each group should provide the subject with one type of feedback: positive, negative, or zero. Observe the student's behavior as people from each group interact with him. At the end of the class session, discuss your observations with the subject of the experiment. What conclusions can you make about each of the three types of feedback?

5. Select a professor who teaches you a subject other than speech communication. Arrange with the other students in the class to provide the professor with positive feedback everytime he walks to the right side of the classroom. What effects did this have on the professor's behavior? Can you explain why the professor reacted as he did?

Theodore Clevenger, Jr., *Audience Analysis* (Indianapolis: Bobbs-Merrill Company, 1971). This is a short but well-written book which focuses on different methods for analyzing an audience.

James C. Gardiner, "A Synthesis of Experimental Studies of Speech Communication Feedback," *Journal of Communication*, 21 (1971), pp. 17-35. This article presents a detailed summary of research findings on feedback and its effects on the communication process.

Kim Giffin and Bobby R. Patton, "Personal Trust in Human Interaction" in *Basic Readings in Interpersonal Communication* (New York: Harper and Row, 1971). This is an excellent discussion of the effects of trust on interpersonal communication by two of the leading researchers in the field.

Carl I. Hovland and Irving L. Janis, eds., *Personality and Persuasibility* (New Haven: Yale University Press, 1959). The editors have compiled some interesting research findings on demographic and personality variables and their effects on the persuasion process.

Gerald Miller and Michael Burgoon, "Inducing Resistance to Persuasion," in *New Techniques of Persuasion* (New York: Harper and Row, 1973), pp. 18-44. This chapter presents a detailed summary of research findings on self-esteem, anxiety, hostility, education and prior attitudes and their relation to persuasibility.

Ralph G. Nichols and Leonard A. Stevens, *Are You Listening?* (New York: McGraw-Hill Book Company, 1957). This book is an excellent introduction to the nature of listening in the communication process by two early research pioneers in the field.

Milton Rokeach, *The Open and Closed Mind* (New York: Basic Books, 1960). Here is a careful consideration of experimental research in dogmatism as well as Rokeach's own theory of the open and closed mind.

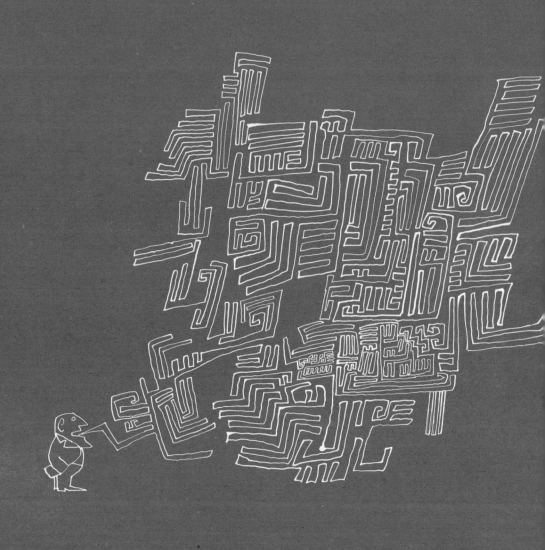

Verbal message variables

Communication has many functions, such as persuading, sharing information, resolving conflict and filling social needs. But most communication research has focused on persuasion. Some experts even maintain that all communication is essentially persuasive. For instance, they argue that a teacher tries to persuade his students to accept certain ideas and that a labor-management arbitrator tries to persuade both parties to agree. They also say that in social communication, a person tries to persuade others that he is a worthwhile human being. While this view of communication may be accurate, it seems rather narrow. Some kinds of communication are clearly more persuasive than others, and persuasion is not the only way to communicate.

Since communication serves many functions, it would seem likely that certain kinds of messages would be more effective in one communication situation than in another. Communication experts often make the distinction between persuasive and informative messages, and we would expect one kind of message to be more effective in a persuasion situation and another kind to be more effective in an information-sharing situation. This chapter discusses the construction of messages to persuade. More traditionally studied aspects of informative messages are covered in Chapter 8; however, many of the suggestions made in this chapter for shaping a persuasive message can be adapted to other nonpersuasive communication situations. A business executive needs to know what kinds of messages are most likely to be accepted and retained by people working for him. Anyone involved in an intimate relationship needs to know that some kinds of messages increase tension, whereas others lessen it. Through practice and intelligent observation, a person can learn to communicate with messages that work.

te:
ght © 1960
 Steinberg.
he Labyrinth,
 & Row, Publishers
ly published
New Yorker.

The components of a persuasive message

Every persuasive message presents an idea or course of action which the communicator advocates; it then suggests the reasons that his listeners should agree to it. In their simplest form, most persuasive messages are made up of three parts or components: claim, warrant, and data.[1] These elements work to reinforce one another.

Claim

A *claim* is any statement, implied or explicit, which a communicator wants his audience to accept or agree to.

A particular claim can serve as the major point of several related arguments; or it may be used by the communicator in one part of his argument to support an assertion (claim) made in another part.

There are several kinds of claims which can be used in a message. In a *policy* claim, the speaker calls for a specific course of action. The statement "Heroin should be available to addicts under medical supervision" is an example of a policy claim. The speaker might make a *fact* claim: "In England, heroin is available to addicts under medical supervision." And he might then make a *value* claim such as, "The English system for treating heroin addiction is superior to that of the United States." Regardless of the kind of claim used, a single claim does not in itself provide a reason for audience acceptance of it.

Warrant

To persuade, the communicator must support each claim with two other message parts: a warrant and data. A *warrant* is a general belief or attitude stated in support of a claim. To be effective, a warrant must be implicitly accepted by the audience; otherwise it remains just another claim. For example, a communicator who says that "Schools should not be racially integrated" is making a claim. He may then support his claim with the general statement, "Blacks are genetically inferior to whites in mental ability." Such a statement would be a warrant. A Ku Klux Klan meeting might accept this warrant, and so accept the claim. But a convention of anthropologists or black intellectuals might not believe the warrant, and so would reject the claim as unwarranted. In this case, the warrant itself (that blacks are mentally inferior) becomes a claim and needs a new warrant to justify it.

---

[1] Stephen Toulmin, *The Uses of Argument* (Cambridge, England: Cambridge University Press, 1959).

Many persuasive messages fail even when the claim is acceptable to the audience, because the warrant is totally rejected. For instance, suppose that a man who believes marijuana to be a dangerous drug goes to see a 1930s movie called *Reefer Madness*. It claims that marijuana is a dangerous drug, a claim he is predisposed to support; it warrants that smoking marijuana leads to mental illness and violent crime. The warrant may seem so absurdly exaggerated that the viewer rejects first it, then the claim, deciding that marijuana couldn't be as dangerous as all that. An inappropriate warrant can actually be counterpersuasive.

Data

Data are specific beliefs stated in support of a claim. Like the warrant, the data must be accepted by the audience to be persuasive. James McCroskey, a leading communication expert, has suggested that there are three types of data: first-order, second-order, and third-order.[2]

First-order data are specific beliefs or knowledge shared by the communicator and his audience. It may be claimed, for example, that all cigarette advertising should be banned. Such a claim might be warranted by the generally accepted belief that cigarette smoking causes lung cancer. The communicator might then offer as data the information that cigarette advertising encourages smoking. The success or failure of this argument depends upon whether or not the data are first-order—that is, whether or not they are a belief or awareness of fact which the audience shares with the communicator. If they are not, the data themselves become a claim which the communicator will have to support by further argument.

Second-order data are beliefs held by the communicator, but not necessarily known or shared by his audience. This type of data is often called *source assertion*, for it asks the audience to accept something just because the speaker, or source, says it is so. The important message component in this case is the warrant that the speaker is a credible source. For example, a speaker might assert that consistently poor nutrition retards the mental development of children. If his credibility is high enough—let us say that the audience knows him to

---

[2] James C. McCroskey, *An Introduction to Rhetorical Communication* (Englewood Cliffs, N.J.: Prentice Hall, Inc., 1968), pp. 84-105.

be an established and respected member of the medical profession—the assertion itself becomes sufficient data. If the audience fully accepts the warrant (often implicit) that the speaker is a knowledgeable source, it will probably accept the speaker's claim without the need for further documentation. In this case, the second-order data, information previously known only to the speaker, become first-order data, which the audience also accepts as part of its beliefs or knowledge, and can be used in documenting further arguments. Of course, if the audience doubts the authority of the speaker, the data are useless.

When the communicator has low credibility and the audience does not share his views, he must often use third-order data to persuade. This type of data is called *evidence*. It comes from a third party, a source outside of the communicator and audience. Here is an example:

1. All cigarette advertising should be banned. (claim)
2. I am a truthful person. (warrant)
3. *The New York Times* said in an editorial that all cigarette advertising should be banned. (third-order data)
4. *The New York Times* is a credible source. (warrant)

As you can see, this example really consists of two separate persuasive messages. The first is:

1. *The New York Times* said in an editorial that all cigarette advertising should be banned. (claim)
2. I am a truthful person. (warrant)
3. I say that I read this editorial in *The Times*. (second-order data)

If that claim is accepted, it can be used as first-order data in a second message:

1. All cigarette advertising should be banned. (claim)
2. *The New York Times* is a credible source. (warrant)
3. *The New York Times* said in an editorial that all cigarette advertising should be banned. (now considered first-order data, because the audience accepts it)

Third-order data ask the audience to accept warrants for two separate claims. The audience must trust that the speaker is telling the truth about what he read in *The Times*, and it must trust *The Times*. If the communicator has low credibility, or if the outside source is disliked or disbelieved by the audience, third-order data are not persuasive. Of course, no amount of credibility will persuade if the audience totally rejects the claim. For instance, an audience of Roman Catholic clergy will probably not accept a claim that abortion should be legalized, no matter how credible the speaker or data.

Factors affecting persuasive message appeals

Aristotle specified three basic appeals which a communicator can make in a persuasive speech. A speaker can use a logical argument (logos), an emotional argument (pathos), or an argument based on credibility (ethos). Some contemporary communication experts distinguish between logical appeals and emotional appeals. A logical appeal is one which presents evidence in support of the acceptance of a claim, whereas an emotional appeal focuses on the consequences which will result if a person accepts or rejects a claim.[3] An advertisement which says that you will save five hundred dollars if you buy a particular kind of automobile during August is making a logical appeal. An advertisement for life insurance which stresses that your wife and children will be without money should you suddenly die is making an emotional appeal.

Clearly, certain messages are more logical or more emotional than others. Nevertheless, logical and emotional appeals should not be viewed as mutually exclusive categories. For example, the car advertisement mentioned above might also discuss the "sex appeal" or "status" conferred upon the owner of such an automobile. Likewise, the insurance advertisement might cite cold statistical evidence to support its claim that many families suffer financially when the husband dies unexpectedly at an early age. Furthermore, the logic or emotion of an appeal is perceived by the receiver, and research shows that an audience is often incapable of distinguishing between the two types of appeals.[4] In fact, some studies have shown that when the members of an audience agree with the conclusion of a message they tend to perceive it as logical, even if it contains faulty reasoning.[5] Despite the difficulties in distinguishing between logical and emotional appeals, there are several factors which will affect the persuasiveness of a message regardless of the type of appeal used.

[3] William J. McGuire, "The Nature of Attitudes and Attitude Change," in Gardner Lindsey and Elliot Aronson, eds., *The Handbook of Social Psychology*, 2nd edition, Vol. III, (Reading, Mass.: Addison-Wesley, 1969), p. 202.

[4] Randall C. Ruechelle, "An Experimental Study of Audience Recognition of Emotional and Intellectual Appeals in Persuasion," *Speech Monographs*, XXV (1958), p. 58.

[5] A. Lefford, "The Influence of Emotional Subject Matter on Logial Reasoning," *Journal of General Psychology*, 34 (1946), pp. 127-151.

Using evidence to persuade

Is it important to present evidence (third-order data) to support a claim? The answer depends on the situation. Research has shown that sometimes evidence is very persuasive, whereas at other times different kinds of supporting material are more effective. It is possible to extract from the research some generalizations about the usefulness of evidence.[6]

If the communicator has high credibility with his audience, he will probably not need to present evidence. For example, suppose the President's chief economic adviser claims that the nation is headed for a depression. If you believe he is a credible source, you will probably accept his statement without hearing his statistics. Citing that evidence would not make him more persuasive to you, because you already believe him; his position convinces you that he is an expert in his field.

But what if the speaker has low credibility? In that case, evidence is persuasive only if the audience was previously unaware of the data. If, in the example above, the economic adviser was a man you considered untrustworthy, you would want to hear his evidence. If he gave convincing statistics that you had not known before, you might accept his claim in spite of his low credibility. But suppose you were a student of economics who had read the same statistics and drawn a different conclusion. In that case, the adviser's use of evidence would not persuade you; it might even make you resist his claim more, because you would suspect him of manipulating the facts. In general, if an audience already knows of the evidence, it has probably made up its mind, and the communicator gains nothing by restating the evidence.

Research has also shown that evidence must be delivered clearly if it is to have maximum persuasive effect. This does not not mean a speaker must use a compulsively logical and straightforward approach, since he may lose his audience by boring its members to death. But if there is no organic unity to his presentation, if statistics are haphazardly thrown at his audience, or if he mumbles words and drones away in a relentless monotone, all the evidence in the world will not help that speaker. A poor delivery will not only make evidence useless, failing to persuade the audience of the particular argument being discussed at the time; it is very possible that it will also reduce the speaker's

[6] For a detailed discussion of evidence see James C. McCroskey, "A Summary of Experimental Research on the Effects of Evidence in Persuasive Communication," *Quarterly Journal of Speech*, 55 (1969), pp. 169–176.

Figure 3-1 *The use of additional visual stimuli may increase the accuracy with which a verbal message is perceived and may also facilitate retention of the material being discussed.*

credibility in terms of future messages he may present.

Apparently a speaker runs risks in presenting evidence. It may have a neutral effect, swaying an audience neither one way nor the other; or it may actually hurt a speaker's chances of successfully conveying his message. What then is the ultimate value of evidence? Studies show that, whereas the immediate effect of evidence can be negligible, the long-rang effects—for both high- and low-credibility speakers—may be important. Over a period of time, audience attitudes may change slowly but decidedly if the listeners receive several doses of evidence in the messages conveyed to them. A good example is the political candidate who begins his campaign months in advance of election day. The cumulative effect of the evidence he presents, especially in claims made against opponents, may eventually alter the attitudes of the voters. Furthermore, this evidence is a kind of "security" against counterclaims. In other words, it may help the audience to resist the views of the candidate's opponents.

Using one-sided and two-sided messages

Most claims are only one side of an argument. The communicator must decide whether or not to cite opposing arguments. In a one-sided message, he makes his own claim and supports it. In a two-sided message, he makes his claim, acknowledges opposing arguments, and gives reasons to justify his claim over the others. The decision to present a one-sided or two-sided message depends on several audience factors.

In some cases in which an audience already agrees with the claims of a speaker, a one-sided argument will immediately increase or confirm that support.[7] In fact, if a speaker has reason to believe that his audience is unaware of counterarguments, he will probably do best deliberately to avoid these arguments. By mentioning them, the speaker might simply persuade his listeners against his own claim. The mayor who cites fifteen instances of alleged police corruption when the public knows only of five is at a disadvantage no matter how well he disproves the accusations; those additional ten examples could convince people that there really is widespread police corruption.

On the other hand, if an audience is hostile, if its sympathies are unknown, or if there is any possibility that an audience is aware of opposing arguments, a speaker is best advised to present a two-sided message. Even when people are in agreement with the speaker, the more educated they are (an increasingly common situation in our society), the more likely such an audience will be persuaded by a two-sided argument.[8] Educated people are usually capable of thinking of at least a few opposing arguments for themselves and therefore might be suspicious of the motives or intelligence of a speaker who does not consider these same arguments.

One also has to realize that great numbers of people are exposed to conflicting arguments on issues through mass media coverage.[9] Suppose a mayor claims that there is no corruption in the city's police department. If the public has already listened

---

[7] Carl I. Hovland, A. A. Lumsdaine, and F. D. Sheffied, *Studies in Social Psychology in World War II*, Vol. 3 (Princeton, N.J.: Princeton University Press, 1949), pp. 201-227.

[8] *Ibid.*

[9] For a detailed discussion of prior information and message-sidedness see John R. Weston, *Argumentative Message Structure and Prior Familiarity as Predictors of Source Credibility and Attitude Change*, Unpublished doctoral dissertation, Michigan State University, 1967.

to television programs highlighting instances of such corruption and read evidence cited in newspaper accounts, the mayor is going to seem foolish and incompetent—or worse. If the public believes the mayor was being dishonest in his message, not only will they fail to be persuaded by his immediate claim, they might also doubt his credibility on other issues.

It would seem, therefore, that in most cases—other than outright propagandizing when the speaker is merely recycling shared beliefs for the benefit of his followers—it is usually better to use some form of the two-sided message. The speaker will have to use his discretion in deciding how much he should say.

Using persuasive messages to inhibit attitude change

Persuasion is often used to change attitudes, but it can also be used in another way: to reinforce existing attitudes, making them resistance to change.[10] One theory regarding this kind of persuasion suggests that the opposition's arguments are analogous to a disease.[11] Just as a person develops antibodies against a disease by receiving a vaccination consisting of weakened doses of the germ, so can an audience be "immunized" by receiving messages that stimulate its defenses (sometimes quite subtly) against opposing arguments.

The "vaccination" can be in the form of a supportive message or a refutational message. *Supportive messages* make statements that endorse the desired belief, or that incline the audience to seek more information to support that belief. *Refutational messages* attack the opposing belief. Suppose a political candidate wants to be sure that voters in a district that previously supported him will not change their minds by election day. If he picks the supportive message, he will emphasize positive things about himself—his excellent record, his experience in politics, his personal charm. If he picks the refutational message, he will attack the opposing candidate, criticizing his record and pointing out weaknesses in his arguments.

To some extent, the effect of supportive and refutational strategies resembles the way message-sidedness works. The

---

[10] For a detailed discussion of inducing resistance to persuasion see Gerald R. Miller and Michael Burgoon, *New Techniques of Persuasion* (New York: Harper and Row, 1973), pp. 18-44.

[11] William J. McGuire, "Inducing Resistance to Persuasion: Some Contemporary Approaches," in Leonard Berkowits, ed., *Advances in Experimental Social Psychology*, Vol. 1 (New York: Academic Press, 1964), pp. 191-229.

supportive message, which seeks to strengthen belief, is much like the one-sided message, which tries to alter belief; both have a minimal effect. It does appear that the refutational message works somewhat better than the supportive. But as in the case of the two-sided message, a combined approach (supportive and refutational) may be more successful than any single strategy. The political candidate mentioned previously would probably be most effective by reasserting the value of his own position as well as attempting to rebut potential claims of the opposition candidate.

Using fear appeals to persuade

Many communicators try to persuade by stimulating fear in their audiences. Public health pamphlets, for example, predict a frightening future of blindness, sterility and paralysis as the reward for sexual promiscuity (or even occasional indiscretions) unless one takes the recommended precautions. Gun-control advocates talk of unleashed violence, and their opponents talk of first steps down the road to totalitarianism. Students in a driver's education course watch a State Highway Department film which graphically portrays the results of reckless or negligent driving, complete with blood and bodies and intimations of one's own mortality. Because people do react strongly to fear in everyday life, much research has been done to see if fear can be used to change attitudes.

A fear appeal says that harm will befall the listener or someone important to him, unless he adopts the claim of the communicator. A strong fear appeal dramatically shows this harm. A film intended to make people stop smoking which shows a close-up of a cancerous lung being removed from a corpse is an example of a high fear appeal. A moderate fear appeal states the same message less dramatically, as in the case of a film which shows people smoking, then coughing. A low fear appeal states the message in a fairly calm way— for example, a printed advertisement claiming that scientists have established a link between smoking and lung cancer. A communicator must decide which type of fear appeal will produce the change he wants.

Research findings on this subject are conflicting. Some studies show that a strong fear appeal is best; others show that a moderate fear appeal is best. Such confusion means that factors other than the fear appeal itself are affecting the receiver's response to the message.[12]

The credibility of the source is one influence on the audience's reaction to a fear appeal. A highly credible source is more persuasive using a strong fear appeal. A less credible source does better with a moderate fear appeal. If a doctor tells you that you will die of heart trouble within a year if you do not stop overeating, that should provide enough incentive for you to take action. If a well-meaning friend tells you the same thing, you may not be so quickly persuaded. Therefore, a communicator who plans to persuade through fear should first attempt to establish his credibility in the eyes of his audience.

When the fear appeal threatens harm to someone important to the listener, a strong fear appeal is most effective. For instance, a claim that children undernourished on sugarcoated breakfast cereal and junk food may grow up with brain damage would be more persuasive than the claim that they grow up failing to appreciate good food. When the fear appeals threaten loved ones, the listener cannot reason that he is only hurting himself by rejecting the claim.

A strong fear appeal with evidence is more effective than one without evidence and is stronger than any mild fear appeal, with or without evidence. In research studies, only the people who heard evidence kept their changed attitudes for longer than two weeks. Those who heard appeals without evidence quickly returned to their original belief. Thus, an opponent of sugarcoated cereal and junk food who wants to change permanently the nutritional attitudes of mothers should make claims that he can support with convincing evidence. If he has no evidence for the brain-damage claim, he would do better with a mild fear appeal, citing evidence which supports the claim that bad eating habits formed in early childhood usually continue in adult life.

Communicators who use any sort of fear appeal should be careful not to frighten the members of the audience so that they reject the threat as absurdly farfetched, or regard it as too unbearable to think about. A public health official who tells a group of pregnant women who smoke that their infants will be addicted to nicotine for the rest of their lives is likely to be unpersuasive because his claim is so exaggerated. However, fears appeals used moderately are effective ways to persuade.

---

[12] For a detailed discussion of fear appeals see Gerald R. Miller, "Studies in the Use of Fear Appeals: A Summary and Analysis," *Central States Speech Journal, 14* (196), pp. 117-125.

Using intense language to persuade

Language intensity can be rated by measuring the distance between a claim and a neutral position. For example, the claim "Unions are *destroying* the newspaper industry" is certainly less neutral than saying that "Unions create *problems* in the newspaper industry." There are two different ways to vary the intensity of language in a message.[13]

The first way is to insert qualifiers. One kind of qualifier expresses probability. Take the statement, "Recent Supreme Court decisions on the rights of accused criminals will *certainly* lead to more violent crime." This statement can be made less intense by replacing "certainly" with "perhaps." Another kind of qualifier expresses extremity. If a Presidential aide tells the press, "The President *vigorously condemns* bias in the news media," the attitude implied is obviously more intense and more threatening than if he says, "The President *frowns* upon bias in the news media."

The second way to increase intensity of language is to use metaphors, especially those with sexual or violent connotations. When a speaker claims, "The President *is raping* the Constitution," "The recent incursion by Russia is a *molestation* of the country's territorial waters," "Public school teachers *suffocate* student creativity," or "Prejudice in the system *has brutalized* the minds of young children," he is going beyond a representation of the facts as they stand and attempting to persuade through the intensity of his images.

Whether such high-intensity language does in fact achieve the speaker's goal is difficult to say. One study showed that a very intense communicator seems more credible, and that his messages seem more clear and intelligent; however, the study did not indicate that such a communicator persuades better.[14] Other research has found that low-intensity language produces more attitude change, whereas highly intense messages may create a "backlash" effect.

One explanation of these findings is that a speaker often uses high-intensity language when his views are very different from those of his audience. Since the members of an audience disagree with him, they tend to contrast the speaker's statement

---

[13] John Waite Bowers, "Some Correlates of Language Intensity," *Quarterly Journal of Speech, 50* (1964), pp. 415-420.

[14] William J. McEwen and Bradley S. Greenberg, "The Effects of Message Intensity on Receiver Evaluations of Source, Message and Topic," *Journal of Communication, 20* (1970), pp. 340-350.

to their own beliefs, refute him in their minds, and thus stay unpersuaded. This contrast can be avoided by using language that is moderate or low in intensity, since listeners are less likely to feel polarized from the speaker. They may be more able to see similarities and to absorb his claims into their own beliefs.

Listeners who are very involved in the topic (for example, reporters listening to an argument against confidential sources) are especially likely to contrast opposing views to their own. With such audiences, a communicator will effect little attitude change with highly intense language. If a topic is less crucial to the audience, more intensity of language can persuade.

Opinionated language is similar to intense language and has similar effects. Generally speaking, opinionated language really expresses two separate messages: the claim and the speaker's attitude toward those who agree or disagree with him. Opinionated language may express rejection of those who disagree, as in the statement, "Only criminals with something to hide would object to being stopped and frisked by a policeman." Or it may praise those who agree with the communicator—for example, "People who favor stop-and-frisk laws are responsible citizens who are willing to put up with a slight inconvenience in the interests of justice." Statements such as "Stop-and-frisk laws are good" are nonopinionated since they merely express a claim.

Research indicates that opinionated rejections are perceived as more intense than nonopinionated statements. They can be used effectively by highly credible sources. Less credible sources, however, do better with nonopinionated language.[15] Also nonopinionated language is likely to be more persuasive with an audience which is involved in the issue being discussed. A neutral audience is more persuaded by opinionated rejections.

Because these findings are so similar to those for contrast effects in the use of intense language, a communicator can draw some general conclusions. When the audience thinks he is credible, he can use intensity to persuade. But when he disagrees with his audience on an issue that is very important to it, he should be less intense. Many people believe, quite intuitively, that a passionate speaker is most persuasive. But this is not

[15] Gerald R. Miller and John Lobe, "Opinionated Language, Open- and Closed-Mindedness and Responses to Persuasive Communications," *Journal of Communication*, 17 (1967), 333-41.

always true. A persuader must use reason and caution in deciding how intensely to state his claim.

Figure 3-2 Although studies have shown that humor does not increase the persuasiveness of a verbal message, it can establish rapport between the source and the receiver which may, in some way, affect the nature of their interaction.

Using humor to persuade

The effect of humor on persuasion has not been examined very thoroughly. An early study showed that humor (puns, turns of phrase and humorous anecdotes) did not significantly increase or decrease attitude change in the audience. Furthermore, humorous and nonhumorous messages were perceived as equally interesting and convincing by the receivers.[16] Similarly, experiments have shown that satire also does not enhance the persuasiveness of a message both immediately and over a period of three weeks.[17]

[16] P.E. Lull, "The Effectiveness of Humor in Persuasive Speech," *Speech Monographs,* 7 (1940), pp. 26-40.

[17] Charles R. Gruner, "An Experimental Study of Satire as Persuasion," *Speech Monographs,* 32 (June 1965), pp. 149-153 and Gary F. Pokorny and Charles R. Gruner, "An Experimental Study of the Effect of Satire Used as Support in a Persuasive Speech," *Western Speech,* (Summer 1969), pp. 204-211.

Although there is no evidence that humor affects persuasion, humor may create a sense of warmth or rapport between the communicator and his audience. Therefore, it is possible that humorous material in a speech may enhance an audience's perception of a speaker's sociability, a dimension of his credibility. For example, many people attribute much of President Kennedy's popularity to his sense of humor, which made him more attractive. Whether a source's credibility is, in fact, enhanced by humor has not yet been supported by experimental studies. This and other questions about the importance of humor in persuasive communication remain to be answered by researchers.

Message discrepancy

While audiences can be persuaded to change their views dramatically, there are limits to their tolerance of opposing views. The distance, or *discrepancy*, between the views of a communicator and his audience can affect his persuasiveness.

For example, suppose a speaker who favors laws requiring journalists to disclose confidential sources to the government or courts is addressing a group of newspaper reporters. This speaker will probably not be very persuasive if he supports his claims with philosophical objections to the idea of confidential sources. He will probably be more persuasive if he asserts the journalist's right to confidential sources and then says that this right must be exercised in a responsible way—that is, it must not obstruct justice in criminal cases. Using this strategy, the speaker allies himself with the audience and gains credibility.

Research shows that a communicator who makes his beliefs sound close to those of the audience will be more persuasive. The farther his message departs from its views, the more the audience will see him as unfair, uninformed, illogical and uninteresting.[18] However, a source with high credibility—for example, a Pulitzer prize-winning journalist speaking to the same group of reporters—will probably be able to depart from his audience's views without so much loss of credibility.

Whenever a communicator is uncertain about how strongly he should present his point, he should try to make his message sound as close to the views of the audience as possible. Usually, the less discrepant message will effect more attitude change than the tough one.

---

[18] William J. McGuire, *op. cit.*, p. 221.

Structuring a persuasive message

The question of whether a well-organized speech is more persuasive than a poorly-organized speech has received considerable attention from researchers in the field of speech communication. Studies have shown that severe disorganization does make a message less persuasive but that moderately disorganized messages are no less effective than very logical ones.[19]

There are several plausible explanations for this result. First, the audience may be capable of organizing information that comes to it in an "illogical" way. Marshall McLuhan, perhaps the most revolutionary communication theorist, claims that the electronic media have created an environment that forces people rapidly to recognize patterns in seemingly random information. Whereas books trained people to think in a logical, "linear" way, electronic media such as television ask us to take in vast amounts of disconnected information, and do the job of ordering it ourselves. If McLuhan is right, people today are used to dealing with information that is presented in a disorganized way. They could easily understand a speaker who did not present his argument in a logical, step-by-step fashion.

A second explanation is that most of the research on the organization of persuasive messages was done with college students. They may be especially skilled listeners, because the college lecture is an especially good example of a disorganized message. Organization might be more important in communicating to a noncollege-educated audience.

A third possible explanation for these research findings focuses on the process of feedback. In face-to-face and small group situations, the amount of feedback is greater than in public address and mass communication situations. A receiver who makes a verbal response to a particular point in a speech is, to some extent, altering or disrupting the logical pattern of the communicator. It would seem likely, therefore, that message organization would become less important as the amount of feedback in the communication situation increased.

---

[19] James C. McCroskey and R. Samuel Mehrley, "The Effects of Disorganization and Nonfluency on Attitude Change and Source Credibility," *Speech Monographs, 36* (1969), pp. 13-21 and James F. Weaver, *The Effects of Verbal Cueing and Initial Ethos Upon Perceived Organization, Retention, Attitude Change, and Terminal Ethos Upon Perceived Organization, Retention, Attitude Change, and Terminal Ethos,* Unpublished doctoral dissertation, Michigan State University, 1969.

In addition to its logical organization, a message also has a psychological structure. The way we order the different parts of a message can make an audience more or less receptive to persuasion. Research on the psychological structure of messages has provided some generalizations which may be helpful when shaping persuasive messages.

Organizing supporting materials

Presenting a two-sided message always involves some decision-making, since there is more than one way to organize the arguments. Suppose a speaker claims that capital punishment should be abolished. He might choose to plow through the opposition's arguments point for point, and only then settle back to a presentation of his own claims. There is nothing wrong with this—except that he may lose the argument.

One reason is that an audience very often reacts defensively toward a speaker who begins his message with a strong offensive, especially if the audience happens to agree with some or all of the opposition's claims. William Shakespeare understood this psychological aspect of audience reaction very well. In *Julius Caesar*, Marc Antony faced a public whose loyalty to Caesar could be severed or reaffirmed by the "right" message. In his speech, Antony gently and unantagonistically described each of Caesar's virtues while at the same time refraining from obvious attacks against Caesar's opponents. Only later in his oration, when he sensed that audience sympathies were won, did he dare to shift the emphasis of his message from positive claims to an outright attack against Caesar's enemies.

If Shakespeare had been a professor as well as a playwright, he might have warned his students that discussing opposition arguments first may invest them with more importance than one ever intended. In other words, the very fact that a speaker gives opposition statements priority in his message may establish a psychological priority in the minds of audience members—even those who were previously uncommitted. As for those who already support the opposing claims, such a message structure may actually reinforce their attitudes, an unfortunate result for the speaker.

If the speaker who is trying to persuade his audience that capital punishment should be abolished pays any attention at all to Antony's speech and to the findings of modern research on the subject, he will decide that a more persuasive method would be to present his own claims first and subsequently discuss, and refute, his opponent's stand.[20]

He could, for example, emphasize the immorality of taking human life, even in retribution; the unconstitutional nature of capital punishment; and the opinions of highly respected citizens who support his claim. Since an audience is often more favorably inclined toward the arguments it hears first, he will already have something of an advantage by the time he begins discussion of counterarguments.

These opposition claims might include the notion that capital punishment is the only adequate deterrent for major crimes. In that case, his refutation could be in the form of third-order data such as statistical figures relating to crime rates. But even if he fails to check the opposition on all points, his arguments will still be more persuasive if they are placed first than they would be if they are placed last.

Identifying the source of evidence

When citing an outside source (third-order data, or evidence), a speaker must decide when to state the identity and qualification of the source. This depends on the source's credibility.[21] If the audience believes the source is highly credible, he can be identified before or after presenting the evidence; it does not matter. However, when the source's credibility is low, it is better to cite the source after presenting the evidence. Thus, an advertising copywriter preparing a book advertisement for a new novel might proceed this way:

NORMAN MAILER SAYS: "This is the best novel I have read in 25 years!"

❖   ❖   ❖   ❖

"A BLOCKBUSTER OF A NOVEL! THRILLING, INCREDIBLY EROTIC, AND POSSIBLY THE GREATEST WORK OF FICTION EVER WRITTEN IN ENGLISH!!"—*The Nowheresville Tribune*

In fact, when the source is cited after the evidence, a highly

---

[20] Norman Miller and Donald T. Cambell, "Recency and Primacy in Persuasion as a Function of the Timing of Speeches and Measurements," *Journal of Abnormal Social Psychology,* 59 (1959), pp. 1-9.

[21] Bradley S. Greenberg and Gerald R. Miller, "The Effects of Low-Credible Sources on Message Acceptance, *Speech Monographs, 33* (1966), 127-136.

credible source is no more persuasive than a low one. Thus, if you do not know how the audience rates a source, you should give the evidence first, then name the source. If, in the example above, the copywriter believed Norman Mailer had endorsed so many bad books that his credibility was low, he might decide to put his quote first, followed by his name.

Revealing your desire to persuade

The question of whether it is wise to tell someone you want to change his mind is complex. If the members of the audience are strongly opposed to your claim, warning them in advance that you intend to persuade them is not effective.[22] A person speaking to a group of radical feminists would be ill-advised to state that he intended to change their minds about job discrimination against women. Or referring once again to Marc Antony's speech, it will be remembered that he told his audience he was there "to bury Caesar, not to praise him." In reality, he was there to bury Caesar's enemies and enhance his own position. But realizing the ambivalence of his audience (and the fact that Caesar's enemies were scattered among the citizenry), he never even implied his intent to persuade.

However, if a speaker and his audience are known to be in strong mutual sympathy (for example, if they are friends), the speaker may be more persuasive if he openly admits his intent. If the audience obviously dislikes the speaker, he will probably do better to keep quiet about his intent.[23] Sometimes an apparent lack of intent to persuade can become a powerful persuasive tool. When someone is led to believe he has accidentally overheard a message, he tends to be persuaded by it.[24] Political gossip columns often work this way. A government official "leaks" information to the columnist, who then pretends it is a secret that has been accidentally uncovered. In such a case, our belief that the official had no intent to persuade us can lead us to accept his claim. However, this strategy can also bolster existing negative attitudes.

---

[22] Jane Allyn and Leon Festinger, "The Effectiveness of Unanticipated Persuasive Communications," *Journal of Abnormal and Social Psychology*, 62 (1961), pp. 35-40.

[23] Judson Mills and Elliot Aronson, "Opinion Change as a Function of the Communicator's Attractiveness and Desire to Influence," *Journal of Personality and Social Psychology*, 1 (1965), pp. 173-177.

[24] Elaine Walster and Leon Festinger, "The Effectiveness of Overheard Persuasive Communications," *Journal of Abnormal and Social Psychology*, 65 (1962), pp. 395-402.

Presenting problems and solutions.

Suppose that a speaker wants to convince people that the problems of mothers on welfare can be solved by government-funded day-care centers. He could structure his message in two ways. He might discuss the problems of welfare mothers and then propose day-care centers as the solution. Or he could discuss the merits of day-care centers and then explain the problems of welfare mothers.

Research indicates that the first pattern is much more effective in changing attitudes, both immediately following the message and over a period of time.[25] The problem-to-solution message is more interesting, and the solution is more understandable when presented as the answer to a specific problem or need. When the solution is presented first, people may not understand its relevance until they hear about the problem. By that time, they may have lost interest.

Stating points of agreement and disagreement

In most persuasive communication situations, the communicator shares some of his audience's beliefs and disagrees with others. When does he discuss the shared beliefs? When does he introduce dispute? Research shows that the best strategy is to discuss points of agreement first, then move on to disagreements.[26] In this way, the speaker captures attention and raises his credibility. That credibility then covers him when he begins to disagree with his audience.

A politician telling reporters about union negotiations often uses this strategy. He points out that he, too, desires a higher standard of living for sanitation workers; that union members certainly deserve higher wages and more benefits for their hard work; and, finally, that he and the union leaders merely disagree on a few "minor" points, such as whether the wage increase shall be five cents or five dollars. This sort of strategy is used to persuade the public that the politician is a warmhearted fellow. However, at the actual negotiating table, one is often expected to exaggerate disagreements at the outset, and then gracefully concede points one by one, as if giving up something.

---

[25] Arthur R. Cohen, "Need for Cognition and Order of Communication as Determinants of Opinion Change," in Carl I. Hovland, ed. *The Order of Presentation in Persuasion* (New Haven: Yale University Press, 1957), pp. 102–120.

[26] William J. McGuire as cited in Arthur R. Cohen, *Attitude Change and Social Influence* (New York: Basic Books, 1964), p. 12.

In such cases, however, both sides understand the implied rules of the game. The general public is not likely to be so sophisticated.

Stating your conclusions

Research shows that most audiences respond favorably to clearly stated conclusions that call for a specific course of action. A speaker who makes an explicit conclusion creates more attitude change than one who lets the audience deduce the beliefs or actions he favors.[27] There are some experts who say that the listener will have more lasting change of attitude if he "participates" in the communication by drawing his own conclusions. But this method is risky, for there is no assurance that the listener will arrive at the conclusion the communicator desires. Thus, in persuasive communication situations, it is always wise for the speaker to state his conclusions clearly and specifically.

---

[27] Gary Cronkhite, *Persuasion: Speech and Behavioral Change,* (Indianapolis: Bobbs-Merrill, 1969), pp. 194-195.

1. A persuasive message presents an idea or course of action which the source advocates and suggests reasons that the receiver should agree to it. Most persuasive messages are composed of three parts: claim, warrant and data. A claim is an explicit or implicit statement which the communicator wants the receiver to accept. A warrant is a general belief stated in support of a claim. Data are specific beliefs stated in support of a claim.

2. Evidence is third-order data from a person outside the communication situation. Evidence seems to have little effect on the persuasiveness of a high credibility source, but it may increase the persuasiveness of a low credibility source if the audience was previously unaware of the data. When in doubt a speaker should use evidence.

3. In a one-sided message, a speaker makes his own claim and supports it. In a two-sided message, the source makes his own claim but also cites opposing arguments and gives reasons to justify his claim over the others. Research has provided some generalizations about the use of one- and two-sided messages: a) If the audience already agrees with the claims of the speaker, a one-sided message will immediately increase his support. b) If the speaker believes his audience is unaware of opposing arguments, a one-sided message is best. c) If the audience is hostile or aware of opposing arguments, a two-sided message is most effective. d) Well-educated people are more likely to be persuaded by a two-sided message than by a one-sided message. e) In general, it is better for a speaker to use a two-sided argument when the sympathies of an audience are unknown.

4. Persuasion can be used to inhibit attitude change. Attitudes may be reinforced through the use of a supportive message or a refutational message. A supportive message endorses the desired belief or inclines the audience to seek additional information to support the belief. A refutational message attacks opposing arguments. A refutational message may be somewhat more persuasive than a supportive message, but a

combined strategy using both types of messages is most effective.

5. A fear appeal is a message which says to the listener that harm will befall him or someone he cares about unless he adopts the claim. The credibility of the source can influence the audience's reaction to a fear appeal. A highly credible source is more persuasive when he uses a strong fear appeal, whereas a less credible source does better with a moderate fear appeal. Strong fear appeals seem very effective when they threaten harm to someone important to the listener. Strong fear appeals are most effective when used with evidence. Receivers who hear fear appeals without evidence tend to quickly return to their original beliefs. A communicator must use caution not to frighten his audience too much, since this may lead them to reject the threat as absurd or too unbearable to think about.

6. Messages containing highly intense language are not very persuasive when the audience is very involved in the topic under discussion. If a topic is less crucial or unimportant to the receivers, highly intense language can be persuasive. Opinionated language may express rejection of those who disagree with the speaker or it may praise those who agree with him. Highly credible sources can use opinionated rejections quite effectively, whereas less credible sources do better with nonopinionated language.

7. Research, though scant, has demonstrated that humor does not significantly increase or decrease the persuasiveness of a message. However, humor may create a sense of rapport between the source and his audience. Further research on the effects of humor is still needed.

8. Message discrepancy refers to the distance between the views of a speaker and those of his audience. Research indicates that a speaker who makes his beliefs sound close to those of the audience will be more persuasive. A source with high credibility will be able to depart from his audience's views without much loss of credibility.

9. Experimental research has provided some generalizations which are helpful when structuring a persuasive message:

a) When presenting a two-sided message, the speaker should discuss his arguments first. b) When citing evidence, the speaker should consider the credibility of the source of evidence. If the source of evidence has high credibility, it is best to cite the source and then the evidence. If the source of evidence has low credibility, it is best to cite the evidence and then name the source. c) A speaker should not forewarn the audience of his intent to persuade unless he is friendly with its members. d) Presenting the problem first and then the solution is more persuasive than beginning with the solution and moving on to the problem. e) A speaker who makes a specific conclusion will be more persuasive than one who allows the audience to deduce the beliefs or actions he favors.

1. Select a persuasive argument to which you have been recently exposed. Diagram the argument by identifying the claim(s), warrant(s), and data.

2. Select a topic in which you have some interest. Write a claim about the subject, then support it with warrant(s), and three different types of evidence.

3. Select an issue which is of campus concern. Design a persuasive message you think would be effective with a one-sided presentation, then create a two-sided message on the same issue. Present each message to a few people. Which was more persuasive?

4. Watch and analyze several television advertisements one evening. Select two which you think were very effective and two which you think were ineffective. Write a brief description of each advertisement, explaining the persuasive techniques used. Did each commercial use evidence? If so, what kind of evidence was used? Did any of the advertisements use a fear appeal or intense language to persuade?

5. The next time you are about to purchase a product from a salesman listen carefully to his "pitch." What verbal message techniques discussed in this chapter did he use to sell the product?

Thomas D. Beisecker and Don W. Parson, "Characteristics of the Message," in *The Process of Social Influence* (Englewood Cliffs, N.J.: Prentice-Hall, 1972), pp. 271-370. This is an excellent discussion of some classic experiments that delineate the effects of specific message variables on attitude change.

Gary Cronkhite, "The Persuader's Choice," in *Persuasion: Speech and Behavior Change* (Indianapolis: Bobbs-Merrill, 1969), pp. 172-211. This chapter seeks to answer three important questions: "What choices must be made by the person who wants to persuade? What are the available alternatives in each case? Under what circumstances should each alternative be chosen?"

Gerald R. Miller, "Studies on the Use of Fear Appeals: A Summary and Analysis," *Central States Speech Journal, 14* (1963), pp. 117-125. This is one of the best summaries of important experimental research on the persuasive effects of fear appeals.

Gerald R. Miller and Michael Burgoon, "Inducing Resistance to Persuasion," in *New Techniques of Persuasion* (New York: Harper and Row, 1973), pp. 18-44. This chapter presents a detailed discussion of numerous strategies to induce resistance to attitude change.

Harry C. Triandis, "Focus on the Message and Channel," in *Attitude and Attitude Change* (New York: John Wiley and Sons, 1971), pp. 182-200. This article discusses the effects that the channel may have on the communicator's message.

"What happens during the unspoken dialogue between two people can never be put right by anything they say." When Dag Hammarskjold made that statement, he probably didn't know he was talking about nonverbal communication. And although his observation is too general, it does provide insight into a frequently overlooked aspect of communication. The messages conveyed by our nonverbal behavior are often much stronger than our actual verbal statements. We attribute much meaning to such things as gestures, glances, touches and voice qualities. In fact, one estimate is that 65 percent of the meaning in an interpersonal interaction is transmitted nonverbally. When people say "his eyes told me what he was feeling" or "I could tell by his voice that he was angry," they are actually responding to nonverbal communication. Truly, "actions speak louder than words."

Despite our great reliance on nonverbal communication, very little time is actually devoted to studying it. Most people spend at least twelve years of school systematically studying verbal language, but almost no time is devoted to studying the syntax or vocabulary of nonverbal behavior. We tend to be only subconsciously aware of nonverbal means of communication, and so our ability to effectively interpret and send nonverbal messages is generally inadequate. Studying nonverbal communication in more detail can therefore be useful in heightening our awareness of the nonverbal code. Our goal should be to make our nonverbal communication intentional, by eliminating unintentional behavior which may be misinterpreted.

Difficulties in understanding nonverbal communication

One of the difficulties in understanding nonverbal communication is deciding which behaviors belong under that label. Should it include only behavior that can clearly be interpreted as a message, or should it be broadened to cover everything that has meaning for a receiver? Do we include only behavior that is intentional, or do we also consider unintentional messages? Can communication only come from a human source, or can the environment and inanimate objects communicate?

When a person intentionally sends a nonverbal message, and the message is clearly received by another, there is no doubt that a nonverbal communication has taken place. If a policeman raises his hand with his palm facing out and cars at an intersection stop, it is a safe guess that a message was sent and received. But what about a case in which a person attempts to send a message, but it does not get through to the intended receiver? For example, one person may try to convey an apology by the tone of his voice, but the injured party may fail to notice this apologetic note. If we define nonverbal communication as anything that affects the interaction between two people, then this situation fits the definition. Both the effort to communicate and its failure will affect the relationship of those two people.

A third kind of nonverbal behavior that should also be included as communication is that in which a receiver ascribes meaning to an unintentional behavior of a source. For instance, the child who slouches in his chair because he is more comfortable that way probably doesn't intend to send a message, but this behavior may be interpreted as indifference or lack of respect by the adult with whom he is conversing. We are interested in this kind of unintentional behavior as well as intentional behavior, because an interaction is bound to be affected by the fact that one person attaches meaning to the behavior of another. If we are to be effective communicators, we must be sensitive to the thoughts that our behavior might be triggering in the minds of others.

The final class of nonverbal communication includes the messages inherent in objects and features of the environment. Objects may convey a message to us about their owner. A carpeted office tells us something about the status of a person within an organization. A man who wears an expensive suit to work is communicating something about his personality. Of course, the actual message received may vary in different contexts. A clerk who wears a two-hundred-dollar designer suit to the office is likely to be perceived as status-seeking, whereas a different interpretation might be made of an executive who is similarly dressed. From another perspective, factors in the environment where an interaction takes place may influence the nature of the verbal communication that occurs. Fewer interactions will take place in a room where people are seated in a row against the wall than in a room where they are seated at round tables. The communication potential of objects and the environment are such that we include these in our consideration of nonverbal communication.

Functions of nonverbal behavior in the communication process

Communication experts have determined that nonverbal cues may serve six functions within the context of a total communication event. The first function is *redundancy*. Nonverbal behavior frequently repeats what is being said verbally. For example, if an instructor tells you that you have five minutes to finish a test and simultaneously holds up five fingers, he is providing nonverbal redundancy.

A second function of nonverbal behavior is *accentuation*, the highlighting or emphasizing of a verbal message or other nonverbal cues. When Nikita Khrushchev pounded a desk top with his shoe during a speech at the United Nations, he was rather strongly accenting a point in his message. On a less dramatic level, moving closer to someone who has expressed interest in you highlights the message of friendliness which may have first been signaled with the eyes.

Figure 4-1 Nonverbal behavior may be used to accentuate a point in a verbal message as this photograph of Richard Nixon and Nikita Khrushchev illustrates.

Substitution or replacement of a verbal message is a third function of nonverbal behavior. If an employee shows up late for work, the glare from his boss can clearly carry several messages. It substitutes for a barrage of verbal criticism and verbal threats about "the next time." Similarly, obscene gestures often replace their verbal complements.

A fourth use of nonverbal communication is *regulation* of the flow of verbal communication. A good example is eye behavior. When you look directly at another person as you complete a statement, you signal that you are open to communication. Conversely, breaking eye contact or orienting your body away from the person may keep him from replying. The familiar expression, "I gave him the cold shoulder," refers to such a use of body language.

Nonverbal communication may also *complement* verbal communication, that is, if it modifies or expands upon the verbal message, it is complementing it. The smiles and gestures of the returning traveler when he is discussing his trip provide added information. The lingering touch after a fight may carry a much stronger plea for reconciliation than the difficult words of apology preceding this nonverbal behavior.

A final function of nonverbal communication is *contradiction* of the verbal message. This contradiction may be intentional or unintentional. If a person sarcastically says, "That is the best program I ever saw," he is intentionally contradicting his verbal message with the tone of his voice. The small child who with a trembling lip claims he didn't break the clock is unintentionally betraying his statements. Many times our attempts at deception fail because our nonverbal behavior, which we are not aware of or used to controlling, gives us away.

The dimensions of nonverbal communication

While it is important to understand the functions of nonverbal communication, there are other useful ways to classify nonverbal behavior. One convenient method which provides insight into this variable of the communication process is to categorize nonverbal behavior according to its modes of expression. For example, all touching behavior can be grouped together, regardless of the functions the touches actually serve. Using this system, it is possible to examine nonverbal behavior along seven dimensions.

Proxemics

Proxemics, or the ways in which man structures and uses space in his daily life, is one of the key dimensions of nonverbal communication. The distances we maintain between ourselves and others, and our reactions to inappropriate spacing, have a potent impact on the communication process. A well-known example that illustrates the importance of proxemics comes from an embassy cocktail party. A newly arrived American diplomat was carrying on a conversation with his Arab host. As was the custom in his country, the Arab moved up very close to the American. This made the American very uncomfortable, so he retreated a few feet. Not used to such a distance, the Arab moved in again, and again the American retreated. This comedy of advance and retreat continued until the Arab had literally chased the American across the length of the room. The American's impression of the Arab was that he was pushy, while the Arab regarded the American as cold and aloof. Clearly, each person had sent unintentional messages through his use of space.

This example highlights one of the underlying concepts of proxemics: man's need for certain amounts of space. Man seems to have two different types of spatial needs, the first of which is *territoriality*. Like animals, man apparently carves out territories. A father's workshop is his territory, just as the kitchen is generally perceived as the mother's territory. Likewise, a family's home and property are its territory, which means that they are not openly accessible to strangers or intruders. Some people demand more territory than others. For instance, the Japanese seem to be satisfied with very little space for their homes, whereas in other cultures, such as our own, people feel hemmed in if they do not have large living space. Perhaps the key variable is not so much the actual amount of space available as it is the individual's perception of the adequacy of that space.

The physical and social effects of inadequate territory are illuminated by various studies of overcrowded conditions. A classic study with rats found that even when there was plenty of food and water available in their environment, the rats became aggressive, neurotic, sexually deviant and ill when their territory was reduced by overpopulation.[1] A French sociological study found similar results among inhabitants of Paris, which

---

[1] J.B. Calhoun, "Population Density and Social Pathology," *Scientific American*, 206 (February, 1962), pp. 139-146.

suggests that an analogous situation may be developing in our cities.[2] The avoidance of communication or heated confrontations that characterize residents of particularly congested areas may be partially attributable to inadequate territory.

Man's other spatial need is for *personal space*. Personal space differs from territory in that it is not a fixed geographic area. Rather, it is an invisible "bubble" of space that the individual carries with him. Depending on the situation, a person's need for space may expand or contract; personal space has no rigid boundary. If a person is in a formal situation, he will probably feel much more need for personal space than if he is in an intimate one. In addition to the degree of intimacy of a situation, a multitude of other factors affect a person's needs or preferences for space.

Determinants of personal space preferences A person's *sex* will partly determine his choice of distance in an interaction. In general, two females will sit or stand closer to each other than they will to males; males in turn will sit or stand closer to the opposite sex than they will to each other. The *race* of the interactants may also affect distance. Not surprisingly, whites and blacks usually maintain greater distance from each other than from people of their own race.

A third factor is *status*. As a sign of respect, we generally stand further away from people who are of higher status. It is easy to tell by watching subordinates approach a seated business executive just what their status relationship is; those who stand in the doorway are likely to be of much lower status than those who walk up to the edge of his desk. Or notice the degree of deference students show professors in the distance they maintain. Closely related to status is the effect of *age*. We often stand closer to our peers than to persons who are older or younger.

Another determinant of our use of space is *personality*. Persons who are extroverted and outgoing are willing to be closer to others than those who are shy and introverted. A recent interesting finding suggests that aggression may be connected to personal space needs. In a prison study, two groups of men were tested on their reactions to people closing in on them. One group of prisoners had histories of violent behavior; the other

---

[2] P. Chombart de Lauwe, *Famille et Habitation* (Paris: Editions du Centre National de la Recherche Scientific, 1959).

group did not. The men were told to stand in the middle of a room, while a person slowly walked toward them. The prisoners were instructed to say "Stop" when they felt that the invader was too close. The men in the violent group kept the invader twice as far away as the men in the nonviolent group. In terms of volume, the violent men required personal space zones which were four times the size of the men in the nonviolent group.[3]

Yet another factor determining spatial preference is *cultural norms*, the standards of behavior which the society considers correct. Anthropological observations suggest that standards of spatial use vary greatly in different societies. For most Americans, the average conversational distance when standing ranges from 18 to 28 inches; distances closer than 18 inches are presumably reserved for intimate interactions.[4] In comparison to other cultures, Americans tend to maintain greater distances from one another. This difference has created some embarrassing situations in the past for American travelers in Italy and Latin America who misinterpreted the friendly advances of the natives. There is some evidence now, however, that these cultural differences are becoming less noticeable.[5] It is possible that international travel and the mass media are helping to standardize cultural norms regarding personal distance.

Overriding many of the above variables is personal attraction. As would be expected, people approach much closer to someone they find attractive; people are also much more willing to tolerate the approach of someone they find attractive. Similar to the effect of attraction is the degree of acquaintanceship. People maintain a greater distance from strangers than from acquaintances, and they come closest to friends.[6] This makes sense, since if we are not attracted to a person, that person remains only an acquaintance or even a stranger. If we are attracted to someone, a friendship usually develops.

Other influences on personal distance are such situational variables as the *topic*, the *social situation* and a person's *psychological state*. All of these factors affect a person's spatial

---

[3] A.F. Kinzel, "Towards an Understanding of Violence," *Attitude I*, No. 1 (1969).

[4] F.N. Willis, "Initial Speaking Distance as a Function of the Speaker's Relationship," *Psychometric Science*, 5 (1966), pp. 221-222.

[5] R.F. Forston and C.U. Larson, "The Dynamics of Space: An Experimental Study in Proxemic Behavior Among Latin Americans and North Americans," *Journal of Communication*, 18 (1968), pp. 109-116.

[6] K.B. Little, "Personal Space," *Journal of Experimental and Social Psychology*, 1 (1965), pp. 237-247.

Figure 4-2 Birds, like many animals, seem to have instinctual territorial needs. Although man too has a need for territory, his use of space seems to be determined by many personal, cultural and situational variables.

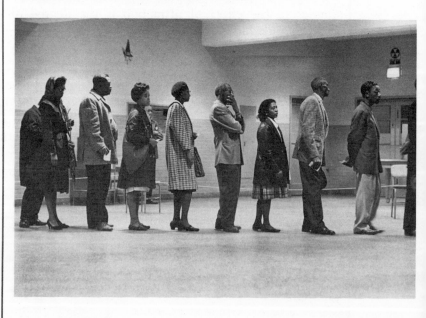

needs at a given moment. One study showed that students expecting to receive praise from a professor sat closer to him than students who expected to receive an unfavorable report of their class progress.[7] Similarly, people are likely to stand closer in an informal situation than in a formal one because the nature of the social event has altered their personal space needs. Most people have experienced moments when they were so upset that they preferred others, even intimate friends, to keep their distance. Of course, in many situations an individual may feel that his personal space has been invaded, that is, he has less space than he needs. To cope with such situations, a person may communicate his discomfort in a variety of ways. Experts have determined that there are several patterns of response to the invasion of personal space.

Responses to personal space invasion You can discover some responses to personal space invasion by conducting a simple experiment: find a fellow student by himself at a large library table, then sit down in the seat immediately next to him. Chances are that the person will first try to counteract your intrusion by avoiding eye contact, shifting his body orientation away from you and creating "barriers" with such objects as books or coats. If that fails, he may glare at you, or perhaps even subject you to verbal abuse. If all else fails, he may take flight. Responses will differ from person to person but nearly all will show signs of discomfort.[8]

In such places as a crowded elevator or bus, a different response pattern is likely to occur. People have learned that in such instances, invasion of their personal space is necessary. They cope with the situation by treating other people around them as nonpersons or objects. The next time you find yourself in such a place, notice the absence of eye contact and the rigid posture of the other people. This behavior helps to reduce some of the tension created by strangers who are in a space zone usually reserved for intimates. As explained by Robert Sommer, an expert in proxemics:

A nonperson cannot invade someone's personal space anymore than

---

[7] W.E. Leipold, *Psychological Distance in a Dyadic Interview*, Unpublished doctoral dissertation, University of South Dakota, 1963.

[8] M.L. Patterson, S. Mullens and J. Romano, "Compensatory Reactions to Spatial Intrusion," *Sociometry*, 34 (1971), pp. 114-121; N.J. Felipe and R. Sommer, "Invasions of Personal Space," *Social Problems*, 14 (1966), pp. 206-214; and J. C. Baxter and B.F. Deanovitch, "Anxiety Effects of Inappropriate Crowding," *Journal of Consulting and Clinical Psychology*, 35 (1970), pp. 174-178.

a tree or chair can. It is common under certain conditions for one person to react to another as an object or part of the background.[9]

The perception of a personal space invasion may also affect the communication interaction between two people. If you invade your neighbor's space, he is likely to show increased arm and body movements, more vocalized pauses ("ums" and "ers"), greater verbosity, more tension and less flexibility in his communication. He may also have a less favorable attitude toward what you are saying. However you may benefit in some respects from your status as an invader. There is some evidence that you will be perceived as more competent, more dynamic and more composed.[10] The overwhelming conclusion to be drawn from all of this is that our use of space is a significant element of nonverbal communication.

Figure 4-3 In overcrowded situations, people tend to treat others as objects. This behavior is often evidenced by lack of eye contact and rigid posture.

Chronemics

An interesting but often overlooked dimension of nonverbal communication is *chronemics,* or our use of time. Our music gives strong evidence of the meanings conveyed by time. Our notions of time, how we "use" it, the timing of events, our emotional responses to time, even the length of our pauses—all

---

[9] R. Sommer, *Personal Space* (Englewood Cliffs, N.J.: Prentice-Hall, 1969), p. 24.

[10] P. Garner, *The Effects of Personal Space on Interpersonal Communication,* Masters thesis, Illinois State University, 1972.

of these contribute to its communicative effect. Just recall a few phrases from some musical favorites: "Time, oh good, good time, where did you go," "Time won't let me," and "I'll stay until it's time for you to go." Or consider such expressions as "dead time," "lead time," "time on our hands," and "making time." Clearly, we are time-conscious and conscious of the meanings conveyed by the way we deal with time.

Our sensitivity to time is partly revealed through our reliance on clocks. Notice how few people you meet in a single day who do not wear a watch. We are so obsessed with time, in fact, that we become genuinely disturbed if a few minutes are "wasted." After all, "time is money." We view time as a commodity to be spent, earned, saved or wasted. We also divide time into small increments; we are even conscious of passing seconds. In contrast, other cultures have less concrete notions of time. To them, time is a vague sense of the present. It is "here and now," and punctuality is not valued. The Sioux Indians have this orientation. In their language, there are no words for "late" and "waiting." Among the Pueblo Indians, things take place "when the time is right," whenever that may be. Such cultural differences in peoples' attitudes toward time have caused many problems for government officials and businessmen at home and abroad. The federal government lost thousands of dollars on construction projects because the Hopi Indians did not have a concept of a "fixed date" by which a house or a road would be completed. Many American businessmen have told angry tales of having to wait a half-hour or longer to see an Arab or Latin American associate. To Americans, a waiting period of this length is an insult, but in other cultures it is appropriate. As noted by J. Horton in his essay "Time and Cool People," young blacks today also have a different sense of time, which they use to communicate their values and attitudes toward white society:

> Negro street time is built around the irrelevance of clock time, white man's time, and the relevance of street values and activities. Like anyone else, a street dude is on time by the standard clock whenever he wants to be, not on time when he does not want to be and does not have to be.
>
> When the women in school hit the street at the lunch hour and he wants to throw them a rap, he will be there then and not one hour after they have left. But he may be kicked out of high school for truancy or lose his job for being late and unreliable. . . .
>
> In the street, watches have a special and specific meaning. Watches are for pawning and not for telling time. . . .

Personal time as expressed in parties and other street activities is not simply deficient knowledge and use of standard time. It is a positive adaptation to generations of living whenever and wherever possible outside of the sound of the white man's clock. The personal clock is an adaptation to the chance and accidental character of events on the street and to the very positive value placed on emotion and feeling."[11]

The ways in which Americans use time can be divided into three sets: technical, formal and informal.[12] *Technical time* is used in certain professions such as astronomy, but the terminology (solar, sidereal and anamolistic year) carries little meaning for the layman. *Formal time* is our traditional conscious time structure. It includes our division of time into days, months, years and seasons. Our uses of cycles of time, such as day and night, our valuation of time, our perceptions of its depth, duration and tangibility are all part of our formal time system. Edward Hall has commented on the importance of formal time patterns to Americans:

The American never questions the fact that time should be planned and future events fitted into a schedule. He thinks that people should look forward to the future and not dwell too much in the past. His future is not very far ahead of him. Results must be obtained in the foreseeable future—one or two years or, at most, five or ten. Promises to meet deadlines and appointments are taken very seriously. There are real penalties for being late and for not keeping commitments in time.[13]

The third system, *informal time*, is the one that causes us the most difficulty because it is loosely defined and out of consciousness. Whereas the vocabulary of informal time is generally the same as that of formal time, its meaning is less clear because it is dependent on the context rather than clear-cut definitions. Moreover, the informal manner in which it is learned means that we are usually not consciously aware of it.

One element of our informal system is the way we communicate urgency through time. If you received a phone call at two in the morning, you would undoubtedly assume that the call was urgent, whereas a call received at two in the afternoon would be routine. Our timing of events is also a part of our informal

[11] J. Horton, "Time and Cool People," in L.A. Samovar and R.E. Porter, eds., *Intercultural Communication: A Reader* (Belmont, Calif.: Wadsworth Publishing, 1972), pp. 84-96.

[12] For a detailed discussion of chronemics see Edward Hall, *The Silent Language* (Greenwich, Conn.: Fawcett Publications, Inc., 1959).

[13] *Ibid*, p. 134.

time system. A hostess may plan a dinner party for a Friday or Saturday night because she and her guests do not have to work the next day. In dating situations, timing can be very critical: when do you first kiss a girl, how far in advance do you call for a date, how late do you keep her out? In our verbal communication, the placement of pauses and climaxes is of equal importance. Most of us are familiar with the importance of timing to the success of comedians such as Jack Benny and Bob Hope.

Americans use of informal time seems to follow two clear-cut patterns. Some people habitually operate in a *diffused point pattern*: they arrive somewhere around the appointed time. They may be early or late, but they have some built-in maximum range of acceptability and are usually consistent in either their early or late arrival pattern. In contrast, those who operate on the *displaced point pattern* see the appointed time as a fixed boundary that cannot be violated. These are the people who usually come at the scheduled time or earlier.

In general, people have tendencies to follow either the diffused or the displaced point pattern; however, the nature of an event may also determine which pattern is used. The diffused point pattern is perfectly acceptable for a shopping trip, but for a business appointment, it is appropriate to arrive early or on time but never late (five minutes beyond the scheduled time being considered late). Conversely, if you are invited to a cocktail party at 6:00, you often aren't really expected until 7:00 or later. However, if dinner is to be served, it is required that you arrive promptly at 6:00 or at the very latest 6:15. Misjudgments and misuses of these informal time systems can lead others to inaccurately interpret our nonverbal behavior. The person who is habitually late on the job expresses disinterest, disorganization and disrespect for his employer. The party guest who stays long after the others have departed may communicate insensitivity and selfishness by his dallying.

Another element of our informal time system is *duration*, a particularly potent element in our culture. Each person has his own definition of what is a short, long or impossibly long period of time. With Americans' heightened sensitivity to the passage of time, forever may actually be a relatively short period, technically speaking. Five minutes may be impossibly long if a person is waiting to see the dentist. Because we attribute meanings to the amount of time we have to wait to see someone, it is possible nonverbally to tell someone what we think of him through this mode. One person who had a keen understanding of this use of time was Harry Truman. When he was President, an important editor who came to see him was kept waiting 45 minutes. When an aide informed Truman that the editor was becoming impatient, Truman replied that when he was junior senator from Missouri, that same editor had kept him "cooling his heels" in the outer office for an hour and a half. As far as he was concerned, the SOB had 45 minutes to go.

Kinesics

A more traditionally studied dimension of nonverbal communication is *kinesics*, or the visual aspects of behavior. Included under this heading are movement and posture, gestures, facial expressions and eye behavior. These modes of behavior have long been recognized as carrying meaning in an interaction. At the turn of the century, a movement even developed—the elocutionary movement—to teach people how to convey emotions through various body positions, facial expressions and gestures. For instance, the upturned palms signified supplication; the outturned hand at the brow showed distress or fear. These artificial behaviors can be seen in the old silent movies. Although people may ridicule such overdramatizing, kinesic behaviors are still being prescribed in speech classes today. Consider a few excerpts from a contemporary public speaking text:

> Stand with the feet no more than six inches apart, with one foot somewhat behind the other. . . .

> Keep the shoulders on a level, and avoid the sailor's roll. . . .

> Keep a hand on the lectern, even though in this maneuver you will be shifting hands at the back corner of the stand as you turn. . . .

> [When gesturing] start the movement by letting the *wrist* lead; the hand *follows* at first and gradually catches up by the time the stroke is reached. . . .

> Keep your eyes on your hearers.[14]

These recommendations underline the belief that kinesic behavior is important, but they fail to point out the impact that these gestures will presumably have on a receiver. Only recently have people begun to scientifically study the effect of kinesic behavior in a communication situation.

---

[14] D.C. Bryant and K.R. Wallace, *Oral Communication* (New York: Appleton-Century-Crofts, 1962).

Figure 4-4 The pointed finger signifying accusation and the clutched hand signifying fear are examples of exaggerated kinesic behavior which were used in silent movies.

Sex and individual differences Much of our kinesic behavior signals our gender. Men and women have characteristically different ways of sitting and standing. Notice, for instance, differences in the way men and women cross their legs. In general, women use fewer gestures than men, but engage in more eye contact.[15] People have strong stereotypes of masculine and feminine behavior. As a result, the man who deviates from the norm may be regarded as effeminate or homosexual, when his kinesic behaviors may actually have been learned because they were appropriate for his ethnic background or because they were comfortable. Similarly, women who deviate may be considered unattractive or domineering.

In addition to basic patterns of kinesic behavior which seem based on sex differences, people do develop their own unique patterns that remain fairly consistent over time. Each person has his own characteristic head and shoulder movements, gestures and gaze patterns. For example, the amount of time a person

[15] For an extended discussion of gestures see P. Ekman and W.V. Friesen, "Hand Movements," *Journal of Communication*, 22 (1972), pp. 353-374. For an extended discussion of eye behavior see P.C. Elisworth and L.M. Ludwig, "Visual Behavior in Social Interaction," *Journal of Communication*, 22 (1972), pp. 375-401.

spends in directly gazing at another may range from 28 percent to 70 percent of the total time of the interaction. Because of wide variations in individuals, it is possible to misinterpret idiosyncratic behavior. A person who yawns when he's anxious may be perceived as tired or uninterested. Thus the wise receiver is cautious in making quick judgments from kinesic behaviors.

Liking, affiliation and affective states Our bodies communicate much about our feelings towards others. If we lean forward or face a person directly, we probably like the person; conversely, if we lean back or turn our face away, we probably dislike the person. People often mirror the sitting or standing positions of someone they like or agree with. Long gazes and less frequent glances are interpreted as liking. A person's degree of muscular relaxation further connotes liking; people are moderately relaxed with those they like.

Our liking of others is additionally reflected in the way we include them within a communication circle. When we wish to affiliate with others, we often use our body to form an inclusive unit. We may cross our legs and orient our bodies toward the person we wish to include. While doing this, we may also use our arms and legs as barriers to others we want to exclude from the interaction. Most people use direct eye contact to further cement the bond. They avoid eye contact with those who attempt to intrude, or alternatively glare at them. As with other dimensions of nonverbal behavior, cultural differences may change the kinesic pattern associated with liking or disliking other people. Some blacks have developed their own effective means of communicating dislike or disapproval: they roll their eyes. Although such behavior may not be noticed by whites, other blacks are usually very aware of it and the meaning of the behavior is clear.[16]

Our emotional states are also revealed through the body, face and eyes. Head orientation is usually an indicator of a person's general mood or gross affective state, whereas the face gives clues to specific feelings. Altogether, there are at least thirty-three distinguishable major head and face movements.[17] Most people are fairly accurate in deciding whether a person feels pleasant

---

[16] K.R. Johnson, "Black Kinesics: Some Non-verbal Communication Patterns in the Black Culture," in L.A. Samovar and R.E. Porter, eds., *Intercultural Communication: A Reader* (Belmont, Calif.: Wadsworth Publishing, 1972), pp. 181-189.

[17] R. Birdwhistell, *Kinesics and Context* (Philadelphia: University of Pennsylvania Press, 1970).

or unpleasant, relaxed or tense. Beyond that, however, it becomes difficult to make accurate judgments. For instance, a person probably cannot distinguish between rage and resentment, happiness and amusement, or pride and confidence.

Figure 4-5 Facial expressions serve as clues to a person's general emotional state. However, it is difficult to distinguish between similar emotions such as joy and pleasure, or grief and despair.

Another source of information about a person's mood is the frequency of his gestures. When we are tired, demoralized or unenthusiastic, we use fewer gestures than when we are excited, happy and refreshed. Similarly, people reduce eye contact when they are criticized and increase it when they are praised or accepted.

Status and background   Kinesic behaviors are cues not only to our situational state, but also to our general status and background. For example, Italian-Americans use different gestures than Mexican-Americans. K. R. Johnson in his examination of kinesic patterns among blacks has commented on the unique walk adopted by some young blacks to signal masculinity and sensuality:

> The young Black males' walk is different. First of all, it's much slower—it's more of a stroll. The head is sometimes slightly elevated and casually tipped to the side. Only one arm swings at the side with the hand slightly cupped. The other arm hangs limply to the side or it's tucked in the pocket. The gait is slow, casual and rhythmic. The gait is almost a walking dance, with all parts of the body moving in rhythmic harmony. This walk is . . . referred to as "walking that walk."[18]

Gestures may also indicate social class. Working class women tend to use more "masculine" gestures, as do working class men.[19] Status is also revealed through the eye behavior of others. The more eye contact a person receives, the greater his power and status is perceived to be.

Interaction controls   A major function that kinesic behaviors perform is controlling the flow of communication. People have several means of indicating when they are willing to listen and when they want to talk. Leaning back may signal that a person is listening, whereas leaning forward signals that he wants to talk. When we use eye contact and a head movement, we tell another person that he may begin speaking. Conversely, looking away or filling a pause with a gesture is a way of preventing an interruption and maintaining control of the conversation. One other way a person may indirectly control an interaction is by using direct, continuous eye contact to signal his desire for feedback and to demand attention. Since the face is such a good indicator of the way someone feels about us, it is natural that we look at the face frequently when we want feedback. This tends to force the other person's attention on ourselves and to induce nonverbal or verbal feedback.

---

[18] K.R. Johnson, *op. cit.*

[19] L. Hamalian, "Communication by Gesture in the Middle East," *ETC.*, 22 (1965), pp. 43-49.

Verbal substitution   Particularly good examples of the way nonverbal behavior may substitute for verbal expressions are gestures. A waving hand means hello or good-by, and a finger pressed to the temple like a gun means suicide. Similarly, eye, face and head movements substitute for words. Lowered eyes, a frown and a shake of the head may all signal "no."

The problem with kinesic behavior as verbal substitutes is that they don't always have shared meaning. One Vice-President learned this when he traveled through Latin America on a good-will tour. As he stepped off the plane in one country, he held up his hand in the AOK sign (thumb and forefinger touching to form a circle) to show that he was happy to be there. To his dismay, the crowd booed him. They were equally dismayed by his behavior. He had made what was considered in their country an obscene gesture.

Contradiction and deception   A final function that kinesic behavior performs is contradiction of the verbal message. The girl who says "no" verbally may actually have "yes" in her eyes. When the verbal message is contradicted by the nonverbal behavior, people tend to believe the nonverbal message.[20] Such contradictions are usually not intentional. For instance, when a person raves about an unwanted birthday present, he does not want the gift giver to suspect his true feelings. But when a person is trying to deceive another, his body may give off totally unconscious cues that betray his true feelings or intent.

For highly perceptive observers, small changes in facial expressions can provide clues to a person's actual feelings.[21] But these are often difficult to observe, since people try to disguise their attitudes by controlling facial expression. Easier to read indicators are hand, leg and foot movements. People are less careful to control these parts of their bodies, because they do not expect them to be noticed. Consequently nonverbal behavior can leak information about the real state of affairs. Jiggling feet and legs unconsciously reveal anxiety, nervousness and fear. When there is an increase in fidgety, anxiety-revealing gestures, there is also generally a reduction in illustrative gestures. An increase in hand shrugs has also been found to occur when people are

---

[20] For partial support see E. Tabor, *Decoding of Consistent and Inconsistent Attitudes in Communication*, Unpublished doctoral dissertation, Illinois Institute of Technology, 1970.

[21] E.A. Haggard and K.S. Issacs, "Micromomentary Facial Expressions as Indicators of Ego Mechanisms in Psychotherapy," in L.A. Gottschalk and A.H. Auerback, eds., *Methods of Research on Psychotherapy* (New York: Appleton-Century-Crofts, 1966).

induced to lie.[22] Deception may further be suggested through a person's eye contact. Since direct eye contact connotes honesty, the person who is lying may avoid eye contact for fear that his eyes will give him away. Others may attempt to maintain a direct gaze, but they are likely to overcompensate. If you suspect someone of lying, look for nonverbal cues, especially from the hands, arms, legs and feet.

Paralanguage

Paralanguage is concerned with the use of the voice in communication. It focuses on how we say something rather than what we say. It is therefore referred to as the *vocal* element of speech, as opposed to the *verbal* element, which is the words and their meanings. Actually, our vocal behavior is often critical to understanding the meanings of words. Consider the following sentence:

"How could she do it?"

Depending on whether the emphasis was on "how," "could," "she" or "do," the sentence would carry different meaning. Thus paralanguage means an accessory to or subsidiary of language. Our vocal behavior is instrumental to understanding our language.

Paralanguage can be broken down into several categories. *Voice quality* is the characteristic tonal quality of the voice, based on such factors as resonance, articulation, lip control and rhythm control. *Intensity* or the pressure of sound waves which are perceived as loud or soft is another area of vocal behavior. *Rate and timing* refer to the speed at which a person speaks and the length and location of pauses. *Pitch*, another element of paralanguage, is the typical frequency and range of the voice. *Vocal segregates* are nonfluencies or irregularities ("ers" and "ums") in our speech patterns. *Fluency* is the term used to describe the absence of distractions such as repetitions, hesitations, stuttering, vocal segregates, and false starts. *Vocal patterns* include inflectional patterns, dialects and other combinations of vocal elements that form identifiable patterns. The final area of paralanguage focuses on *vocal characterizations*, such things as crying, laughing, yelling, sneezing, sighing and snorting.

The combination of all these elements should produce in each of us a unique voice. Who could question the uniqueness of the

---

[22] P. Ekman and W.V. Freisen, *op. cit.*

voices of Everett Dirksen, Marlene Dietrich or Howard Cosell? The fact that the FBI has begun using voice prints along with finger prints to identify criminals confirms the singularity of our vocal behavior. However, our voices are not often perceived by others as unique, but are rather used to place us into stereotyped categories. Both our personal characteristics and our personalities are stereotyped on the basis of our voice.

Personal characteristics and personality stereotypes A person listening to our voice without seeing us can pick up fairly accurate cues to our age, sex, race, height, weight, body type, status, occupation, education and regional dialect. One extensive study found that listeners could distinguish between male and female, black and white, and big and small speakers.[23] They could differentiate among 20- to 30-, 40- to 50-, and 60- to 70-year-olds, and among those with less than a high school education, high school graduates and college graduates. They also identified regional dialects. Another study on height, weight and body type found the extremes were more accurately judged.[24] People are surprisingly accurate in determining status.

We have developed strong stereotypes of personality based on voice quality. Males and females with flat voices are both perceived as cold, sluggish, withdrawn and masculine. Persons with nasal voices are seen as whiney, nagging and unpleasant. Males with a breathy voice are perceived as young and artistic; breathy females are seen as feminine, petite, pretty, high strung, shallow and not very intelligent. Males with a throaty voice are regarded as mature, well-adjusted and sophisticated, whereas females with a throaty voice are considered masculine, stupid, boorish, lazy, dull and ugly. Stridency in a voice signals mental illness. Except for the latter, many of these stereotypes may be inaccurate. A variety of studies have found mixed results on the accuracy of vocal cues as predictors of personality traits.[25]

Related to personality is the judgment of a person's credibility. Recent studies of responses to dialects are beginning to reveal that a person does perceive others differently because of their

---

[23] G.P. Nerbonne, *The Identification of Speaker Characteristics on the Basis of Aural Cues*, Unpublished doctoral dissertation, Michigan State University, 1967.

[24] P. Fay and W. Middleton, "Judgments of Kretschmerian Body Types From the Voice as Transmitted Over a Public Address System," *Journal of Social Psychology*, 12 (1940), pp. 151-162.

[25] See Mark L. Knapp, *Nonverbal Communication in Human Interaction* (New York: Holt, Rinehart and Winston, 1972), pp. 151-155.

dialect.[26] For example, the female New Yorker is seen as more dynamic but less sociable in comparison with the female Southerner, who is seen as the least composed of any of five regional speakers. The New York and Central American dialects are perceived as indicators of more competence than the Northeastern, Southeastern and Southern dialects. Other studies have dealt with ethnic dialects. Both Jews and Gentiles rated a speaker with a Jewish accent low on leadership and good looks, but Jews also rated the speaker high on humor, kindness and his ability to entertain.[27] Such studies provide further testimony to the impact of voice in characterizing individual traits and personality.

Emotions   A person's vocal behavior may provide clues to his emotional state. For instance, a loud, high-pitched, irregular, clipped voice may communicate anger, while a slow, slurred, soft voice with irregular pauses and downward inflections may signal sadness.[28] Yet many individual differences exist in communicating the same emotion. Moreover, the same emotion can be expressed in different ways at different times. A person may shout one time when he is angry and whisper intensely another. Persons also differ in their sensitivity and accuracy in judging vocal cues. Consequently, no firm statements can be made about which vocal behaviors signal which emotions. We only know that emotion is being conveyed.

The findings on vocal cues as stereotyped indicators of personal characteristics, personality and emotion all view paralanguage from the source's point of view in the communication process. Another approach is to consider the effects of vocal behavior on the receiver. Do certain kinds of vocal behavior increase comprehension in the receiver? Can vocal behavior enhance the possibility of persuading another person?

Comprehension and persuasion   It has generally been presumed that rapid speech, poor vocal quality and nonfluencies interfere with comprehension of what a person is saying. Studies on intelligibility have found that highly intelligible speakers use

---

[26] J.K. Tomb, J.Q. Quiggins, D.L. More, J.B. MacNeill and C.M Liddell, *The Effects of Regional Dialects on Initial Source Credibility*, Paper presented at the International Communication Convention, Atlanta, Georgia, April 1972.

[27] M. Anisfeld, N. Bogo and W. Lamert, "Evaluation Reaction to Accented English Speech," *Journal of Abnormal and Social Psychology*, 65 (1962), pp. 223-231.

[28] J.R. Davitz, *The Communication of Emotional Meaning* (New York: McGraw-Hill, 1964).

longer syllable duration, greater intensity, less pause time and more pitch variety.[29] Nevertheless, research has also shown that listeners are highly adaptable to differences in vocal presentations. For example, a rapid rate of speaking with little pause time does not seriously hurt comprehension.[30] In fact, as long as a speaker is understandable, poor vocal quality, pitch variety and fluency do not reduce comprehension in a receiver. Surprisingly, it has been found that stutterers may be more effective speakers because people pay closer attention to what they are saying.

Little is known about the effect of vocal behavior on persuasion. It is known that voices with more intonation, more volume, faster rate and more fluency are perceived as more persuasive.[31] Yet to the contrary, one study showed that speakers with large numbers of nonfluencies were as persuasive as speakers with few nonfluencies.[32] Although this latter finding is consistent with other findings that vocal cues affect credibility, there is no evidence to make conclusive statements about the direct impact of vocal cues on attitude change.

Haptics

Haptics, or our use of touch in the communication process, is just beginning to receive attention from serious researchers. Our need for touch seems to be powerful. We know, for instance, that monkeys raised without any contact with other monkeys will spend hours clinging to a cloth-covered wire figure preferring it to an uncovered figure that supplies food. This need for contact can also be seen in babies raised in orphanages and institutions. In many orphanages, babies are left for hours by themselves, lying in their beds in an environment with almost no sensory stimulation. They are rarely touched or held for any length of time. Such babies first become apathetic and lifeless, then develop bizarre behaviors; many even die. If human contact is so essential in early life, it seems reasonable to conclude that touch can have significant communicative value.

Yet in our culture, touch is discouraged as a mode of

[29] N.W. Heimstra and V.S. Ellingstad, *Human Behavior: A Systems Approach* (Monterey, Calif.: Brooks/Cole Publishing, 1972).

[30] D.B. Orr, "Time Compressed Speech—A Perspective," *Journal of Communication, 18* (1968), pp. 288-292.

[31] A. Mehrabian and M. Williams, "Nonverbal Concomitants of Perceived and Intended Persuasiveness," *Journal of Personality and Social Psychology, 13* (1969), pp. 37-58.

[32] G.R. Miller and M.A. Hegwill, "The Effect of Variations in Nonfluency on Audience Ratings of Source Credibility," *Quarterly Journal of Speech, 50* (1964), pp. 36-44.

communication. Our clothing styles and taboos about revealing our bodies reflects our inhibited view of touch. Boys learn at an early age that touching is not masculine, especially among males. This may explain the great attraction of contact sports for boys; it is one of the few situations in which body contact is condoned. The rituals of huddling in close contact and slapping on the basketball court demonstrate the recognized value of touch in communicating solidarity, supportiveness and enthusiasm.

For girls, touching is more acceptable. A girl may hug her father or mother without disapproval. It is permissible (though uncommon) for girls to hold hands or put their arms around one another, but unfavorable insinuations would be made about boys who did the same thing. It is possible that all findings on proxemic preferences, especially on sex differences, really indicate our fear and avoidance of touch. Thus males sit the farthest apart from each other because touching would be inappropriate.

This avoidance of touch is taught at an early age. As children, we are frequently told not to touch other objects, "improper" parts of Mommy's and Daddy's body and even parts of our own body. To compensate for reduced tactile stimulation, we formalize

Figure 4-6 In American society, touching, especially between men, is discouraged. However, in many other cultures, touching is an acceptable form of communication as this photograph of two rugby players illustrates.

acceptable forms of tactile interaction. The handshake, social dancing, the perfunctory kiss: all of these are acceptable means of communicating by touch. Touching certain parts of the body is also acceptable, if the touches are not prolonged. Brushing an arm or putting a hand on someone's shoulder is permissible, but touching his abdomen or thigh is not, except in overtly sexual situations.

Many of our touching taboos have evolved out of our sexual mores or moral attitudes. Touching in our culture carries with it sexual overtones. Since we are not a sexually free society, touching is frowned upon. Adolescents are taught not to touch their dates. Parents frequently avoid intimate contact in front of their children for fear of providing a "permissive" model of interpersonal behavior.

As a result of our disapproval of intimate behavior, we deny ourselves a meaningful avenue of communication. Touch can be an effective means of expressing understanding, sympathy, affection and interest. In one hospital, nurses who touched their patients found the patients had better attitudes toward them and increased their verbal output.[33] Encounter groups emphasize touching as a way of breaking down communication barriers. Through touch, members become more aware of each other and supposedly more sensitive to each other's needs. By allowing others to touch them, they make themselves vulnerable, which is a prerequisite to building trust.

If touch is so potent, why has it been so suppressed in our society? One explanation is that as societies progress, they substitute for touch other signs and symbols, such as language. From this perspective, touch, like drums, is regarded as a sign of a primitive society; refinement and "sophistication" thus dictate a reduction in such personal, ambiguous forms of communication as touch.

But our society is not likely to totally eliminate haptic communication. The recognition by clinical psychologists of the value of touching, the increasing popularity of the encounter movement, and the changing sexual mores of young people may instead contribute to an increasing acceptance of touching behavior. It may become possible for men openly to display affection through touch, as is already done in other cultures. And perhaps even the phrase "a touching scene" will take on a new meaning.

---

[33] D.C. Agulera, "Relationships Between Physical Contact and Verbal Interaction Between Nurses and Patients," *Journal of Psychiatric Nursing*, 5 (1967), pp. 5-21.

Physical appearance and adornment

Another dimension of nonverbal communication is the *physical appearance* of the human body. Our preoccupation with appearance was insightfully noted by the Earl of Chesterfield in the late eighteenth century:

> Women who are either indisputably beautiful, or indisputably ugly, are best flattered upon the score of their understandings; but those who are in a state of mediocrity are best flattered upon their beauty, or at least their graces; for every woman who is not absolutely ugly thinks herself handsome.[34]

We are very conscious of our appearance and that of others. Our body shape, height, weight, hair, dress, accessories and cosmetics are all read as clues to our personal characteristics, personality and attitudes.

Body shape, height and weight   Our bodies may be categorized as one of three general types: (1) the endomorph, which is soft, round and fat; (2) the mesomorph, which is bony, muscular and athletic, and (3) the ectomorph, which is tall, thin and fragile. Research has clearly shown that people stereotype our personality on the basis of our body types. Some personality attitudes connected with the endomorph are sluggishness, tolerance, affability, warmth, affection, generosity, complacency and kindness. Adjectives applicable to the mesomorph are dominant, cheerful, reckless, argumentative, hot-tempered, optimistic, enthusiastic, confident and efficient. The ectomorph is characterized as detached, introspective, serious, cautious, meticulous, thoughtful, sensitive, tactful, shy and suspicious.

Our body height and weight are also used by others to assess our competence. Endomorphs are frequently discriminated against in seeking jobs, whereas tall men seem to consistently win out over short men for jobs.[35] In fact, a University of Pittsburgh survey of graduates found men over 6'2" receiving higher starting salaries than men under 6'.

Body shape, height and weight all seem to be related to physical attractiveness. Our stereotyped image of the hero is someone who is tall and athletic, rather than short and fat. The stereotyped heroine is moderately tall and sleek. These stereotypes are perpetuated by the mass media in their selection of people who fit the "image" of a movie or TV star. Persons

---

[34] P.D. Stanhope, Earl of Chesterfield, in a letter, September 5, 1780, in J. Bartlett, *Familiar Quotations* (Boston: Little, Brown and Company, 1955), p. 323.

[35] Mark L. Knapp, *op. cit.*, p. 73.

who deviate from these images may therefore be perceived as less attractive. Since physical attraction is a key element in interpersonal attraction, this may explain the discrimination against short, fat, or overly thin people.

Hair   The current popularity of long hair and beards seems to have opened up a new means of nonverbal communication. Most bearded, long-haired men can testify to experiences of discrimination because of their appearances. Whether or not such an appearance is intended as defiance or rejection of society's values, it is interpreted as such by older generations. The reaction to long hair has been so strong that at times violent incidents have been known to occur. One study done by two college students tested the effects of hair and dress on people's willingness to sign a harmless petition. In one situation, the male student had long hair and a beard, and the female experimenter wore long hair; both had on "hippie" clothing. On the second occasion the male cut his hair and was clean shaven, the female wore her hair up, and both dressed "conservatively." Not surprisingly, significantly fewer people signed the petition of the "long hairs."

Dress and accessories   The test by the two college students gives a clue to the impact of dress on others. Numerous studies have been done on the effects of clothing. When persons are previously unacquainted, dress is a major influence on the first impression developed. Clothing has been found to be significantly related to the perceived status and social roles of others, to the social acceptability of high school students and to perceived political philosophies of the wearers. In a study limited to college students, persons dressed "less conventionally" have been classified as radical, pro-black, against the Vietnam War, left-wing and prone to marijuana use. Conversely, figures dressed "conventionally" have been perceived as career-oriented and favoring the traditional "fun and football" culture.[36] It should be noted, however, that once individuals become acquainted, dress seems to have no effect on their judgments. This may indicate that dress is used as a stereotypic guide to response only until first-hand personal knowledge provides a substitute.

The way we dress is consistently perceived by others as an indicator of certain personality traits. Girls rated high on good

---

[36] J. Kelly, *Dress and Non-Verbal Communication,* Paper presented at the Annual Conference of the American Association for Public Opinion Research, May 1969.

appearance were seen as more sociable and more intelligent.[37] Clothing preferences and awareness are also fairly stable aspects of dress. This consistency enhances the symbolic value of clothing. A person's typical dress is interpreted as a message about his life style, values, personality and attitudes toward others. An employer is likely to pick up signals of disrespect from the employee who always shows up in jeans, or signals of availability from the female secretary who wears short skirts and tight-fitting sweaters.

Accessories may also carry meaning. The presence or absence of jewelry and its style may indicate age, wealth and status. The style of a person's glasses may tell you something about his personality. Just the wearing of glasses has its effects: persons with glasses are rated more intelligent, dependable, industrious, conventional, shy and religious but less attractive and sophisticated.

Cosmetics   Intuitively, people perceive differences in women who do and do not wear makeup. A 1959 study found that women who wore lipstick were perceived as more frivolous, less talkative, more placid, more conscientious and, surprisingly, less interested in the opposite sex.[38] Today it is more likely that lipstick and other makeup would be a sign of greater interest in the opposite sex. Certainly cosmetic ads are predicated on this assumption. A recent phenomenon seems to indicate that cosmetic products are becoming more important for the American male. While sales of cosmetic goods for women have continued to rise in the past few years, the largest area of growth has occurred in products for men, including such items as skin toners, colognes and hair sprays.

Environment and objects

The last dimension of nonverbal communication that deserves mention is the environment and our use of objects. A person's office or home and its furnishings carry messages about him. Further, surroundings can significantly affect verbal interactions. The lighting, temperature, ventilation, size and architectural

[37] S.S. Silverman, *Clothing and Appearance; Their Psychological Meaning for Teen-age Girls*, Research monograph, Bureau of Publications, Teachers College, Columbia University, 1945.

[38] W. McKeachie, "Lipstick as a Determiner of First Impressions of Personality: An Experiment for the General Psychology Course, *Journal of Social Psychology*, 36 (1952), pp. 241-244.

style, color, furnishings and attractiveness of the environment are all important factors.

Consider some different settings. A bar or restaurant is dimly lit, with subdued colors. It features comfortable, intimately arranged chairs and tables to encourage its customers to linger. An office is usually brightly lit, properly ventilated, kept at a slightly cool temperature, painted in neutral (nondistracting and nonirritating) colors and furnished with functional chairs and desks that are not conducive to relaxation. A church sanctuary has lofty inspiring ceilings, subdued colors that set an atmosphere of peace and reflection, or reds and purples that are rich in religious symbolism, and stiff uncomfortable pews to force attention to the minister. Each setting conveys a message about the kind of activity and interaction that is acceptable in that atmosphere. The owners or designers can thus manipulate settings to suit their preferences. The restaurant owner who wants quick turnover in clientele will raise the lights and purchase less comfortable furniture. One businessman has been designing chairs explicitly intended to discourage people from sitting too long. A famous hotel replaced all its comfortable lobby furniture with hard benches and chairs to encourage people to circulate among its shops rather than sit. The same principle is employed in airports.

In this manner, the environment we control becomes an extension of ourselves. Our furnishings reflect our personalities and tastes. Persons who decorate in green say something different about themselves than persons who decorate in pink. The memorabilia that populate people's desks or rooms, even their stationery, give clues about themselves. Status can be clearly communicated by the elegance of a person's office and its location. For instance, offices in corners with windows and those with their own private door have more status than those located in the middle of a large room. Employees with large wooden desks clearly have more status than those with small metal ones. Business executives who recognize this can use office location and furnishings to motivate their workers.

Placement of furniture within a room may also carry a message. Notice, for example, where professors place their desks within their offices. Those who have their desks betwen themselves and the doorway have established a barrier that reduces their accessibility to students. The placement of furniture in a public setting can do much to increase or decrease interaction. Studies in hospitals and other public institutions, where chairs have been lined up along the walls for the convenience of janitors, have found very little interaction. Similarly, in a classroom with fixed rows of chairs, there is less overall interaction than with a circular arrangement. Conversely, in bars, where people are seated at tables in close proximity and in intimate arrangements, interaction is frequent and personal.

Other features of the environment that have an impact are its attractiveness and the degree of sensory stimulation it provides. In one study, subjects rated photographs of people's faces significantly higher in attractiveness when the subjects were in a "beautiful" room than when they were in an "ugly" room.[39] Unattractive rooms are seen as fatiguing and displeasing, whereas attractive rooms tend to create feelings of well-being. The degree of sensory stimulation can further contribute or detract from the atmosphere of a setting. There is a good deal of evidence to suggest that both understimulation and overstimulation are undesirable.

Our environment both communicates and impinges upon the communication process. The way we design and use the elements in our environment transmits messages about ourselves. Objects may also serve as symbolic communication. The use of flags, arm bands and campaign buttons are examples of the way people use objects to replace verbal communication. A fitting conclusion to this section is the story of a frustrated Californian who had tried in vain to receive compensation for his faulty new automobile. The dealer and the manufacturer both failed to respond satisfactorily to his claims. Realizing the futility of his efforts, he resorted to symbolic communication to protest his treatment: he painted big yellow lemons on the sides of his car and parked it in front of the dealer's office.

Nonverbal communication: A global approach

As knowledge of the individual elements of nonverbal communication is refined, experts are beginning to study them not separately but in combination. This global approach has been limited so far by the inability to determine which of several factors is producing a given effect. Nevertheless, to illustrate this kind of approach, let us conclude with a discussion of a form of interaction relevant to all people: quasi-courtship behavior.

---

[39] N.L. Mintz, "Effects of Esthetic Surroundings: II. Prolonged and Repeated Experience in a 'Beautiful' and 'Ugly' Room," *Journal of Psychology, 41* (1956), pp. 459-466.

In a series of interesting studies, A. E. Scheflen, a psychologist, has demonstrated that there are consistent patterns of human courtship behavior.[40] The term "quasi-courtship behavior" refers to the flirting games that go on between men and women, whether or not they are interested in each other. In many instances, it is merely a ritual in which both parties agree implicitly that it will not go beyond an understood point. They simply engage in the behavior to assert their own sexual attractiveness. In other instances, it serves as a prelude to more intimate relations. Quasi-courtship behavior then becomes a means of determining another's availability and approachability.

Figure 4-7 Some preening behavior of male psychotherapists
   A) Tie preen
   B) Sock preen
   C) Hair preen

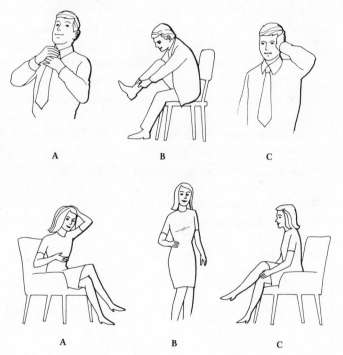

A   B   C

A   B   C

Figure 4-8 Appealing or invitational behavior of women patients
   A) Presenting the palm with hair press
   B) Rolling the hip
   C) Presenting and caressing the leg

---

[40] A.E. Scheflen, "Quasi-Courtship Behavior in Psychotherapy," *Psychiatry*, 28 (1965), pp. 245-257 and "The Significance of Posture in Communicative Systems," *Psychiatry*, 27 (1964), pp. 316-331.

The ritual frequently begins with extended, penetrating eye contact, which creates emotional arousal. Women hold their thighs together, walk with their upper arms against their body and tilt their pelvises slightly forward. Men stand with their thighs apart, hold their arms away from their body, swing them as they walk, and carry their pelvises slightly back. Attraction is further evidenced by heightened muscle tone and erect postures. Men pull their stomachs in, whereas women throw their chests out to emphasize their breasts. Both sexes engage in preening behavior: tugging at socks, rearranging clothes and makeup, stroking hair and glancing in mirrors. If women are open to a man's advances, they may cross their legs to expose a thigh, unfold their arms, engage in flirting glances and roll their hips. Both men and women may open more buttons on their shirt or blouse than they usually do.

In the advanced stages, men and women may invade each other's personal space. This also has an arousing effect. If seated, they will close others out by their shoulder and leg positions. Once an intimate distance has been established, touching is likely to occur. Men may brush a woman's arm; women may touch a man's thigh. If contact progresses beyond this stage, chances are it is no longer "quasi-" courtship behavior.

When nonverbal elements are viewed in this global sense, their communication potential is significantly increased. Out of context, a single behavior may be misinterpreted; placed in the context of a given location and type of interaction, nonverbal behaviors take on more accurate meaning. When the message transmitted by one behavior is echoed by that of another, we can better interpret its meaning.

1. Nonverbal communication includes any intentional or unintentional nonverbal behavior which affects the interaction between two people. Objects and features of the environment which convey meanings about their owners may also be included in a discussion of nonverbal communication.

2. Nonverbal behavior seems to serve six functions in the communication process. It may repeat, highlight, replace, regulate, complement or contradict the verbal message.

3. Nonverbal communication may be classified along seven dimensions or modes of expression: proxemics, chronemics, kinesics, paralanguage, haptics, physical appearance and adornment, and environment and objects.

4. Proxemics is the study of the ways in which man structures and uses space to communicate. Man has two spatial needs: territoriality and personal space. Sex, race, status, age, personality variables, cultural norms, personal attraction, and situational variables all effect an individual's space needs. People resent invasions of their personal space and have developed several response patterns to deal with such invasions.

5. Chronemics is the study of the way man uses time. American use of time falls into three categories or sets: technical time, or scientific breakdowns which have little bearing on nonverbal communication; formal time, or the traditional, conscious divisions of time such as years, months and days; and informal time which is dependent on the context of a communication situation for its definition. American use of informal time follows two patterns: the diffused point pattern in which people arrive somewhere around the appointed time, and the displaced point pattern in which people arrive at or before the appointed time.

6. Kinesics, or the visual aspects of behavior, has long been

recognized as carrying meaning in a communication interaction. Sex often influences kinesic behavior; however, every individual develops his own unique kinesic patterns. A person uses his body to communicate much about his feelings toward others. A person's emotional state may be revealed through body, face, eye movements and gestures. Kinesic behavior may also serve as clues to an individual's status and background.

7. Paralanguage is the study of the vocal (as opposed to verbal) aspects of speech. Research has shown that a person's voice can provide clues to his age, sex, race, height and other personal characteristics. People have also developed strong stereotypes of personality based on voice quality. A person's dialect may, in fact, affect a receiver's perception of his credibility. Little is known about the effect of vocal behavior on persuasion, but research has shown that listeners are highly adaptable to different vocal presentations. Poor vocal quality does not seem to reduce the receiver's comprehension as long as the speaker can be understood.

8. Haptics is the study of man's use of touch. Touch has significant communicative value, but in our society it has been discouraged as a mode of communication except in intimate relationships.

9. Our physical appearance may also carry messages to another person. People tend to stereotype our personalities on the basis of our body type. Research indicates that people may perceive our weight and height as indicators of our competence. In addition, hair, dress, accessories and cosmetics are often used as indicators of certain personality traits. Dress is most typically seen as a message about a person's lifestyle. However, once people are acquainted, dress seems to have no effect on their judgment.

10. The physical characteristics of the environment can affect the nature of the communication activities which take place in it. Linear arrangements of furniture tend to inhibit communication interaction. The furnishings of an environment often serve as clues to an individual's personality and status. Objects in the environment such as flags may function as symbolic communication.

1. The next time you are engaged in a conversation, move as close as you can to the other person. Observe and later record the other person's reaction to your behavior. In what ways did the other person indicate his discomfort?

2. The next time you are in an uncrowded elevator stand as close as you can to a stranger. Observe the stranger's reaction to your behavior. Compare the stranger's behavior with that of your friend in the exercise above. In what ways were their reactions similar? In what ways were their reactions different?

3. Recall a personal incident in which you used time to convey a message to someone or one in which another person used time to convey a message to you. Compare experiences with other members of the class.

4. Choose a newscaster whom you consider to be an excellent speaker. What vocal elements contribute to his excellence? Contrast the newscaster's vocal qualities with a person whom you consider to be a poor speaker.

5. During the course of a week, observe several of your professors to determine how they use kinesics to emphasize, clarify or contradict their verbal messages. Record two examples of each of these functions of kinesic behavior, then compare the kinesic patterns of your professors.

6. For a week keep a record of how many times you touch others and they touch you. In what way do sex differences contribute to the amount and type of touching behavior?

7. During a conversation, stare directly at the eyes of the other person for a long time. What reaction does your behavior produce in the other person?

8. Select someone with whom you are friendly and observe their living quarters. What furnishings, objects or features of the environment reveal something about your friend's personality?

Robert L. Birdwhistell, *Kinesics and Context* (Philadelphia: University of Pennsylvania Press, 1970). This book is a collection of many of the original research articles by one of the early pioneers in the study of kinesics. It is difficult reading, but it may provide the reader with helpful insights into how people use gestures, eye movement and other kinesic behavior to communicate.

Abne M. Eisenberg and Ralph R. Smith, Jr., *Nonverbal Communication* (Indianapolis: Bobbs-Merrill Company, 1971). A brief but well-written book which focuses on paralanguage, kinesics and proxemics. Chapter 5 on the social functions of nonverbal communication is particularly worthwhile reading.

Edward T. Hall, *The Hidden Dimension* (Garden City, New York: Doubleday and Company, Anchor Books, 1969). Dr. Hall, a leading anthropologist and expert in nonverbal communication, presents a detailed account of man's use of space and its affects on communication. His cross-cultural approach makes this an important and fascinating book to everyone interested in the subject of proxemics.

Edward T. Hall, *The Silent Language* (Garden City, New York: Doubleday and Company, Premier Books, 1959). In this earlier book, Hall convincingly presents the thesis that culture is communication. Chapters 1 and 9 provide some interesting insights into people's use of time.

Mark L. Knapp, *Nonverbal Communication in Human Interaction* (New York: Holt, Rinehart and Winston, 1972). This is probably the most comprehensive and readable summary of research in all areas of nonverbal communication with the exception of chronemics which is not covered. If you wish to read just one book on the subject, this is the one.

Obstacles to effective communication

Communication is a personal process and, to some extent, all communication problems can be traced back to this fact. Indeed, if we probe more deeply into the perceptions, attitudes and psychological make-up of the people involved in the process, and the way they use language to express themselves, we may wonder if communication can succeed on anything but the most elementary level. For even when people share a language and a common cultural background, they are ultimately isolated from each other's "reality" by differences in their personal histories and by the feelings and expectations they associate with words, the symbols of this reality. Each person is an unique organism who uniquely responds to unique stimuli in his unique environment in an unique way. The qualifications may be a bit overwhelming, but they point to a sobering fact: communication, at best, involves a compromise of meaning between people.

One would expect to be able to establish enough "conventional" symbols to suit any communication situation. But words do not have any meaning apart from the background of the people who create and use them. And people are not governed by objective and immutable laws of logic; they are not a community of computers but of psychologically different beings. People often do not know exactly what they think or believe and so their communication attempts may inaccurately represent their own feelings. In addition, people are often afraid of listening to what others think or believe because it may require a re-orientation of their existing values—some of which were formed in their earliest experiences. People often prefer to "trust their instincts." As one psychiatrist put it:

> The primary trust we have in instinctual reactions, our fear of revelations about ourselves, the suspicion that new realities will be impossible to live with, the painful effort it takes to develop our powers of reasoning makes an enemy of anyone who questions our assumptions and makes us think.[1]

If we acknowledge that thinking is integral to communicating, we can readily see how people create their own obstacles in the communication process.

---

[1] V.M. Victoroff, "The Assumptions We Live By," *ETC.*, XIV (Autumn, 1958), p. 20.

The problem is further complicated by the fact that language itself may facilitate miscommunication. For example, people like to label and file away anything which seems to threaten their complacency about attitudes they have held for a long time. It is infinitely easier to pigeonhole what someone else says than to experience the difficulty and anxiety of trying to be receptive to the other fellow's point of view and to determine how and in what ways that viewpoint differs from our own. But it is language itself that makes it so easy to "give a name" to, and summarily categorize, the communication of others. And it is language too which leads us to view words themselves as the final reality rather than as imprecise symbols of reality. This problem of "words" and "things" led one communication expert, T. Clifford Allbutt, to warn:

> If we give no heed to our symbols—to our means of conceiving, recording, and formulating the conditions under which we have to design our world . . . we shall be drawn almost inevitably into error as if our observations were themselves erroneous.[2]

In this chapter, therefore, we will try to examine the paths to error, those personal limitations which create obstacles to effective communication. Awareness and understanding of these problems is an obvious prerequisite to our ability to overcome them.

Selectivity in communication

Most people are unaware that communication is a very selective process, and they are unaware that selectivity greatly affects the nature of their communication activities. The significance of selectivity becomes apparent when we consider a common communication situation, such as watching the evening news.

For the sake of clarification, let us focus for a while on a hypothetical man, Mr. Smith, at home on a Tuesday evening at 7 P.M. Having finished dinner, Mr. Smith decides to relax and turn on the evening news. Of course, he has a choice among several networks but like most of us, he prefers one over all the others. In making his decision, Mr. Smith is selectively exposing himself to just one of a number of possible news programs. Having selected which station to watch, Mr. Smith

---

[2] T.C. Allbutt, "An Address on Words and Things," in Irving J. Lee, ed., (San Francisco: International Society for General Semantics, 1967), p. 304.

may pay attention only to certain news stories. He may, for example, attend to only the political and economic news of the day, avoiding sports, entertainment and the weather—all of which bore him. Of those messages to which Mr. Smith pays attention, he will perceive and interpret each in a very personal way. For instance, being a liberal Democrat, he may interpret a story about a Republican-sponsored bill to increase federal expenditures for highway construction as just another indication of Republican insensitivity to the needs of the city dweller. Mr. Smith's selectivity does not stop here. On the next day and those which follow, he will retain just a few of the messages which he received during the news program.

While highlighting the importance of selectivity in communication, the example of Mr. Smith also points out the stop-gate nature of these selective processes. In short, we cannot pay attention to a message to which we are not exposed; we cannot perceive and interpret a message to which we have not attended; and we cannot retain a message which we have not perceived. Clearly, the subject of selectivity deserves careful consideration in any discussion of effective ways to communicate. Fortunately, experimental research has provided some helpful insights into the processes of selective exposure, attention, perception and retention.

Selective exposure

It appears that people tend to choose from the variety of communication experiences available to them so that they are exposed to ideas and attitudes which reaffirm their own, thereby bolstering their image of themselves and what they "know." Such behavior is founded on a basic aspect of human nature: the rationale behind almost all human activity is the strong need to protect, maintain and enhance one's self-concept or image. In a study conducted during the 1940 Presidential election, it was determined that more Republicans than Democrats exposed themselves to the campaign messages of Willkie (the Republican candidate) and that more Democrats than Republicans followed Roosevelt's campaign.[3] Another study showed that the people who followed a media campaign designed to enhance attitudes toward the United Nations already had favorable opinions about the organization and its operation.[4]

[3] J.T. Klapper, *The Effects of Mass Communication* (New York: The Free Press, 1960), p. 20.
[4] *Ibid.*, p. 21.

Similarly, a series of radio programs intended to teach tolerance of other nationalities by discussing the cultural contributions of different ethnic groups was listened to mainly by people of the particular ethnic group being praised.[5]

Since research clearly demonstrates that a person tends to selectively expose himself to messages which support his self-image, we would expect the converse of this principle also to be true—that is, a person tends to avoid messages which challenge his preconceptions. For example, we would expect a person who has very traditional attitudes about the roles of men and women to avoid listening to the messages of feminist supporters, because they are a threat to a self-concept which has been reinforced since childhood. Some evidence from experiments does confirm this idea. For instance, in the 1940 Presidential study previously mentioned, the researchers found that very partisan Republican and Democratic voters tended to insulate themselves from the messages of the opposition candidate, more so than less partisan voters. However, some experts challenge the idea that people intentionally avoid exposure to messages which are unfavorable to their self-image. Indeed, evidence is scant and, for the moment, all that can be said with certainty is that people selectively expose themselves to messages which reinforce their already existing attitudes.

Selective attention
Information theorists tell us that although the eye can handle about five million bits of data per second, the brain is able to "compute" the information at the rate of about 500 bits per second. Obviously, at any given time, a person must select the information to which he will give his active attention or else nothing will make sense.

The information received is usually held for a short time in what may be called "short-term sensory storage"—something like a short-term memory bank—from which the person draws according to his capacity to process sensory input. When he does draw from it, the person may either respond to the data immediately or transfer the information to a more permanent memory bank.[6] For example, let us say that you are reading a newspaper and have focused almost all your attention on

---

[5] *Ibid.*

[6] H. Egeth, "Selective Attention," *Psychological Bulletin*, 67, No. 1 (1967), pp. 41-57.

an article which interests you a great deal. If a friend sitting nearby happens to say a few words to you, you will probably continue to focus on the article. However, the stimulus provided by your friend's voice has not been totally neglected; it may simply have been transferred by your sensory receptors to the memory bank. Minutes later, when you have completed the article, you will have the capacity to draw the message (simply that "someone" said "something" to you) out of storage and attend to whatever your friend had been trying to convey. Clearly, a person can only give his attention to a limited number of stimuli at one particular time.

There are several factors which may interfere with a person's ability to attend to stimuli in his environment. The most obvious obstacles are caused by certain physiological impairments, such as poor eyesight, poor hearing or color-blindness. A person with normal vision, for example, turns his attention to the color of the traffic light before he crosses a street. A person who is color-blind, however, will attend to different stimuli in the same situation. In all likelihood, he will check to see which light is the brightest—the top or the bottom. If it is the top light, he will conclude that the light is red.

Certain physiological needs can also interfere with interpersonal communication. Suppose you are having an extremely busy day at the office, with no time for anything but a few quick coffee breaks. Immediately after work, you are required to attend a seminar featuring several speakers discussing their view on modern business management. The topics may be of interest to you; in fact you may be seeking specific information which you know they can provide. But try as you will to listen to what is being said, you can think of nothing but the dinner that is to follow. In such a case your physiological need (hunger) has forced you to selectively focus on "food" as the most important stimulus in your environment. This need has impaired your ability to attend to other desirable stimuli. To some extent, training facilitates our ability to attend to certain stimuli which we know we will need at a particular moment. An aeronautical engineer at the Kennedy Space Center is faced with an awesome array of dials, graphs, buttons, toggle switches and computer read-outs. Unless he knows what to look for—that is, unless he consciously selects certain stimuli (a process of selective attention which seems impossible to the untrained observer)—effective communication with co-workers will be impaired. On a less sophisticated level, a key-punch operator who works for a department store may be trained to attend to certain facts, such as the customer's name and address, his account number, the price of items purchased, the amount of payments made and the date.

Figure 5-1 This photograph of a busy street corner illustrates the nature of the selective attention process. A person who is hungry might focus on the restaurant on the corner; a numismatist might attend to the sign on the coin shop; and a woman looking to buy a pair of stockings might notice the Hosiery store.

Sometimes our past experience forces us to focus our attention on certain stimuli in our environment. This is fortunate for us, or like Nero we might be fiddling while our own house burns. Stimuli that imply an immediate danger often narrow our attention in this way. If someone shouts "Watch out for that car," we would not have to consciously choose to attend to that warning rather than choose to watch the dog dig up the lawn across the street or to look at an attractive sunset on the horizon. Through past experience and familiarity with similar information, we automatically select the warning as the most important of all stimuli available to us.

Sometimes, however, familiarity with certain information tends to make a person negligent in his conscious selection of data. If a student is familiar with the material being discussed in a lecture, he might be less attentive to the professor's words than if he had no knowledge of the subject. The professor's attempt to communicate is thus foiled by the student's assumption that he already knows what the professor intends to say; the student's attention to the professor's message is limited to "one-ear listening."

A sender may employ various techniques to gain a receiver's attention. For many years, the volume level of television commercials was markedly higher than the volume of regular programming. To some extent, this focused viewer's attention on the advertiser's message. Consequently, the FCC outlawed this practice. Sometimes breaking the flow of one communication with another sender's message may mitigate the effectiveness of either message. Consider, for example, a television documentary on poverty which is interrupted by a commercial that urges the viewer to "live the good life" by vacationing on some Caribbean island. The airline's message may permanently disrupt the viewer's thoughts about the documentary message, and this may annoy him to the point that he refuses to focus his attention on the commercial message. There are, of course, some viewers whose attention may wane after the first five minutes of a program. In such cases, a commercial break may serve to draw back their attention from incidental stimuli— family, friends, a snack or a beer—to the electronic messages on the television.

Some communicators also create obstacles by focusing our attention on some things to the exclusion of others. For example, when a salesman emphasizes the solid construction of a car, its 2000cc overhead cam engine, fully synchronized four-speed transmission, rack-and-pinion steering and award-winning design, he is riveting attention on what he considers the most important—and salesworthy—features of the car. However, in doing so, he is diverting attention from what may be the most practical consideration: will the car fit the garage? If not, the customer who buys it may regard the salesman's message as a failure because it did not provide him with an essential bit of information. From the salesman's perspective, the communication will be viewed as a great success, unless of course, the customer returns to the showroom with angry words on his lips and murder in his eyes.

Sometimes noise will affect our attention in a communication situation. Experiments in which subjects were orally instructed to attend to only certain stimuli in the environment confirm this fact. In one series of tests, subjects simultaneously received two or more auditory messages. It was found that a message can be most easily heard in noise when the message and the noise come from two different locations.[7] It was also demonstrated that the differences in the intensity of sounds aid in selectively attending to one message among several —even if the relevant message is softer.[8]

Some of this data is borne out by our everyday experiences. For instance, two messages produced very close to each other and of equal volume intensity usually cancel each other out. One example is the mother who is trying to decipher the screams and protests of her two children, each of whom is accusing the other of spilling a glass of milk. In moments of high debate when the voices of two opposing groups are spiraling to an incredible noise level, it is often the softer words of some less emotional person that pierce through the noise and hold our attention.

Selective perception

Perhaps the most workable definition of perception is that it is "the process of making sense out of experience—of imputing meaning to experience."[9] However, the process of perception is not as simple as this definition may at first seem. To begin with, different people do not experience the same stimuli in exactly the same way. Differences in environment; differences in sensory receptors; differences in internalized values, goals and attitudes—all contribute to differences in the way a person perceives reality. Furthermore language—the process by which we impute meaning—compounds the problems caused by these physiological and psychological differences. No two people invest a particular word with exactly the same meaning.

[7] I.J. Hirsch, "The Relation Between Localization and Intelligibility," *Journal of the Accoustical Society of America*, 22 (1950), pp. 196-200.

[8] J.P. Egan, E.C. Carterette, and E.J. Thwing, "Some Factors Affecting Multichannel Listening," *Journal of the Accoustical Society of America*, 26 (1954), pp. 774-782.

[9] William V. Haney, *Communication and Organizational Behavior* (Homewood, Illinois: Richard D. Irwin, Inc., 1967), p. 52.

To one person, the word "happy" may mean not being depressed; to another person, it may mean being overjoyed at some wondrous event which has taken place. The communication problems which result from these individual differences are often intensified by the fact that people tend to be unaware that differences do, in fact, exist. In short, we think that what we perceive is reality—how can there be differences?

Most people have experienced moments when their perceptions of a particular person, or situation, or object, differed greatly from the perceptions of other people. For example, Dr. William Jones may be perceived as an excellent surgeon by a man whose life was saved by a delicate heart operation which the doctor performed. The husband of a woman who died under Dr. Jones' scalpel may perceive the doctor as a quack whose license should be revoked. Dr. Jones' wife perceives him as a sensitive and dedicated professional and a loving husband. His children view him as a strict father whose gaze makes them uncomfortable. Will the real Dr. Jones please stand up? Of course, the point is that there is no real Dr. Jones. Each person thinks his private perception of Dr. Jones is the real man.

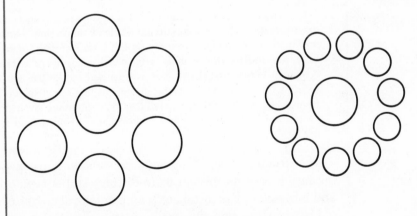

Figure 5-2 Environmental factors may affect a person's perception of stimuli. Do the center circles in these figures appear to be the same size?

A person's past experiences and expectations will affect the way he perceives stimuli in his environment. For example, if a critic you respect writes a brilliant review of a new film, the review is likely to create a favorable image of the movie in your mind. More important, this favorable impression will affect your actual perception of the film—if you expect to like the movie, you probably will like it. Many experimental studies have confirmed the powerful impact which past experiences and expectations have on a person's perception of a message. In one study, people who were exposed to a neutral statement on school busing tended to perceive it as "anti-busing" when the message was attributed to George Wallace and "pro-busing" when it was attributed to Martin Luther King.[10] Ninety-five percent of the subjects in another test judged "cookies" excellent to good until they found out the cookies were made of dog biscuits.

People often forget that words, which function to define, label or categorize, restrict our perceptions of other people, things and situations. For example, in one study two groups of subjects were shown identical drawings of ambiguous shapes, and each group was given a different "label" for the same drawing. When asked to reproduce the shapes, the subjects consistently drew the shapes more in accordance with the words used to describe them than with the actual shapes they saw (see Figure 5-3.) William Haney, in his book, *Communication and Organizational Behavior*, has commented on the way words narrow people's perception of reality:

> One cannot help wondering how long progress has been retarded by the assignation of inappropriate names. How much time was lost and how many lives were squandered by the term *malaria?* Contracted from the Italian words *mala aria* ('bad air'), it perpetuated the erroneous notion that the disease was caused by the bad air of the swamps. . . . And how many bright and willing scientists were inhibited from even dreaming of the possibility that the *atom* (from the Greek for *indivisible*) *could* be split largely because its *name* said it could *not* be divided?[11]

The structure of our language can sometimes cause problems because it does not permit us to distinguish between observations and inferences. For instance, John can look at my fifteen-year-old sister, Mary, and through a process of selective perception (primarily employing sensory receptors), he can say to me "Mary is holding a package of cigarettes." But what if he says, "Your little sister smokes!" Even though he may never have seen her purchase a package of cigarettes or actually smoke one, I will probably perceive his inference as a

---

[10] J.W. Koehler, J.C. McCroskey, and W.E. Arnold, *The Effects of Receivers' Constancy-Expectation in Communication*, Research monograph, Department of Speech, Pennsylvania State University, 1966.

[11] Haney, *op. cit.*, p. 413.

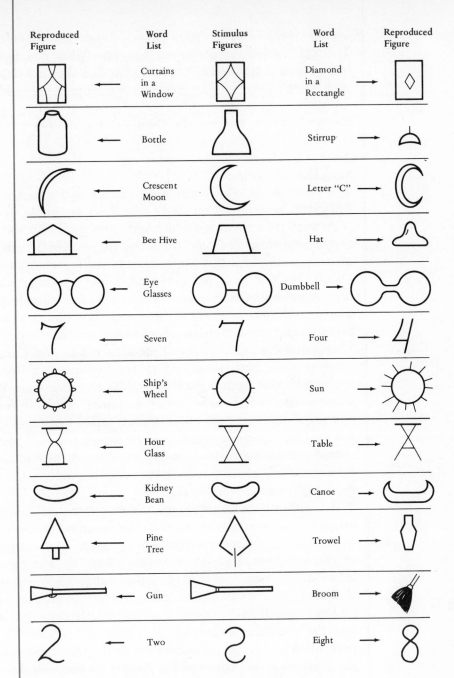

Reproduced Figure	Word List	Stimulus Figures	Word List	Reproduced Figure
	← Curtains in a Window		Diamond in a Rectangle →	
	← Bottle		Stirrup →	
	← Crescent Moon		Letter "C" →	
	← Bee Hive		Hat →	
	← Eye Glasses		Dumbbell →	
	← Seven		Four →	
	← Ship's Wheel		Sun →	
	← Hour Glass		Table →	
	← Kidney Bean		Canoe →	
	← Pine Tree		Trowel →	
	← Gun		Broom →	
	← Two		Eight →	

Figure 5-3 These figures drawn by subjects in an experiment demonstrate that language may affect a person's perception of stimuli.

statement of fact. Nothing in the language he uses—the syntax, grammar, pronunciation or inflection—distinguishes his statement of observation from his statement of inference. The real problems in communication arise when people begin basing their actions on the false notion that they are dealing with facts rather than inferential statements. Approaching my sister with angry words may delay me in finding out that she was, in fact, holding the cigarettes for another person.

Selective retention

The principle of selective retention states that a person more accurately remembers messages which are favorable to his self-image than messages which are unfavorable. In short, people remember the good times and forget the bad. An amazing example of this can be seen in the fact that former inmates of Auschwitz actually hold reunions, during which they grow sentimental over remembered jokes, sounding just like old fraternity brothers at the annual class dinner. A few experimental studies have also confirmed this hypothesis. In one study, a pro-Communist message and an anti-Communist message were both presented to two groups of college students.[12] One group had favorable attitudes toward Communism and the other group had unfavorable attitudes. Not surprisingly, the members of each group more accurately retained the message which was in agreement with their attitudes than the message which challenged their attitudes. Likewise, each group forgot the unfavorable message more quickly than the favorable one.

It is rather difficult to discuss selective retention apart from attention and perception, since all are functions of the same basic process. In fact, sometimes it is virtually impossible to assign degrees of importance to each function. For instance, let us say a person is exposed to a political message and shortly thereafter presents an incomplete or distorted report on what he has heard. Was the "data" itself incorrectly perceived, or was the retention incomplete or distorted? Or were both perception and retention inaccurate? If the time lapse between the perception and the report is lengthy, it becomes even more difficult to answer these questions.

The scarcity of research makes it difficult to make many conclusive statements about the retention process. It does seem that retention of at least part of a message is improved if intense

---

[12] J.M. Levine and G. Murphy, "The Learning and Forgetting of Controversial Statements," *Journal of Abnormal Social Psychology*, 38 (1943), pp. 507-517.

sensory stimuli accompany the message. Teachers, for example, often use visual aids to help the student remember the message he is listening to. Sometimes increasing the motivation for retention is helpful. Thus, if a professor tells his students that remembering that day's lecture will assure them of passing the next exam, the students will probably be more mentally receptive, will concentrate more deeply, and thus will remember the lecture more fully and accurately. However, if the lecture seemed confusing to the students or involved material with which they had no prior contact, the degree and accuracy of the students' retention (and the success of the professor's communication) will be limited.

It would seem that retention in conjunction with other selective processes can be quite detrimental to effective communication. Our perceptions, as we have said, are in part influenced by our memory of past experiences and messages. If we do not retain messages which conflict with our basic self-image, or these messages become distorted in memory with the passage of time, our future perceptions will be narrowed or distorted. The cycle of behavior which results may be a difficult one to break, and consequently our communication efforts may be greatly hampered.

Frozen evaluation

People often feel most comfortable when they can slip their perceptions beneath a label or into a category. Language, of course, facilitates this process. Furthermore, once an evaluation has been made, people do not like to modify it. It is easier for a person to perceive no changes, to believe that once another person or situation or thing is "pigeon-holed," it is forever. A consideration of a simple word such as "river" illustrates the pervasiveness of our frozen conception of reality. The word itself does not suggest the fact that the river is in a state of constant change. Instead, the word makes us perceive the river as a static, changeless object. Nothing—not even a brick—is changeless, and no description applies forever. Each thing has a history and our descriptions of things should reflect this fact. Yet consciously and unconsciously, in our language and in our thinking (which affects and is affected by language) we often disregard change and the fact that all things are in process. The assumption of "nonchange" can have more serious implications and be more detrimental to our ability to communicate than the example of a river may suggest.

Frozen evaluations may have devastating effects on other people's lives. For example, criminals who have served their prison sentences and seek to begin a new life often find themselves imprisoned once again—this time within the frozen evaluations of friends, relatives and employers who think "once a crook, always a crook." Many officials who control penal institutions also disregard the potential for change. Prison conditions perpetuate the image of being a criminal rather than helping to create a new image for the prisoner's future life. In some cases, a prisoner's acceptance of this frozen evaluation of himself causes him to live up to the term "hardened criminal" in an almost self-fulfilling prophecy. Indeed, label is libel.

When words are confused with reality they become burdensome weights that anchor past evaluations within our minds. They can in fact lend support to the rationale for preserving such evaluations. Women, for example, were formerly referred to as "weak-minded," "fragile," "emotional," "passive," and "immature." Certainly that was good enough reason to consider them inferior! In the nineteenth century the word "woman" suggested about as much of process and change as the word "table." Men could *become*—statesmen, lawyers, philosophers and doctors; women simply were—women. Members of one-half the population reveled in the language of change while members of the other half remained suspended within a frozen evaluation.

For women, the momentum of past evaluations proved an irresistible force, one that was impervious to the contradictions of experience. Women who had actually changed their lives still remained trapped within the assumption of nonchange; and the discrepancy between new experience and inherited evaluations created a strain that was physically and mentally disruptive. The momentum was halted, finally, when women stopped compiling evidence of equality and simply assumed it. The insight which opened a new level of communication between women was quite simple: women's old image was "ersatz" reality, a man-made product; women could not deny this past reality but they could reevaluate it, discard the language biases which supported it, and thus create a whole new reality for both men and women.

The why of frozen evaluations, the reason for holding onto assumptions which no longer mesh with experience, is rather difficult to pinpoint. The passage of time often invests these evaluations with the authority of tradition to which people consciously and unconsciously yield control of their lives. Frozen evaluations can make our world seem more stable, more secure; but they can also make it seem dismally fated. We would despair of solving the social, economic and political problems we face if we communicated solely on the basis of past assumptions about reality.

Polarization

Communication and problem-solving are obstructed not only by frozen evaluations but also by too few evaluations. The complexity of experience and the inevitable process of change require us to make more subtle and more numerous distinctions than are found in simple "either-or" evaluations. Perceiving the world in terms of contradictory opposites, or *polarities*, saves time and certainly simplifies life; but it is an illusory and potentially dangerous simplification which can create lines of battle and destroy lines of communication.

Polarization occurs when a person fails to distinguish between a true dichotomy and an artificial one. A true dichotomy exists when there are in fact only two alternatives, or two values, to describe a situation. Something which is "A" cannot at the same time be "not-A"; if you are 30 years old, you cannot at the same time be 40 years old. There is, in other words, no middle ground. Artificial dichotomies, however, imply the existence of only two alternatives or values, when in fact there may be several alternatives or gradations between polarized values. We refer to someone as being either sane or insane, happy or unhappy, a success or a failure, assuming there is no middle ground. We arbitrarily polarize values and create either-or situations when in fact the experiences of our lives suggest a multitude of "in-betweens."

Polarization implies a limitation of choices: if you regard your way of handling a problem as the "right" way, then another person's way of handling the problem must be the "wrong" way. Your delusion of only two alternatives is the real limitation, since there can be many ways of handling a problem. Even if your way seems absolutely right for you, that is no justification for self-righteously polarizing yourself from another person's method. Furthermore, people's methods may intersect or overlap at some point, suggesting a synthesis of values rather than a polarization.

Perceiving the world in terms of polarities can lead to many types of negative behavior, detrimental to ourselves and others. By suggesting an unbridgeable gap between any two values, rather than an unbroken continuum of values connecting people with different ideas and experiences, polarization creates unnatural rifts between people and may foster antagonism and irrational hostilities. History has shown us the devastating effects of such polarizations; yet they are still allowed to control much of our behavior as the following news items demonstrates:

> James Michener, one of the most successful and popular novelists of our times, interviewed a mother who lived near the Kent State campus for his book, "*Kent State: What Happened and Why*," published this year (1971) by Random House.
>
> In it Michener records the following dialogue:
>
> Mother: Anyone who appears on the streets of a city like Kent with long hair, dirty clothes or bare feet deserves to be shot . . . it would have been a lot better if the guards had shot the whole lot of them.
>
> Michener: But you had three sons there.
>
> Mother: If they didn't do what the guards told them they should have been mowed down.
>
> Professor of psychology: Is long hair a justification for shooting someone?
>
> Mother: Yes. We have got to clean up this nation. And we'll start with the long hairs.
>
> Professor: Would you permit one of your sons to be shot simply because he went barefooted?
>
> Mother: Yes.
>
> Professor: Where do you get such ideas?
>
> Mother: I teach at the local high school.
>
> Professor: Do you mean that you are teaching your students such things?
>
> Mother: Yes. I teach them the truth. That the lazy, the dirty, the ones you see walking the streets and doing nothing ought all to be shot.[13]

If they are not for us then they are against us; if they are against us (meaning "different" from us in one or several of their values and beliefs) they are against all that is "right" and "good"—and therefore any action taken against them is justified.

---

[13] From "Keeping Up," Parade Magazine, *Long Island Press*, Sunday, November 21, 1971.

Figure 5-4 *To some extent, this photograph of federal troops and a peace demonstrator symbolizes the polarization which the Vietnam War caused in the United States.*

Sometimes polarizations are not inadvertently, but deliberately, used to bend the thinking of an audience, to affect emotions and to direct behavior. In fact, polarizations are one of the most common affective elements in writing and speaking. One way that a speaker may polarize "his" side from "theirs" is by arbitrarily assigning different values to equivalent or similar behavior. This type of polarization occurs not only on a national or political level, but also in daily interpersonal communication. Mother does not approve of Sharon's boyfriend Jose, but she thinks that Barry is just fine. So when Jose phones Sharon, Mother says, "Why does that boy always tie up our phone? He's so annoying, doesn't he have any work to do? He talks on and on like an old housewife!" But when Barry calls, Mother says, "Isn't that nice? He's so attentive. Probably taking time out from his studies to see how you are. I'll bet he's interesting to talk to!"

Mother's attempt to sway Sharon's emotions is a comparatively harmless use of polarization, although Sharon might disagree. But in the *wrong* hands (excuse the implicit polarization) this manipulation of emotions can be dangerous. People are not inherently weak-willed or stupid, nor will they normally accept the exhortations of just any street-corner reformer. But life's problems can seem dreadfully complex, and so it is sometimes difficult to resist the communicator (especially an authoritative one) who simplifies it. Fortunately, many speakers have the integrity and respect for truth to qualify polarizations by pointing out, for example, what is wrong with their side. Others however are blinded by their own polarizations and their desire to control.

Some scientists have suggested that man's biological composition causes people to think in either-or terms. Although this hypothesis has not been in any way confirmed, it is clear that language plays a role in creating polarizations. For one thing, the grammatical structure of our language does not distinguish between true and artificial dichotomies. Both types of statements use the either-or form. For example, an employer tends to rate his employees as either "good" workers or "bad" workers. Few are willing to say that an employee is sometimes good at one task and sometimes bad at other tasks. Linguistically, people are encouraged to simplify their thinking into such terms, since there is a lack of quantifying substantive words in our language to express the degrees between polar words such as "good" and "bad." It is almost second-nature, linguistically speaking, to opt for the polar word than to use adjectival and adverbial modifiers or descriptive phrases.

The pace and style of life in our society also condition us to polarized behavior and thinking. Business transactions often require immediate either-or decisions, and the "philosopher-businessman" who muses over the infinite complexity of any situation may find himself a full-time unemployed philosopher. Careful contemplation and reflection, even in areas involving complex social problems, are not highly valued commodities. Action, not thought, receives the praise in an industrial society, and action often demands clear-cut polar decisions. The Good Products Company will either market a new toothpaste or it will not. Of course, this is not to imply that all such decisions are detrimental. If the alternatives for any action are consistently updated to accommodate changing conditions, polar decisions actually facilitate progress. But if the polarizations blind us to new sets of alternatives, we may simply shuttle back and forth within the same two-valued response.

Social conditioning unfortunately tends to reinforce the same polar values system that constricts individual development. Not long after children learn the basic tools of communication, they are taught the basic polarities such as success-failure, happy-unhappy, rich-poor, young-old. Commercial advertising reinforces the polar self-image with products that imply "success," "happy," "rich," and "young"; if we are unsure at which end of the pole we are hanging, a purchase (a lifetime of them) may insure us of being at the "right" end. Pop culture also steps in with its own polar trap: "where-it's-at" versus "nowhere."

Bypassing

Many times, in the process of communication, words are like "ships passing in the night." Or, to use another trite expression, the meaning a sender intended his words to have "goes right over the head" of the receiver. Effective communication does not take place when sender and receiver are at different levels of understanding. Perhaps the people involved are using the same words to mean different things, in which case they may believe they agree about the meaning intended when in fact they do not. Or perhaps they are using different words to represent the same thing—which may lead people to believe they disagree about meaning when in fact, they do not. In both cases, communication problems occur because the receivers assume that their word uses are also the word uses of the sender of the message. Communication fails because word meanings bypass each other.

At the root of the problem of bypassing is the assumption (consciously or unconsciously made) that words themselves have meaning; that if I, for example, say the word "cat" to you, it is somehow equivalent to handing you the concrete thing itself. But the words are not the things themselves; they are symbols of things. It is people who create these symbols and invest them with meaning. Thus, if I say "cat" there is no guarantee that the word alone will convey the exact image of a green-eyed tiger-striped cat that I have in mind. You may have learned the word under different conditions than I did, so the symbol evokes for you the picture of a large, fluffy white Persian cat. The word itself has no fixed meaning; its meaning lies in the way I use it and you perceive it.

Words also have no fixed usage. Since there are only a finite number of words to represent an infinite number of "things" (objects, facts, experiences) the same word may be used in a variety of ways, and thus may be interpreted in a variety of ways. Bypassing is often the result of failing to consider this multiple usage of words in the process of communication. A classic example of this involves two producers, one American and one British, who jointly financed a new play. When the drama opened in London, it received rave reviews, and the British producer quickly sent a telegram to his American counterpart. The telegram read "Posting notices tomorrow." The American was very disappointed, for to him the phrase meant the show was closing the next day. To the British producer, the message meant he was sending the reviews by mail in the morning.

Word usage is dependent on several other factors. One is simply the passage of time. Some words drop out of popular usage: "icebox" and "parlor," for example, have been replaced in most people's vocabularies by "refrigerator" and "living room." A person may, of course, still use the older terms; but many people will not understand what he is talking about, since they have had no experience with these symbols. Other words, such as "cool," have not only remained a part of working vocabularies but have acquired several new usages with the passing of the years. For this reason, a communicator must indicate the usage intended by the context in which he places the word.

Another factor in multiple usage is the regional variation given to certain words. A pizza at the Staten Island ferry terminal in Manhattan means a thin crust of dough, with heaps of tomato sauce, plenty of cheese and unconscionable amounts of olive oil. A pizza at Hampton Beach, New Hampshire, means a thick hunk of bread with an almost negligible layer of tomato sauce on top. The word is the same but, depending on the location, it represents very different realities.

A third factor which increases the potential for word bypassing is the common and technical interpretations given to the same words. To a composer, the word "bridge" means a transitional passage between two musical movements; to a dentist, it means a replacement for one or more (but not all) a person's natural teeth; to a sailor, the word refers to the steering platform above the main deck of a ship; and to an electrician, it represents a special kind of circuit. If specialists are working together in the same field, communication problems are minimal since word usages are already agreed upon. But if specialists in different areas are required to work together, there must be some prior orientation to each other's vocabularies if communication is to be effective. Miscommunication is even more likely when a specialist speaks to a layman, since many technical terms have very different meanings in common usage.

All the problems of usage can be dealt with if the parties involved genuinely desire to perceive each other's meanings. But we cannot dismiss the idea that bypassing may be intentional. In politics, for example, the person running for election wishes to attract as many votes as possible. For this reason he may limit his statements on controversial subjects to broad or ambiguous terms which can be interpreted in several ways. The candidate becomes "all things to all men." Advertisers also count on misinterpretation by the public. When a commercial claims that nine out of ten doctors recommend Aunt Mary's Nose Drops, the advertiser may literally mean nine out of a single group of ten doctors. But he expects that the audience will bypass this meaning and perceive it as "nine out of *every* ten doctors."

Words can be manipulated to represent whatever a person wishes. The motivations for this intentional bypassing are varied. They are not necessarily completely honorable or completely dishonorable, but the result is the same: words become further divorced from the reality for which they stand. The problem of bypassing on the national level inspired the novelist Norman Mailer to propose a "fifth estate"—a group of people who would test the statements made by our government to see if they corresponded with the reality of the government's actions and policies. But the idea was considered unrealistic, if for no other reason than that people often prefer to be bypassed rather than risk confrontation with an unpleasant reality.

Allness

Our knowledge of reality can be neither total nor infallible. The selective processes indicate that our knowledge of anything at any one time can only be partial. The nervous system responds to a limited number of stimuli from any particular environment; the sensory receptors, which vary in sensitivity from person to person, modify those stimuli which are perceived; and past experiences and memories shape our reactions to the stimuli. Our perspective on a particular "thing" further modifies our knowledge of it. A person who observes an accident between the drivers of two cars from the window of a nearby building would receive a very different impression of the situation than an observer who was walking down the street. Finally, there is the time factor: we cannot know all that a "thing" was or all that it will be, nor the entire pattern of its interrelationships with other things in the world. Our observations are limited to the present tense.

Yet even when they are aware of these rather obvious limitations, people tend to behave as though their knowledge of a subject were absolute. Examples of such behavior are countless: the person who confidently claims he knows all about the news after reading *Time* magazine; the man who claims there is no other "true" religion but his own; the worker who claims he knows all about his fellow workers because he shares a nine-to-five job with them; the historian who declares that Germany caused the First World War; the "revisionist" who claims the Allied Powers were to blame. The list can go on indefinitely.

The problem of allness arises when people fail to remember that their responses to reality are simply abstractions. Irving J. Lee, an important figure in the field of general semantics, states the point most lucidly in his book *Language Habits in Human Affairs*:

> Whenever we respond we abstract some details from a total situation, so that some others must be left out. Every way of looking brings with it some areas of blindness.[14]

This process of abstracting is not only characteristic of our nervous system responses but also of the structure of our language. Even if a person perceives a multitude of details, his description will necessarily focus attention on only a limited number of them. If a person says, "Vanessa Johnson is black, tall and attractive," his words are creating a picture which focuses on certain details about this person. But it is an *abstract* picture in that it neglects numerous other details which might also "be" Vanessa Johnson. She might also be a doctor, a wife, a Baptist, an excellent cook. People cannot avoid abstracting when they use language and, in fact, it helps them to order their thoughts. The danger is that people often regard abstractions (and the labels that they affix to people and

---

[14] I.J. Lee, *Language Habits in Human Affairs* (New York: Harper and Brothers, 1941), p. 57.

situations) as all that can be known, or is important to know, about the thing they are describing.

The assumption of allness can create substantial barriers to effective interpersonal communication. When Patricia says, "Frank is a creep," she is basing her statement on a limited perception of the young man. Yet her judgment will probably prevent her from viewing Frank in any other light than that of a creep. Patricia, in all likelihood, will deny Frank an opportunity to express other aspects of his personality. The person to whom Patricia made her allness comment may also close off opportunities to interact with Frank. Clearly, allness can have a devastating effect on communication at the personal level.

The problem of allness is not limited to interpersonal communication; it may affect any social organization or system. If government leaders regard their nation's way of life (goals, ideals, political creed) as the "final word" rather than an abstraction from a multiplicity of possible ways of life; or if they allow labels such as "communist" or "capitalist" to represent all that is important to know about the people who exist beneath these abstract terms—then communication becomes a pointless charade. Nations have fought in the past, and continue to enter into conflict, under assumptions of allness.

1. All communication involves a compromise of meaning between people, since each person is a unique individual who perceives the world in a very personal way. Although language provides us with a storehouse of conventional symbols, each person invests a word with different meanings. Language may also facilitate miscommunication, since it leads us to view words as reality rather than as imprecise symbols of reality.

2. The selective processes of exposure, attention, perception and retention affect the nature of our communication activities. Selectivity in communication tends to work in a stop-gate fashion: a person must be exposed to a message or he cannot attend to it; he must attend to a message or he cannot perceive it; and he must perceive a message or he cannot retain it. Various factors such as physiological impairments, psychological and physical needs, cultural background and prior attitudes will all affect each stage of this selective process.

3. Research has shown that a person tends to selectively expose himself to messages which reinforce his self-image. One cannot say with certainty if a person tends to avoid messages which challenge his preconceptions, although some research indicates this might be the case.

4. At any one time, a person selectively attends to only a limited number of stimuli available to him. The information is initially stored in a short-term memory bank from which a person draws according to his ability to process the stimuli. Physiological factors, psychological needs and past experiences affect a person's ability to attend to stimuli in his environment. Other variables that affect attention are the quantity and quality of incoming stimuli.

5. Perception is the process of imputing meaning to experience. Physiological, psychological, experimental and semantic factors all impinge on a person's perception. No two people perceive the same stimuli in exactly the same way.

Furthermore, there is nothing in our language that enables us to differentiate between observations and inferences. Sometimes confusion between these two types of statements cause communication problems.

6. A person more accurately retains messages which are favorable to his self-image. A person also tends to forget unfavorable messages more quickly than favorable ones. The retention of at least part of a message seems improved if intense sensory stimuli accompany the message. This selective retention works to bolster one's self-image.

7. People often treat words as if they were reality instead of symbols which represent that reality. Language enables us to pigeon-hole experiences and, to some extent, facilitates our perception of the world as a "frozen" reality. People assume "nonchange" in a world of "process" or constant change, and frozen evaluations may have devastating effects on their communication efforts and their daily lives. Members of racial minorities, for example, frequently suffer from the frozen evaluation of unfavorable racial stereotypes.

8. Polarization occurs when a person fails to distinguish between a true dichtomy and an artificial one. A true dichotomy is a situation in which only two alternatives exist. An artificial dichotomy implies the existence of only two alternatives when in fact there may be several. Often polarizations are inadvertent, but sometimes they are deliberately used to bend other people's thinking. Since the structure of our language does not distinguish between true and artificial dichotomies, it facilitates the polarization process. Perceiving the world in terms of polarities is a convenient process but one which may create obstacles to effective communication, for most situations offer a wide range of viable possibilities rather than only two.

9. Bypassing occurs when the source and the receiver impute different meanings to the words of a message. The assumption that words themselves have meaning is at the heart of the problem of bypassing. In fact, the meanings of words are in the people who use them. Of course, multiple usage based on cultural, regional, temporal and technical factors

contribute to the problem of bypassing and result in miscommunication.

10. "Every way of looking brings with it some areas of blindness." This statement to some extent sums up the problem of allness. In other words, a person's knowledge of reality can never be total, yet people often behave as though their knowledge of a subject was absolute. The problem of allness may create substantial barriers to effective communication on the personal level, but it may also affect the communication of any organization, institution or system. Nations have entered into wars on assumptions of allness.

1. Make a list of all the important concepts discussed in this speech communication course. Compare your list with those of your classmates. How can you explain the differences in the lists?

2. As a class, select a controversial television program to watch. At the next class session, compare what you saw, believed and remembered with your classmates? How many members of the class would not have watched the program if it had not been a class assignment? Why?

3. Select a product or idea and imagine that you are planning a persuasive campaign to sell it. What strategies would you use to overcome the selectivity obstacles?

4. Select a public or campus figure and make a list of all the words that describe this person. How many of the words on your list represent frozen evaluations?

5. Select a friend or a relative and for a day pay careful attention to everything this person says in your presence. How much of this person's language consisted of polarized terms.

6. Discuss a situation in which bypassing or allness made you a less effective communicator? Compare your anecdote with those of your classmates.

7. Much of the humor in contemporary society is based on the obstacles to communication discussed in this chapter. Find examples of jokes or cartoons which are related to two of the obstacles you have studied.

Herbert G Alexander, *Meaning in Language* (Chicago: Scott, Foresman and Company, 1969). This book presents a detailed analysis of the ways in which meaning is created and expressed. It contains an excellent discussion of how linguistic structure orients meaning and the problems involved in interpreting messages.

Charles T. Brown and Charles van Riper, *Speech and Man* (Englewood Cliffs, N.J.: Prentice-Hall, 1966). This well-written account is a highly readable general introduction to speech communication. Chapters 2 and 4 provide especially good coverage of many of the communication problems discussed in this chapter.

William V. Haney, *Communication and Organizational Behavior*, 2nd Edition (Homewood, Illinois: Richard B. Irwin, Inc., 1967). This book contains excellent chapters on perception, inference-observation confusion, bypassing, allness, polarization and frozen evaluation. The case studies which supplement each chapter make enjoyable reading and provide insight into the way these problems operate in our daily lives.

Irving J. Lee, *Language Habits in Human Affairs* (New York: Harper and Brothers, 1941). For many years the author worked with Alfred Korzybski, the founder of general semantics. In this book, Lee presents an interesting and well-written account of many of Korzybski's ideas.

Magdalene D. Vernon, *The Psychology of Perception* (Baltimore: Penguin Books, 1963). This book contains a detailed summary of some of the important psychological theories of perception. It is a valuable aid in understanding how the perception process affects our view of others and ourselves.

4 *The variables*

part 2

The structures
of the communication process

6 *Face-to-face communication*

Of all communication situations, there is none as commonly innocuous, as potentially threatening, and as frequently and highly effective and satisfying as dyadic, or one-to-one, communication. Unlike public communication, in which, initially at least, one person transmits a message while an audience of more than one person somewhat passively receives it, dyadic communication involves an alternating flow of messages and responses between two people—that is, it is generally a face-to-face interaction in which two parties are directly and actively involved.

Nearly all communication goals can be achieved in a dyadic situation, regardless of the simplicity or complexity of the interaction. For the sake of discussion, dyadic situations can be divided into two classes, "casual" and "interview." Within these rigid classifications, however, there are numerous types of dyadic communication, similar in behavioral patterns, effects and outcomes.

Casual interactions happen in a broad range of settings and communicate diverse messages. They may include anything from intimate confessions to superficial exchanges such as "Hello, how are you today, nice weather, isn't it?" Casual dyadic communication is often ritualistic and incidental, like a brief conversation carried on with a co-worker, a telephone operator, or a corner hot-dog vendor. Sometimes it is one-to-one interaction in the midst of an organized social gathering such as a party, where the content of communication is limited by unspoken rules of propriety and by a natural reticence to discuss personal feelings with a mere acquaintance. At other times casual dyadic communication involves highly personal interactions with friends or family members with whom we feel it is safe to risk intimate disclosures and with whom we can expect a reciprocal candor. Almost all casual dyadic situations, however, are characteristically informal, nonpurposive and unplanned.

The interview, on the other hand, is more formally structured and is usually devised to fulfill a specific purpose. Perhaps the most familiar example is the television interview between a news commentator and a politician or between a paid interviewer such as Dick Cavett and a celebrated actor or actress. In both cases, at least one member of the dyad is specifically manipulating the conversation toward certain premeditated topics and questions. This is not, however, the only interview format that is possible. Any of the casual interactions mentioned in the previous paragraph can move from a rather spontaneous exchange to a more structured discussion. Casual interaction between employees, for example, may become purposive and goal-directed if a specific job problem has to be solved. The sharing of personal problems becomes less casual and involves a projected strategy of some sort when it is conducted in a therapist-patient situation rather than a friend-to-friend communication setting.

Both casual dyad and interview situations probably offer the maximum opportunity for information exchange, interpersonal understanding, mutual influence and persuasion, and a level of self-expression that transcends the barrier of reserve and caution often confronted in large group communication. Yet there is no guarantee that the people involved in a dyad are always capable of utilizing this tremendous opportunity. In fact, the one-to-one nature of dyadic interaction may in itself create obstacles to effective communication. In order to understand and cope with these obstacles, to narrow the gap between the communication potential and the sometimes less dramatic reality of dyadic interaction, one needs to examine those factors operative in the dyadic communication process, the different kinds of dyadic behavior that affect the people involved and the functions of dyadic communication in interpersonal relationships.

Factors affecting dyadic communication

Our communication with others on a one-to-one basis would be easy to describe and comparatively simple to control if each dyadic interaction were isolated from the presence of other people, if our personalities conformed to a single pattern of role behavior, and if our present behavior were not influenced by learned responses and past perceptions. However, in reality, we often find it impossible to preclude others (and thus their direct or implied influence) during interpersonal communication. As socialized beings, we normally play many different roles in our lifetime; and, as the previous chapter explained, we are influenced, and to some extent controlled, by our past perceptions and previous interactions with other people. Furthermore, even if we could miraculously shed our role-playing patterns each time we entered into one-to-one communication, the generally high level of feedback would probably serve to instantly condition our responses while the interaction was still in progress. For instance, if something I say provokes your hostility, my initial approach to you will undergo changes even before the communication is completed.

Degree of perceived privateness

When a person has total privacy, he is generally able to give free rein to his thoughts and emotions. His thinking is spontaneous and largely uncontrolled by outside forces. As one would expect, this interior monologue is quite different from interpersonal dialogue. As soon as another person arrives on the scene, people normally modify their thoughts and responses to accommodate the demands of dyadic communication. It is not surprising, therefore, that any one-to-one interaction is going to be modified either by the actual presence of a third person (or group of persons) or by the implication that anything one says in the dyadic interaction will eventually be revealed to others.

In special instances, both these threats to privacy are precluded. For example, in the confessional booth, the church member assumes that his disclosures to the priest will not be overheard, and also that the priest will not relate them to anyone else. This high degree of perceived privacy—based on both actual physical isolation and the sacrosanct status of confession— contribute to a proportionately high degree of honesty.

Sometimes two people share a degree of privacy even in the midst of a large group. The "barriers" between those in the one-to-one interaction and the rest of the crowd are noise level and other interfering stimuli. At a party, or at similar casual gatherings of people, the noise level is usually high enough so that any messages exchanged between two people in close proximity will be somewhat insulated from those outside the dyad. Furthermore, at such gatherings there are usually a number of distracting stimuli that reduce the chance of being overheard. At a party, for example, other people are preoccupied with their own conversations, with getting food and drink, with listening to music, or with simply observing the furniture, paintings and other objects in the room. Selective perception, sometimes an obstacle to effective communication, in this case facilitates dyadic interaction. Nevertheless, the content of the interaction is usually less personal than it might be in a situation in which privacy is assured.

Figure 6-1 At a large social gathering, noise level and body position often help people to maintain the privacy of a face-to-face interaction.

In other dyadic situations, privacy is assured, even though others may be present. It is based on trust in the discretion of those who overhear the conversation or in a specific (though sometimes unspoken) code of behavior that governs those who are present. For example, the privacy of interactions between diplomats and statesmen, as at the Paris Peace Conference, is strictly maintained until it has been determined that public disclosure will not deter the progress of negotiations. A similar code of ethics protects the private interactions of all high-ranking government officials. And in the field of journalism, the privacy of the communication between a reporter and his source has, at least until recently, received governmental sanction. However, devious invasions of protected one-to-one interactions, the most flagrant example of which is "bugging," have more or less made a joke of "perceived" privacy—and have made part-time paranoics of some public officials and private citizens.

Role behavior

A child growing up, or an adult transplanted to a society different from the one he grew up in, becomes socialized; that is, he learns the kinds of behavior society expects of him in different situations. He also learns the kinds of behavior that will best fill his own needs in those situations. He organizes this information, decides "who" he must be in order to meet social and personal needs, acts like the "who," and receives feedback about the effectiveness of his behavior. This "who," a conceptualized and acted-out identity, is his role in a given situation.

By structuring our social interactions, role behavior helps make life more predictable and safe. Without roles, we would not know what to expect of anyone and would be unable to test the reality of our perceptions of ourselves. For example, a butcher who saw himself as a competent, friendly man who provided customers with good advice on choosing cuts of meat would be confused if some customers started treating him as if he were a psychotherapist or asked him to help with their children's math homework.

Role behavior can be divided into three types: role-taking, role-playing and role-figmenting.[1] In role-taking, a person acts according to an identity that he sees himself as having. For instance, someone who believes himself to be a warmhearted,

---

[1] John E. Horrocks and Dorothy W. Jackson, *Self and Role: A Theory of Self-Process and Role Behavior*, (Boston: Houghton Mifflin Co., 1972), p. 94.

loving person, and acts out that belief by seeking friends
and treating them with affection, has taken a particular role.
In role-playing, a person acts according to the expectations
or demands of others—which may not align with his notion of
himself. A man may play the role of a tightfisted money
manager at work, a loving husband at home and a volunteer
fireman on Saturdays. In role-figmenting, a person imagines
an identity he knows he does not have, and acts accordingly.
A child playing doctor, or a man having Grand Prix fantasies
while driving his 1958 sedan too fast, is role-figmenting.

The nature of communication is to some extent fashioned by
role behavior. Flexibility in assuming roles has become more
necessary as our interactions with others have become more
numerous; and most people quite automatically assume
a variety of roles in the course of a single day. The behavior
associated with our roles—and our perception of the role
behavior of others—neither necessarily hinders nor improves
the effectiveness of dyadic interaction, though it carries
the potential for doing both.

In an analysis of a conversation transcript, role behavior was
observed to be an integrative link in an apparent rambling
discussion, affecting the direction of the total interaction and
the dynamics of one-to-one communication. Topic shifts,
for example, were explained as the result of changes in the
different roles of the speakers.

> These roles give them certain responsibilities to fulfill, so that each
> speaker takes the opportunity when it arises to contribute to the
> discussion his specialized knowledge.[2]

The topics are in fact interrelated, and it is "the different
goals of the speakers that cause the subject of discussion to
shift in a repetitive, rather cyclical manner." Furthermore, the
roles assumed by the speakers enable each one of them to
integrate and sustain his own particular thinking and behavior
despite interruptions by other speakers.[3]

However, if people are locked into a single conception of
their role, or if they similarly "freeze" their perception of the
other person's behavior within a single role pattern, they may
severely limit the flexibility of dyadic interaction. If you
know, for example, that a friend is politically conservative, then

---

[2] Patricia Clancy, "An Analysis of a Conversation," *Anthropological Linguistics, 14*
(March 1972), p. 82.

[3] *Ibid.,* p. 84.

to any discussion the two of you have, you bring the expectation that your friend will always take a conservative role, no matter what he actually says. The classification of his behavior is helpful to the extent that it gives you a perspective on what he says; but it is detrimental to the extent that it may interfere with your perception of the content of his message.

Unfortunately, people often do accept preconceived roles as a substitute for spoken communication. The policeman's military-type uniform, for example, creates role expectations not only in citizens but also in the policeman himself. Obedience and respect often degenerate into fear and distrust, simply because dyadic interaction is obstructed by the "voice" of the uniform. In an experiment in one police department, the authoritarian uniform was replaced with an olive blazer, dark trousers, dress shirt and tie and a name plate over the breast pocket (instead of the badge and the symbol of rank). The officers carried their revolvers inside their blazers and did not carry nightsticks. The results of this radical change were reported by Dr. John H. Tenzel, a psychiatrist at the University of California:

> Stripped of their usual sources of authority the police department had to find its support in the community. They developed new styles of communications and new patterns of relating to the community both on and off the job.[4]

Relationships with the young and with minority group members improved because the perception of mutual needs and goals was drawn from actual experience and dialogue, not from assumptions. The old uniform had previously controlled the pattern of interaction, the perception of relationships and the motivation and goals behind communication; the new uniform shifted control to the actual people involved.

Previous interactions

Although it is possible in dyadic communication to surmount the limitations of role behavior, it is quite difficult to avoid the influence of past interactions. In fact the apparent effortlessness and speed that characterize our daily one-to-one interactions are based on the fact that associations and information from past conversations are automatically triggered by clues in the present interaction. Incoming messages

---

[4] Arthur J. Snider, "Policemen Without Uniforms, *The Herald News*, Passaic, N.J., Saturday, June 2, 1973, p. 10.

are related to previous experiences and memories of similar messages, and responses are shaped by past evaluations.

> In other words, in an operational sense, the listener in any everyday two person conversation would seem to have a small and finite number of interpretative and response choices once verbal input has initiated one of his cognitive structures.[5]

This automation of the communication process increases the efficiency of interpersonal communication, since the people involved do not have to spend time sifting through an infinite number of memories and ideas in order to understand and respond to each other. Furthermore, familiarity with the subject of a conversation eliminates the necessity for "spelling out" every detail of what one wishes to say; communication becomes a kind of verbal shorthand. When sets of information are drawn from shared interactions in the past, rapid changes in topic do not result in any serious disorientation or misunderstanding. For example, two students can discuss last week's test, the basketball game they attended and the price of textbooks all in a matter of minutes. A conversation that appears to be a series of nonsequiturs to someone outside the dyad is, in fact, connected by unspoken feelings and thoughts that each student assumes the other shares from previous interactions.

Dyadic interaction that is purposive—problem-solving, for example—also relies on this ability to draw forth associations from past experience. However, going beyond these experiences to generate new ideas and new ways of handling old information is also vital to problem-solving. In this sense, past interactions may limit dyadic communication, especially if the parties involved are unwilling to shed previous conceptions that are not pertinent to the dynamics of the new interaction.

Availability of feedback and method of interaction

In general, feedback is more available in a dyad than in any other communication situation. Feedback contributes to and sustains the dynamic nature of face-to-face interaction; and because this feedback is usually more specific than in other situations, it enables two people to "zero in" on confusions or misunderstandings and guides them in modifying or redefining their messages until each other's meanings are understood.

---

[5] Michael T. McGuire, "Dyadic Communication, Verbal Behavior, Thinking and Understanding," *The Journal of Nervous and Mental Disease*, 152 (April 1971), p. 227.

However, since there are numerous types of dyadic situations, the level of feedback cannot be treated as a constant.

In face-to-face interaction, the two parties are provided with both verbal and nonverbal feedback, so that it is comparatively easy to make a variety of judgments about the other person's emotions, attitudes and comprehension while the conversation is in progress. If in response to Thomas' declaration of love Ann says, "I love you, too," but with a smirk on her face, a disconcerting impassivity in her eyes and a mocking tone in her voice, this nonverbal feedback will immediately correct any misconceptions Thomas might have drawn from the content of the message. Or, for example, if you are trying to explain your conflicts about living in a politically oriented commune to a friend who is unfamiliar with your ideas about political and social reform, the friend can immediately explain that he has not seen you for five years, knows nothing of the issues involved and cannot comprehend your conflicts until he learns more about you and the ideology involved. After clearing up this disparity in experience, you can both move toward mutual understanding.

The visual element is missing in one-to-one communication over the telephone, but this form of dyadic interaction may have its own advantages. For one thing, it is often simpler and more feasible to phone than to actually meet. This is especially true, for example, of the daily communication between businessmen. Also, some people find that over the phone, with no visual information involved, they can be more intimate in their disclosures or more easily sustain a train of thought. Many friends stay on the phone for hours, yet find that when they meet, they have nothing to say to each other. Perhaps in "live" confrontation some people feel too shy to express themselves, or perhaps the personality or physical bearing of one person overshadows or intimidates the other member of the dyad. Furthermore, superfluous visual stimuli may distract from the verbal interaction.

Both audio and visual elements are missing in written interactions; but like the telephone, this form of communication has special advantages. Some people simply find it much easier to express themselves in writing. Distracting stimuli can be reduced until one is left with unencumbered thoughts; and there is no pressure to "think on one's feet" or keep up with a conversation. The main disadvantage of writing is the lack of spontaneous and immediate feedback. Though a

writer may intend one meaning in the tone and structure of his
message, a receiver often reads in very different meanings; and
the delay in feedback may simply enhance the misunderstanding
and further obstruct effective communication.

Understanding self and others

Feedback is helpful in any communication situation
only if the people involved know the way to use it; and they
can know the way to use it only as they gain understanding of
themselves and others. Dyadic interaction probably offers
the best opportunity for increasing such understanding. Casual
interactions (ones that are unplanned and nonpurposive,
or that at least seem so to the people involved) provide an outlet
for the natural and strong desire to share ideas, feelings
and problems, and create an ambience favorable to the growth
of interpersonal trust and mutual receptivity. However, as we
also noted earlier, there are no guarantees implicit in the
design of dyadic interaction. Consciously or unconsciously,
people may work against self-knowledge and self-disclosure;
and even the most private, relaxed and apparently spontaneous
dyadic interaction may, under careful analysis, prove
to be a failure in communication.

Sometimes a person deliberately avoids self-analysis because
it can be a painful process. It is difficult to accept that one
has certain unlikeable or negative qualities, just as it is easy to
believe that there is something wrong with the other people
with whom one communicates. Because it is often unpleasant
and inconvenient to change, some people will go to great
lengths to confirm their deluded self-image and avoid honest
self-appraisal—witness the many historical examples of
government leaders who surround themselves with "yes" men,
subordinates who did not dare to contradict the leader's
ideas about himself and his behavior, no matter how inaccurate
his perceptions. Hitler, as an extreme example, wished to
believe that he himself was invincible and infallible. The history
of Nazi Germany was, in one sense, that of a monologue,
uninterrupted by any feedback that did not sustain Hitler's
self-image.

Some people manipulate their lives in order to achieve
popularity, power and success; they treat themselves as objects
by masquerading in roles that are unrelated to the true needs

of the self; and they are sometimes left with fragments instead of the full and meaningful life they expected to achieve:

> When one treats oneself as a tool or as a thing, one treats others in the same way. This objectifying of the self is accompanied by self-concealment, or the repression of one's being and experiencing. This, in turn, results in what has been called self-alienation.[6]

When a person becomes self-alienated, he no longer knows what he really wants and what will truly satisfy him. His interactions with others become a travesty of real communication. Yet, at the same time, serious attempts at interpersonal communication may be the only hope for integrating the disparate elements of a fragmented self.

Interpersonal self-disclosure:
Benefits, risks, and obstacles

When people seek interactions merely to enhance their own images, they are usually very careful to reveal only those aspects of their feelings and thoughts that will serve such premeditated goals, and can rarely just be themselves. Yet most people seek interpersonal relationships for this very opportunity to relax and open themselves to others.

Functioning in a complex and competitive world often involves numerous exposures to impersonal interactions, frequently requires the suppression of true feelings, and commonly results in a sense of isolation from others even in the midst of a crowd. Thus people are forever seeking others to whom they can relate deeply, from whom they can receive acceptance and understanding, and with whom they can share their respective solitudes. The desire to penetrate to the real person hidden behind the social mask and the need to interact meaningfully with this other is poignantly reflected in "Effort at Speech Between Two People" by Muriel Rukeyser:

> What are you now? If we could touch one another if these our separate entities could come to grips, clenched like a Chinese puzzle . . . yesterday I stood in a crowded street that was live with people, and no one spoke a word, and the morning shone. Everyone silent, moving . . . Take my hand. Speak to me.[7]

When people do speak to each other, openly and spontaneously, they can learn many things not only about others but about themselves as well. Sidney Jourard, a noted professor of

---

[6] Sidney M. Jourard, *The Transparent Self*, (Princeton, N.J.: D. Van Nostrand Company, 1964), p. 184.
[7] Muriel Rukeyser, "Effort at Speech Between Two People," in *Theory of Flight* (New Haven: Yale University Press, 1935), pp. 18-19.

psychology, suggests that interpersonal disclosure and identification may actually be a prerequisite to understanding oneself:

> Through my self-disclosure, I let others know my soul. They can know it, really know it, only as I make it known. In fact, I am beginning to suspect that I can't even know *my own soul* except as I disclose it. I suspect that I will know myself "for real" at the exact moment that I have succeeded in making it known through my disclosure to another person.[8]

Thus a person must actively and consistently work at expressing his thoughts and feelings in order to strengthen and sustain his self-identity—or in order to avoid self-alienation.

Isolated from meaningful interactions with others, a person can become prey to delusions and fantasies about himself in relation to the rest of the world, since his knowledge is fed by a single and certainly not infallible source—his own perceptions. Through interactions with others, a person can become aware of the multifaceted and multivalued nature of reality; he can learn to modify his self-image so that it more truly corresponds to his real (not imagined) capacities and limitations; and he can gradually build and rework a personal system of values that is affirmed by his deepest convictions and is not subject to the distortions of superficial role-playing. Through the whole process of meaningful one-to-one communication, a person creates a basis for realistic action and facilitates the integration of all aspects of his life.

It is true, of course, that a person needs to share his worries and problems as well as his dreams and aspirations. These needs can be satisfied, to some extent, by identifying with a group—whether it be a formal and organized structure such as a political party, or a group consciousness as implied in the term "Woodstock Nation." Yet group identity does not sustain a person in all his needs, nor is it always consistent in its support. Being a member of the New Jersey Democratic political caucus, for example, will not help a person who is grieving over a death in his family. One-to-one communication, on the other hand, is almost always accessible and is more or less the "perfect food" for nourishing the self and its needs. Furthermore, although group identity can help to break a person's isolation from others, it can also create unnatural polarizations from those outside the group. On the other hand dyadic

---

[8] Jourard, *op. cit.*, p. 10.

interactions that involve open and honest self-revelation can cross all group lines and unite people in the similarity of their needs.

In view of all these general benefits of dyadic communication, we may wonder why some people do not use this vital resource, why others only tentatively and fearfully dabble in self-disclosure, and why many attempts at such interactions are prone to failure.

We might first consider the nature of personal hesitancy toward self-disclosure:

> Don't say anything, because I see that you understand me, and I am afraid of your understanding. I have such a fear of finding another like myself, and such a desire to find one! I am so utterly lonely, but I also have such a fear that my isolation be broken through, and I no longer be the head and ruler of my universe. I am in great terror of your understanding by which you penetrate into my world; and then I stand revealed and I have to share my kingdom with you.[9]

These lines, taken from a prose by Anais Nin, suggest the ambivalence we all feel, in varying degrees, toward self-disclosure. Sometime the reasons for reticence are only vaguely apparent. Sometimes they are based on childhood experiences that have handicapped one's ability to relate meaningfully, to accept the help of others and to offer support in return.

There are some real and common risks involved in self-disclosure. One of these is the risk of moral judgment and criticism, an especially inhibiting risk if there are no presumed limits or qualifications to that judgment.[10] For example, someone who goes to a sex therapist has at least a vague idea that the risks of self-disclosure will be limited. He knows the therapist will not castigate him for being inadequate or punish him for his behavior. Furthermore, he is spared the sense of being personally criticized, since the therapist's function is to provide objective information, sympathetic understanding and help rather than harsh judgments. And even if the therapist does offer some criticism, the professional context makes it more acceptable and less fearsome than criticism from wife or friends.

However, in dyadic situations in which roles are not so carefully defined, or in which role attitudes cannot be presumed, a person faces different problems. He may not be sure whether

---

[9] Anais Nin, *House of Incest* (Chicago: The Swallow Press, Inc., 1958), p. 46.

[10] Jourard, *op. cit.*, p. 3.

the other person's response will be compassionate or critical. And he knows that in any event it will be a personal judgment for which there are no rules of "crime and punishment." Thus he may have to cope with a perpetual uneasiness in the presence of the other person, since the matter is never officially resolved and since he may not be able to atone for or justify his disclosure to the satisfaction of the other person. ("What do you want me to do, kill myself?" is a commonly heard response to excessive criticism.)

The receiver risks finding out things that he may not want to or be able to handle:

> Some people are unable to cope with another's tears, some cannot handle another's anger, some cannot deal with another's sexuality, and still others cannot tolerate spontaneous expressions of despair.[11]

The response to this risk of "learning too much" may be to behave in a way that discourages interpersonal self-disclosure.

Another risk that is related to the fear of judgment is the risk of being "betrayed." The risk is supported by the fact that some people deliberately cultivate another's trust and confidence in order to manipulate and use that person. Sometimes the betrayal involves ridicule or indiscreetly passing on confidences that were assumed to be private. These are not always deliberate and purposive actions, but are often a result of thoughtlessness, insensitivity and a lack of respect for the integrity of another person's selfhood.

People would be more naturally inclined toward making self-disclosures if it did not go against the grain of their social conditioning. When we are children, we learn to distinguish between behavior that pleases our parents and behavior that invites punishment or disapproval. An unfortunate and not uncommon side effect of developing this social conscience is that the child may become compulsively driven to express only the part of himself that wins the approval of others. As he matures into adulthood, he learns the finer points of social duplicity— including the notion that one does not reveal real thoughts or feelings but only those things others want to hear. And of course, as a person matures, the motivations for such duplicity grow stronger; tangible rewards, such as money and social position, are offered to people who satisfy the expectations of others.

Thus, one gradually learns from interaction with others the

---

[11] *Ibid.*, p. 113.

way to categorize or stereotype people. This learning is not in itself disastrous—indeed, it can be helpful in superficial social relationships, in which it would be unreasonable and uneconomical to squander the intensity and energy needed for close relationships. But duplicity usually pervades all relationships, limiting self-disclosure even when it is crucial. Sincerity and openness cannot be turned on and off at will, nor does one suddenly develop naturalness in communication with others. The ability to open ourselves and to be receptive to the self-disclosures of other people is the result of constant and consistent practice.

Conditions for effective self-disclosure

To be totally honest in our communications, to reveal all that we feel, think and experience, is an impossibility. Even "professional disclosers" such as writers often remark upon the frustrations of trying to tell the whole truth of even a single perception or episode, let alone a life. Much modern literature is an effort to capture the overtones and nuances that constantly elude someone who is trying to capture the truth. Yet dyadic communication does not have to be absolute or totally uninhibited in order to be therapeutic and effective. All healthy relationships, regardless of the degree of intimacy, can increase the potential for human growth and for more successful and meaningful dyadic communication. In this section we will discuss some of the conditions that are most conducive to healthy—and thus mutually beneficial—relationships.[12]

One of the most important factors is the desire to understand oneself and others. This involves a genuine interest in the other person and his message—and thus a genuine willingness to listen. Obstacles are created when a person assumes the content of another's message before it is even spoken or when he does not allow the other person sufficient time to gather his thoughts. Probably everyone has encountered the sort of person who stops you in mid-sentence, nods omnisciently, and says, "I know *just* what you mean." He then proceeds to relate an experience that bears only the most peripheral similarity to the message you have been trying to convey.

Intelligent listening would indicate to this person not only similarities in your thinking, but important differences as well, so that communication might lead to an understanding, rather

---

[12] For an excellent discussion of these conditions see Carl Rogers, *On Becoming a Person* (New York: Houghton Mifflin, 1961).

than a bypassing of meanings. Both receiver and source must strive for clarity and accuracy. No effort at listening will be fruitful if the messages are vague and ambiguous—often the case in initial attempts at honest self-disclosure, since people are just beginning to plumb their true thoughts and feelings.

Listening and speaking are more or less mechanical factors that influence dyadic communication. No less important are certain affective elements that set the tone of the relationship Behavior that is consistently sympathetic and inspires trust reduces the possibility of defensive reactions that can obstruct the flow of communication. A person is much more relaxed and articulate when he perceives attitudes of warmth, sincerity, respect and concern. Although it is important that a person indicates an acceptance of the other person for what he is, it is equally vital that he learn to treat himself with respect and acceptance.

Figure 6-2 Face-to-face interaction offers a good opportunity for personal self-disclosure and the development of mutual trust, important prerequisites to the maintenance of any deep friendship or intimate relationship.

When a person cultivates self-esteem, he enters into dyadic communication with the expectation of being liked and understood, an attitude frequently perceived by the other. Furthermore, he feels secure enough in himself to maintain his separateness from the other member of the dyad. This does not mean that he remains alienated from the other, in which case there would be no effective interplay of feelings and thoughts. Rather, he remains strong enough not to submerge his own personality in that of the other person. And he remains clear about his own feelings, instead of distorting them for the sake of agreement and approval.

Self-deprecating behavior prevents effective dyadic interaction just as decisively as alienating behavior does. Because self-deprecation indicates that a person expects to be contradicted, misunderstood or disapproved of, it often invites these reactions. Surmounting this potential obstacle involves nonevaluative behavior, one of the most difficult aspects of dyadic (or any other) communication. The self-deprecating individual who hesitates openly and freely to disclose himself to another has often experienced negative feedback in the form of a direct and penetrating stare. If he could engage in dyadic interaction with someone who is understanding and nonevaluative in his responses—someone, in other words, who is secure enough in himself to allow others to be different without having to label their behavior and responses—then he could learn to exchange caution and timidity for spontaneity and a healthy confidence.

Nonevaluative behavior, then, encourages others to be communicative and to risk allowing themselves to be known. But in order to be genuinely nonevaluative, we must learn to understand another person from his own frame of reference and perspective on the world. In other words, we must learn to see, feel and think as he does. This is not only difficult; it is also risky. For in stepping outside one's own perceptual framework and opening oneself to another's private world, a person risks being changed—something we all fear.

The rewards, however, are undoubtedly worth the risk. At its best, nonevaluative behavior is the ideal lubricant for dyadic communication and for personal growth. It allows one to move beyond the boundaries of past attitudes, perceptions and experiences; to understand and treat others as complex and dynamic human beings, not static "things"; and to understand the many facets of one's own personality.

Interpersonal needs and dyadic communication

Communication studies have attempted to bring a degree of scientific precision to a complex and often unpredictable social phenomenon. The data that have been gathered using this approach provide at least a partial framework within which various aspects of the communication process can be examined. Yet it is one's own individual experiences in interpersonal communication that most fully lead one to understand and appreciate the nature of the process and its ability to satisfy such important individual needs as affection, affiliation and control.

Affection
Someone who has at least temporarily lost the ability to understand himself truly, and to make his true self known to others, is likely to be someone who cannot feel a simple and natural affection for others.

> . . . I am led to propose that when poets speak of love as a case of giving one's heart and soul to another, they are speaking, among other things, of this prosaic thing, self-disclosure.[13]

Because the self-alienated man cannot love himself for himself— that is, the person he is when stripped of artificial roles and the status they have brought him—he usually does not believe that others could like him for himself either. Furthermore, he has received sought after approval by deliberately not disclosing his deepest feelings and thoughts. As a result, he receives reinforcement for his belief that his real self is unworthy.

However, affection does not automatically come with meaningful one-to-one communication. Interactions can remain on the level of impersonal information sharing and still be effective and worthwhile. Those relationships that do become more dynamic and more personal often take considerable time to reach that point; and in the process, communication can be marred by conflict, hostility and misunderstanding. But as people gain a more accurate perception of themselves and others, as they overcome their mutual fears and anxieties about becoming "known," and as they grow toward a mutual respect and a stronger sense of self-esteem, they become more capable of giving and receiving affection.

---

[13] Jourard, op. cit., p. 14.

Affiliation

Some people join groups as a way of building or reaffirming their own identities and of satisfying the need for affiliation. The need for affiliation, however, is probably most often satisfied through interactions, whether or not they actually occur within a group setting. One reason is that feedback indicating a successful association with others—for example, expressions of interest in who we are or in what we are saying—can be most directly and intensely communicated when we are face-to-face with one other person. If the relationship becomes increasingly intimate in terms of self-disclosure, the sense of affiliation with another becomes proportionately stronger.

It should be noted, however, that people do not all exhibit the same level of need for affiliation, nor do they all choose the same situations and "significant others" through which to satisfy that need. For example, people with a low affiliative need may limit most of their relationships to very casual exchanges. At the other end of the emotional spectrum are those who consistently seek many intimate (even sexual) relationships in order to affirm the interest, and thus affiliation, of others. Some seek interactions with persons of the same age or profession.[14] Others, however, are more strongly oriented toward association with persons from different generations and backgrounds than theirs. In this latter case, perhaps it is the difference itself which initially arouses interest in the other and thus creates the motivation for affiliation.

Control

To some extent, each person seeks to define and control a given interaction in order to draw favorable attention to himself. However, the method used to achieve that control and the definition given to "favorable attention" may vary considerably among individuals.

In a particular situation, for example, a person may wish above all else to have someone like him. Depending upon his personality, background and previous experiences in interacting with others, he will behave in a way he thinks will control and shape the other person's perception of him. Perhaps he will behave very kindly and generously or will seek to enhance the other person's self-image in order to draw similar behavior toward himself.

---

[14] Michael Argyle, *The Psychology of Interpersonal Behavior* (Harmondsworth, England: Penguin Books, Ltd., 1967), p. 24.

Another person may wish to control a situation in order to win someone else's respect or admiration. Once again, he will shape his self-presentation toward achieving the desired response. One difference from the former example is that the desired goal is less subtle and more impersonal than affection or liking.

It should be noted that in all cases, whatever the reason for seeking to control an interaction, a person must consider the background and personality of his partner in choosing the appropriate behavior. For example, discussing one's job promotion and high salary may leave another person totally unimpressed; and so the need for admiration or respect— and thus control over the other person—will be frustrated.

It should be emphasized that the other person in the dyad may not actually feel that he or his responses are being controlled—possibly because he is too concerned with his own attempts to draw attention toward himself. The sense of "being in control" (in terms of some desired goal) is often simply the perception of the person seeking it, and may not be overtly apparent to anyone else.

And finally, as with the need for affiliation, the level of need for control is not constant among all people. The tendency to dominate may be more prominent in some because of their upbringing and because their relationships have primarily been with those people whose behavior elicited the response of dominance.[15] The tendency toward dominance may actually be an asset in purposive dyadic communication; but it is detrimental to mutual self-disclosure to the extent that it suppresses other aspects of the personalities of both interactants in the dyad. Thus the need to control must itself be controlled, for the sake of self and interpersonal growth.

---

[15] *Ibid.*, p. 26.

1. Dyadic communication involves face-to-face interaction between two people. There are two kinds of dyadic communication: casual and formal.

2. The degree of perceived privacy, role behavior, previous interactions, availability of feedback and method of interaction are all factors that will affect dyadic communication. A history of frequent interactions may facilitate communication between two persons by fostering trust and providing a common frame of reference. However, previous interactions may result in frozen evaluations, thus hampering effective communication. Role behavior in dyadic communication may serve an integrative function, unifying the disparate elements of a conversation or allowing topic shifts without disorientation. The roles a person plays may also narrow dyadic communication if they are too rigid. The extent and frequency of feedback is modified by different forms of dyadic communication. Face-to-face communication is potentially the most dynamic of all methods of dyadic interaction; it provides the greatest opportunity for verbal and nonverbal feedback. Certain methods of interaction, such as telephone conversations and written communication, eliminate all visual feedback.

3. A person's self-image is greatly dependent on the feedback he receives from others. Because it facilitates self-disclosure and mutual trust, dyadic communication may help a person to understand himself, to be understood by others and to understand others. Fear of criticism and betrayal of confidence may restrict the self-disclosure of a person engaging in dyadic communication. The society in which a person lives tends to condition him to be selective in his revelations, disclosing only attractive traits and ideas and concealing less accepted ones. A genuine willingness to listen to others, to strive for clarity and accuracy in one's own expression, to behave sympathetically toward others, to avoid self-deprecating behavior, to maintain nonevaluative attitudes towards people and ideas are all important conditions for effective self-disclosure.

4. Face-to-face communication may satisfy several important interpersonal needs. To differing degrees, each person has the need to receive and give affection, to feel a sense of belonging or affiliation and to control others. Dyadic communication is able to satisfy these needs better than any other communication situation, because it is both dynamic and intimate.

1. Often an individual will disclose intimate personal information to a stranger sitting next to him on an airplane. How would you explain such apparently contradictory behavior? What variables lead to this self-disclosure? Can you think of other situations in which this type of self-disclosure occurs?

2. Have the class select two members who seem to disagree on many issues. Ask each of the two to play the role of the other in a discussion about a specific topic of disagreement. Describe the result. Based on your estimation of their true attitudes, were the two class members able to accurately take each other's role? Do you think that most people can take the roles of another person?

3. Divide the class into pairs. Each pair should choose a topic to discuss. One member of the dyad should give no feedback to the other member. Roles should be reversed after five minutes. What happens to the discussion when no feedback occurs? Can people really not provide any feedback?

4. Write an anecdotal description of a recent dyadic interaction in which you participated. In what ways were your personal needs for affection, affiliation and control satisfied? In what ways did you satisfy the other person's same needs?

Erving Goffman, *Interaction Ritual* (Garden City, N.Y.: Doubleday and Company, 1967). This enjoyable book focuses on face-to-face interaction, discussing the verbal and nonverbal behavior that people use to "act out" roles in particular social contexts.

Albert H. Hastorf, David J. Schneider, and Judith Polefka, *Person Perception* (Reading, Mass.: Addison-Wesley, 1970). The authors of this brief text examines the psychological processes involved in developing perceptions of other people. The sections on accuracy of perception and impression formation are especially worthwhile.

Sidney M. Jourard, *The Transparent Self* (Princeton, N.J.: D. Van Nostrand Company, 1964). This book presents a detailed discussion of self-disclosure and its effects on interpersonal interactions.

R. Wayne Pace and Robert R. Boren, *The Human Transaction* (Glenview, Ill.: Scott, Foresman and Company, 1973). This text discusses the functions and outcomes of dyadic communication. Special attention is given to the effects of perception and language on interpersonal interactions.

Small group communication

If you counted the groups you have been involved in or influenced by since birth, the number would probably be in the thousands—family, classes, committees, clubs, study groups, athletic teams, political organizations and so on. Like any reasonable persons, you would probably lose patience long before the list was completed. Given the amount of time people spend in small group communication, an inevitable question comes to mind: Why are groups so omnipresent? The answer is at once both simple and complex. Groups perform many important functions, enabling their members to satisfy personal and societal needs. The exact nature of different kinds of groups, the functions they perform and the needs they satisfy are complex aspects of this answer that deserve careful consideration.

Small group communication can be defined as face-to-face interaction by a number of individuals who regard themselves as a group. This definition excludes collections of individuals who are not in close proximity, such as members of a national organization of antique furniture distributors who only correspond by newsletter. It excludes aggregations of people who do not communicate with one another. For instance, four swimmers who happen to be near each other in a large lake on a hot August day would not qualify as a small group. Then, too, this definition excludes a collection of persons who have no sense of group identity. Commuters who happen to ride the same Long Island Railroad train from Little Neck to New York City five days a week do not form a small group, although the cliques of commuters who frequent the bar car every week night may, in fact, fit this description. Indeed, the sense of group identity among a collection of individuals is more important than an outsider's observation that a small group does or does not exist. A ticket collector on the Long Island Railroad may perceive the commuters who board the train in Little Neck at 7:31 as the "7:31 Little Neck group." These commuters would not constitute a group according to the definition because even if there was an exchange of pleasantries while waiting for the train, there would be no common awareness of belonging to such a group.

There are two additional elements implicit in defining a

small group as a collection of persons who engage in interpersonal communication and feel a sense of group identity. Although face-to-face communication may be nonverbal, generally verbal communication must occur if a group is to exist. Customers who shop at the same A & P every Thursday night between 6:30 and 7:30 may smile and nod at each other, but they cannot be considered a small group nor are they likely to consider themselves one. In other words, verbal communication is a necessity for a small group; it helps the members recognize the group's existence. Small group communication is also a frequent, ongoing activity, rather than a one-time event. The members of the New York Mets or Oakland Athletics baseball team would classify as a small group, whereas members of the American or National League All-Star team who play together once a year would not. Like the verbal communication that takes place, the frequency of interaction helps to establish a sense of group identity among the individual members of a small group.

Beyond these essentials of frequent face-to-face interaction and group identity, there are other qualities that distinguish a small group from other communication situations. Small group communication allows less opportunity for individual participation than dyadic communication, but much more than public speaking or mass communication situations. Like dyadic communication, small group interaction is dynamic, spontaneous and transactional in nature. It is a continuous process in which each member may act as both a source and a receiver. But small group communication differs from dyadic communication in that it is somewhat structured. A conversation between two people usually does not follow specific guidelines, whereas a small group generally operates according to some explicit or implicit rules or principles. Of course, the structure of a small group may vary in terms of its formality or informality. It may be very formal as in the case of a monthly meeting of top executives that follows a prearranged agenda, or it may be informal as in the case of a group of high school cheerleaders that practices together twice a week.

Small group communication also differs from dyadic, public address and mass communication situations in the quantity of feedback. Feedback is highly restricted or nonexistent in public and mass communication, whereas it is a frequent and vital part of face-to-face and small group situations. Feedback is especially critical to small groups if they are to attain their objectives. In fact, small group communication without feedback is almost inconceivable; it is an integral part of the multiple interaction of group members. The interaction of persons in a small group is more complex than in other communication situations because of the number of people who are actively communicating. Each person added to a group multiplies the number of channels along which communication can travel. In a group with three people, there are three channels. In a group of four persons, there are six channels. In a five person group, there are ten channels (see Figure 7-1).

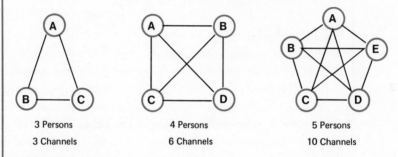

3 Persons   4 Persons   5 Persons

3 Channels   6 Channels   10 Channels

Figure 7-1 Channels of communication.

    As the number of channels increases, so does the potentiality for error and conflict. Just as each group member has his own needs, goals, attitudes, language habits and idiosyncracies, so must he cope with these varied characteristics of all the other members of his group. At the same time, added channels of communication work in a synergistic fashion; the range of inputs and opportunities for problem-solving are likely to be increased. Five persons working together are likely to produce more solutions to a problem than seven persons working individually. Thus, in small group situations, there seems to be a trade-off: what is lost in terms of communication accuracy may be balanced by an increase in the amount and quality of inputs. The ultimate goal of any group is to maximize communication effectiveness while obtaining the optimum range of differences. A group that is too small and whose members are too homogeneous may breed stagnation, whereas a group that is too big and whose members are too dissimilar may breed conflict and confusion. The optimum size of a group and the optimum dissimilarity among its members must be dictated by the group's purposes or functions.

The functions of small groups

Groups exist because they serve some function for society, for the group or for the individuals in the group. Often a group serves more than one of these functions and may, at times, fulfill all three simultaneously. For example, a jazz quartet may contribute to the society's cultural life, accrue publicity and status for the group itself and benefit the individual musicians with financial or aesthetic rewards. In most instances, however, one function predominates. Of course, each function satisfies particular needs and has particular effects on the nature of communication within the group.

Social relationships

Sometimes social relationships are the main focus of a small group. Four or five friends who regularly get together to "shoot the breeze" are an example of this type of group. Likewise, a club for ballroom-dancing enthusiasts is primarily concerned with social relationships. However, other kinds of groups also provide social relationships as a secondary function. Even the most task-oriented group, such as a construction gang, may provide its individual members with opportunities for relaxation, rewarding interpersonal relationships, conversation and entertainment—if only at lunch hour.

How social relationships satisfy personal needs

Small-group interaction can satisfy several personal needs.[1] One such need is the simple desire for affiliation—for joining with others to find the pleasures of friendship and belonging. Man is basically a social animal, and consequently he is motivated to escape loneliness and isolation. In our rapidly changing industrial society where such traditional groups as the family and the church have less of a hold over the individual, membership in small groups can provide a sense of identity and a sense of belonging through close, meaningful relationships with other members of the group.

In seeking affiliations, people also express needs for acceptance and liking. A person's self-image and self-esteem are highly dependent on the opinions of others and much human behavior is directed toward winning approval. Groups serve as an

---

[1] For a discussion of various human drives and motives see Norman W. Heimstra and Vernon S. Ellingstand, *Human Behavior: A Systems Approach* (Monterey, Calif.: Brooks/Cole Publishing, 1972), pp. 225-233.

effective way to teach people how to behave in a way more acceptable to others by rewarding and reinforcing behavior approved by the group. A person who conforms to the standards and expectations of groups that are important to him is rewarded with liking and acceptance. The groups that most influence a person's behavior become reference groups for him —groups with whom he shares his own values, attitudes and beliefs. Groups which function as reference groups are influential because they provide a standard against which an individual can compare and modify his own value system. Naturally, people will chose different groups as reference groups. One college student may join the Students for a Democratic Society, another may join the John Birch Society.

Groups may also provide a person with opportunity to satisfy his needs for achievement and recognition. In the United States and other highly industrialized societies, people learn the desire to accomplish difficult tasks, rival and surpass others and be recognized as successful. These values can be very strong, and group membership offers excellent means to fulfill them. Members have the chance to take on challenges and be recognized as a group—for example, world's champion ping-pong team or best collegiate debating team. Members are also offered the opportunity to compete within the group and can attain recognition for their abilities as first string pitcher, or prima ballerina or concertmaster.

Two other needs, those for dominance and autonomy, can be satisfied in groups but may also undermine the development of social relationships. The desire to be dominant, to influence, direct and control others, can be fulfilled through group leadership which can, in turn, facilitate the achievement of the group's goal. But dominance, if it is too excessive, can also hinder interpersonal relationships by causing defensive communication and conflict among group members. The "bossy" individual who claims to know all the right answers and demands that things be done his way is likely to polarize group members, thereby decreasing the possibility of effective communication. Another potentially negative factor in social relationships is the need for autonomy. To differing degrees, each individual has a desire to be independent of others, to do things his own way. As a person withdraws from other group members and rejects them to maintain his own autonomy, his potential for developing close personal relationships is reduced.

Societal functions can also be fulfilled by social relationships developed in groups. Cohesive groups, in which each member feels personal satisfaction, help make society more stable and orderly. Political, religious, business and cultural groups are strengthened as people join together to overcome the limitations of individual action. Some social scientists even argue that man is basically fallible, weak, dependent and evil, and that groups provide the necessary restraint, organization and rules for the continued existence of society. While many sociologists, political scientists and communication theorists counter that this is an extreme position, it does highlight an important function of group behavior.

Social relationships and communication   The social relationships that spring up in a small group influence the nature of the communication that takes place within the group. And that communication, in turn, affects the nature of relationships among group members. Thus, within any group that satisfies personal needs for social relationships (and every group does, at least on a secondary level), certain communication patterns are likely to occur.

One of the likely outcomes of small group interaction is an increase in attraction between group members.[2] Interpersonal attraction refers to a person's perception of his similarity to, familiarity with and liking for another person. Two factors tend to increase interpersonal attraction in a small group. First, attraction naturally increases as the frequency of interaction increases. As noted earlier, people who communicate on a regular basis tend to develop a liking for each other. Frequent interaction also tends to make people homophilous. Since groups by definition involve frequent and extended interaction, it is only logical that attraction between group members is usually great. Secondly, attraction may also increase when group members share a common fate, that is, all members are dependent on one another and share the consequences of each other's actions, as in a football team or a labor negotiation group. Because groups are formed and sustained on the basis of some similarities, whether it be common fate, common goals or similar interests and attitudes, the existence of groups serve to intensify attraction between members.

Group membership can also satisfy a person's needs for achievement, recognition and dominance through the

---

[2] Barry E. Collins and Harold Guetzkow, *A Social Psychology of Group Processes for Decision-Making* (New York: Wiley, 1964).

establishment of credibility and status. A person who has high credibility generally has more status, and status is often equated with power. Thus, the status or power relationships among group members, to some extent, may govern the communication that occurs within a group.[3] A person who is trying to gain status usually engages in "campaigning" behavior; he communicates mainly with low status people who are more likely to find him credible and attractive. He rewards them with praise, recognition and acceptance. Once he has won status, he interacts primarily with high status people, seeking feedback only from them. In this way, he satisfies his own needs for achievement, as well as for praise, recognition and acceptance. Further, because a high status person generally sends and receives more communication and is more successful at influencing others than a low status person, the high status person's dominance needs are also satisfied. However, if power within the group becomes too concentrated in only a few high status people, lower status members will have less potential for satisfying their own needs, and communication will be less successful. Also, too much status can isolate a powerful group member from the feedback he needs to maintain his status and power. Critics of the Nixon Administration have said that the President cut himself off from important interaction with lower status members of government, thereby making the Watergate scandal and other corruption possible. And Robert Townsend, the former head of Avis, has pointed out that a battery of secretaries and an aura of fear can separate a high exective from the information he needs to make effective decisions. Thus, certain kinds of status and power relationships can turn a functioning group into an inefficient, useless or even corrupt mechanism.

The social relationships within a small group are also affected by the degree of cooperation or competition among group members (intragroup) and between group members and other groups (intergroup). Group members are generally more satisfied if they compete with other groups and cooperate with each other than if they compete among themselves and cooperate with other groups.[4] The competition with "outsiders" satisfies the achievement and recognition needs of group

---

[3] For a delineation of propositions on the relationship of power to communication see Collins and Guetzkow, *op. cit.*

[4] James W. Julian and Franklyn A. Perry, "Cooperation Contrasted with Intra-Group and Inter-Group Competition," in R.S. Cathcart and L.A. Samovar, eds., *Small Group Communication: A Reader* (Dubuque, Iowa: William C. Brown Company, 1970), pp. 82-102.

members, while reinforcing the group identity. The intragroup cooperation helps to maintain a pleasant social atmosphere, making the group a rewarding experience for its members and enhancing its cohesiveness.

Education

Another function of groups is education. Groups may formally or informally work to achieve and exchange knowledge. A college class is formally and almost exclusively devoted to this function. However, among members of a bridge club or a bird-watchers group, learning may be an accident, a by-product or a preliminary to the group's main purpose.

Education fulfills individual, group and societal needs. For individuals, it satisfies curiosity—clearly a potent human drive, as the behavior of children shows. Education may also satisfy a person's desire for competence, or the achievement of expertise and knowledge in a particular area. For the group, certain levels of knowledge may be essential if the group's tasks are to be adequately performed. Thus, the members of an environmental group must first determine the effects that construction of a highway will have on the ecology of an area. Only then will the group be able to complete its task: to decide whether or not to oppose the project. Education is not restricted to task-oriented groups; even the members of a socially-oriented group learn from each other. At the societal level, the values of education are overwhelming. Individuals and groups must learn the ways to create and run the basic machinery of society—they must learn to produce goods and services—if the society is to continue functioning and benefiting its members.

Whether or not education is successful within a small group depends on several of the same communication factors operating in other situations. For example, the processes of selective attention, perception and retention will affect a receiver when he is in a face-to-face, small group, public address or mass communication situation. The clarity, meaningfulness, familiarity and vividness of information presented will also detemine how much a receiver understands and learns, as will the amount of redundancy built into the message he hears.[5]

There are, however, three factors unique to the small group situation that may facilitate or inhibit learning within it.

---

[5] M. Daniel Smith, *Theoretical Foundations of Learning and Teaching* (Waltham, Mass.: Xerox College Publishing, 1971).

These are the amount of new information contributed, the number of persons in a group and the frequency of interaction between group members. Group learning can be very effective if each member brings useful knowledge to the group. If none of the members have new knowledge to contribute, nothing is gained.

The size of a group can make a difference to the learning that takes place in it. The larger the group, the greater the potential for a diversity of ideas and knowledge. However, the group may become so large as to be unwieldy. Each person will have less of a chance to participate and receive feedback. Some ideas will necessarily be overlooked and some people ignored.

Figure 7-2 *The boys in this mathematics lab are eager to ask one another questions and compare ideas. The small group can be a very effective setting for learning.*

If each member brings something to the group and the group is of optimum size, then the degree of interaction becomes important. Members in such a group can correct each other's errors, add much information and create an energetic atmosphere that stimulates learning. Many businessmen recognize this principle by placing employees in task forces to study a problem or by holding "brainstorming" sessions which often result in fresh insights that one individual could not have developed on his own. That is why the degree of interaction among group members is so important. If all members participate, then the group can weed out and integrate the mass of information that results. A small group functioning in this way is an effective instrument for education.

Persuasion

In many situations, it is not easy to separate persuasion from education. A tennis pro teaching a novice how best to grip the racquet may use some persuasion in the form of subtle threats—for instance, "If you don't do it the way I'm telling you, you'll get a sore wrist." And a door-to-door salesman trying to persuade a customer to buy a broom may use education as part of his appeal—"Electric vacuum cleaners contribute to the energy crisis by using unnecessary electricity." The thin line separating education from persuasion is probably thinnest in a small group setting, where members rarely state the exact purpose of their communication.

A person who engages in persuasive attempts in a small group situation may have much to gain, but he may also have much to lose. The satisfactions and risks of using persuasion in a small group are illustrated by the "backroom" discussions that go on when a presidential nominee must select his running mate. An advisor to the nominee may satisfy his own need for dominance and achievement by persuading other advisors to back the vice-presidential candidate of his choice. But a group member who advocates attitudes and behavior that deviate significantly from the group's norms will find himself subjected to pressures to conform.[6] A Southerner who advocates the selection of a Southern governor to run with a Southern senator picked as the presidential nominee will undoubtedly find himself pressured to conform to the group's desire for a more "balanced" ticket. If the Southern advisor has high status and is likely to make bad publicity for the party by denouncing the group's proceedings to the press, he will receive increased communication as the group attempts to keep him within the fold. But if he has low status, or if he maintains his deviant position for a long time, he may receive less communication and eventually be isolated or rejected.

Whether or not a group member chooses the role of advocate for a single position depends, to some extent, on how much

---

[6] Collins and Guetzkow, *op. cit.*

information he has.[7] If he has an abundance of information and alternatives to offer, he will be more likely to adopt a neutral role and simply present all the alternatives. A member who has little information will probably choose one position to defend—perhaps because limited knowledge has made it easier for him to make a choice prior to the group discussion. For instance, the presidential nominee's campaign manager will probably investigate all vice-presidential possibilities and draw up a list, noting the advantages and drawbacks of each. Special interest advisors, however, such as a feminist, a labor leader, a civil rights worker or a campaign aide who has been spending all his time analyzing public opinion polls from major cities, will be more likely to advocate a particular candidate because of limited information.

As research indicates, persuasion in a small group setting can be risky. The group member who attempts to persuade must realize that his position will probably not be accepted without qualification. If his persuasive attempts are too discrepant from the group's values, he may create conflict, thereby jeopardizing his own position within the group. A clear understanding of problem-solving and decision-making in small groups can help a persuader to maximize the results of his efforts.

Problem-solving and decision-making

Many groups function in order to solve problems and make decisions. These functions are really two parts of a single, continuous process. Problem-solving involves discovering previous unknown alternatives or solutions, whereas decision-making involves choosing between two or more solutions. Thus, problem-solving generates the material on which decisions are based. For instance, a chess club may study all the possible responses that White can make in response to a move by Black in order to find out which moves lead to a winning position. That is problem-solving. The choice of White's best response from all the possibilities is decision-making. Sometimes only the first part of the process is necessary; the chess club may discover that there is only one response that will not lead to disaster for White.

Problem-solving and decision-making address rather obvious individual, group and societal needs. People and institutions continually face questions that need answers, problems that need solutions, conflicts that need resolution. Often a group

---

[7] *Ibid.*

effort is the most efficient, creative and satisfying way to meet these needs. For instance, the Bobby Fischer-Boris Spaasky chess match sent an unprecedented number of experienced and beginning players flocking to chess clubs, where they could work together to anticipate the moves and develop the best strategies for their favorite player. The group sessions often came up with correct lines of play long before the two individual players did.

This greater productivity of group effort is called the assembly-effect bonus. If a group's product is greater than the combined product of the same number of people working alone, the extra product is the bonus. Take, for example, the task of listing uses for brown paper bags. One would not expect an immense bonus of creativity to burst forth during this particular challenge. But, in fact, if five people working alone came up with a total of eighty uses, the same five people working in a group might generate a list of two hundred uses, and chances are, their list would be more creative as well as longer. One member might mention that he had seen paper bags used as masks by players in a children's theatre in San Francisco which might remind a second that a paper bag over the head can stop hiccups. This might lead a third member to free associate to other household uses—say, degreasing chicken stock. The spontaneity, creativity and diversity of small group interaction make it an excellent tool for problem-solving and decision-making.

Stages in problem-solving and decision-making The movement from problem-solving to decision-making does not occur in one single, swift jump. In his theory of reflective thinking, John Dewey, suggested that rational thinking involves six phases.[8] These stages have traditionally been regarded as the most logical and orderly process for individual or group problem-solving and decision-making. The first phase is recognition of a difficulty; the individual or group confronts some problem or uncertainty that is causing frustration. In phase two, the person or group defines or clarifies the exact nature of the problem that he or it faces. This phase leads to the third: developing criteria for solutions. In phase four, possible solutions are suggested and rationally explored. After adequately studying the possibilities, the individual or group enters phase five: selection of the

---

[8] For an extended discussion on the reflective thinking process see John Dewey, *How We Think* (New York: Basic Books, 1910).

optimum solution. This is followed by the sixth phase: putting the plan into action.

Research into group problem-solving and decision-making has shown that at least three stages, roughly corresponding to those of Dewey, occur.[9] The first phase is called the orientation stage: members ask for and exchange information; they then classify, confirm and repeat it, among themselves. In the second stage called evaluation, group members seek out and discuss their opinions, analyses and personal feelings concerning the problem. In the third phase, known as the control stage, members ask for and exchange suggestions, directions, solutions and possible plans for action.

From Dewey's work and that of his followers, a standard agenda has evolved; it is the most commonly used order for analyzing problems in groups and can be adapted to any problem-solving situation.

> Standard agenda
> I. Definition of the problem.
>   A. Definition of terms
>   B. Definition of scope
> II. Analysis of the problem
>   A. History and causes
>   B. Effects and extent
> III. Criteria for solutions
>   A. Generation of criteria
>   B. Ordering of criteria according to priority
> IV. Possible solutions
>   A. Generation of possible solutions
>   B. Evaluation according to criteria
> V. Selection of the optimum solution
> VI. Plan for action

This agenda approach requires the group to define at the outset the exact nature of the problem it is confronting. Usually, the group should begin by stating the problem as an open-ended, unbiased policy question. A good example would be, "Should the government regulate marijuana?" If the question were worded, "How can the government eliminate marijuana?," the discussion would be biased by the untested assumption that marijuana is harmful to the public. Similarly, the question, "Should marijuana be legalized or not?" builds in

---

[9] Robert F. Bales and Fred L. Strodtbeck, "Phases in Group Problem Solving," *The Journal of Abnormal and Social Psychology*, 46 (1951), pp. 485-495.

bias, allowing an either-or answer, with no possibility for exploring other policies, such as penalizing dealers but not people who grow marijuana only for personal use, or allowing sale but not advertising. Either-or questions close off alternatives rather than encourage a free flowing discussion.

Once a group has clearly stated its problem, it must define all terms in the question and any other terms likely to turn up in discussion. This step is needed so that group members do not hold widely varying assumptions about what the terms mean. For example, in the marijuana question, does "government" mean federal, local or state government? Does "regulation" only mean outlawing, or does it encompass a spectrum of controls? Does "marijuana" include hashish, a derivative of cannabis resin, or only cannabis leaves?

While the group is defining terms, the scope of the problem must be narrowed to manageable proportions. The question, "What should be done about drugs?" would include too many divergent subjects to allow an orderly discussion. A better strategy for group problem-solving of complex problems is to break them down into smaller segments that can be dealt with one by one.

Before a group tries to analyze a problem, it must gather enough information so that it can fully discuss the causes and effects of the problem and its past and present extent. A decision based on inadequate knowledge is no better—and may be even worse—than no knowledge at all. Furthermore, uninformed people tend to cling to one position instead of being neutral, thus causing conflict and dead-end discussion. For instance, the National Commission on Marijuana and Drug Abuse hired scores of experts to research different aspects of drug use and regulation. If it had not, the Commission's members would certainly have become bogged down in ideological arguments; instead, presented with the researchers' information, many of them realized how little they had understood the issues and developed objective, open-minded attitudes.

Once the problem has been fully analyzed, the group moves into a stage that is crucial to decision-making—the development of criteria, or standards, for judging possible solutions. These criteria might be based on such factors as time, money and other resources, ethical and value judgments and any other considerations that the group feels are important. In developing criteria for proposed action on marijuana regulation, one group might decide: Any action must be implemented at once; it must cost less than present regulatory programs; it must not encourage the use of marijuana by minors; and it must not create a profit motive for black marketeers. Another group might choose different criteria: Cost is no object; any solution must discourage marijuana use while clearly differentiating between marijuana and narcotics; and action must not expand the federal drug-regulatory bureaucracy or further crowd the courts. The group must then weigh the importance of each criterion and decide which ones have priority. In this way, alternatives that meet different criteria can be compared according to how well they rank in priority.

After the criteria have been chosen and ordered, all the possible alternatives are explored. Each is evaluated according to how well it meets the criteria. Its benefits are compared to its costs and disadvantages. If no proposed solutions satisfy the criteria, the group must look for more solutions or revise its criteria. The solution or combination of solutions that best meet the criteria is chosen. Thus, the first group in the marijuana example might choose to allow the possession and sale of marijuana under regulations similar to those for alcohol. The second group, using different criteria, might decide against direct control of marijuana, and instead call for a national program to educate people about transcendental meditation and other alternatives to drugs as means of altering consciousness.

In the last stage of decision-making, group members must determine the best way to implement the proposal. The group must decide what resources are needed, who will take responsibility for putting the plan into action, when it will begin and so on. Once the plan has been implemented, its effects must be observed and evaluated. If it is a success, with no undesirable side effects, the process is complete. If the plan is not working, however, the group must revert to earlier stages of the problem-solving process, reanalyzing the problem, generating new criteria or solutions or finding new ways to implement the original solution. Long-range plans generally require continued observation and revision.

While the agenda outlined above has been advocated by many as the most effective, there are many other strategies. One technique that looks especially promising is derived from computer science and is called Backtrack Programming.[10] A group

---

[10] For a brief description see Michael D. Scott and Edward M. Bodaken, "Backtrack Programming: A Computer-Based Approach to Group Problem Solving," Contributed Paper, International Communication Association Convention, Montreal, Quebec, April, 1973.

using this method must first set up rigid criteria for the
solution. Then the major problem is broken down into
subproblems, each of which is solved before the next is
considered. For example, if too many airplanes are landing and
taking off at an airport, causing congestion and delays,
Backtrack Programming would break down this problem into
subproblems based on the sources of the traffic and availability
of other landing and takeoff sites. Subproblem One might be:
Different airlines schedule flights to the same places at the same
times and do not fully load their planes. Subproblem Two might
be: There are no other airports within a radius of five hundred
miles. This process continues until the group has defined all the
subproblems at work in this particular situation. The group
considers the subproblems one at a time, beginning with
whichever seems to be the most logical starting point. Solutions
to the first subproblem are compared to the criteria. The
best is chosen, and the group moves on to the next subproblem,
building solutions to it based on the solution to the first
subproblem. If at any point the group cannot find a solution to
meet the criteria, it backtracks to the previous subproblem
and changes the solution that is causing the trouble. Backtrack
Programming forces consideration of the criteria at each stage
in the process, thereby producing an ultimate solution that
deals consistently with all the subproblems. Such a systematic,
deliberate approach is especially helpful for groups facing
complex issues.

Conflict resolution
Because problem-solving and decision-making in small groups
are complex processes, they do not always succeed. One of the
unsuccessful outcomes may be conflict within the group, in
which case the group must either disband or perform another
function: conflict resolution. Conflict in a small group may
arise for many reasons. It may grow out of a competitive
atmosphere in which individuals or subgroups are more
concerned about their own needs than the group's goals. It may
arise because status differences or cliques threaten low status
members. Or it may simply be the irrational product of a
member's desire for recognition or dominance.

Once conflict develops, resolution gets increasingly difficult.
People shout, use emotional language and grow defensive and
distrustful. But there are ways for a group to resolve its
conflicts. Some of the strategies are illustrated in Jim Bouton's

book *Ball Four*, an account of life on a professional baseball team.
Strategy: Stress a higher-level goal that all members share.

> "We had a visit from Commissioner Bowie Kuhn today. . . . The
> Commissioner said that baseball is a tremendous, stupendous game. . . .
> One of the things that none of us should do, he said, is knock the
> game. He said if we were selling Pontiacs we wouldn't go around
> saying what a bad transmission it has. In other words, don't say
> anything bad about baseball.
>
> He said he was pleased with the settlement that had been made
> with the players but he felt there was too much bitterness in the dispute.
> I felt there was an unspoken warning there to be careful of things
> we said that could be interpreted as bitterness toward the owners."[11]

Strategy: Reestablish trust by engaging in some cooperative or
compromise behavior.

> "Why should I be one of the boys? Why should I yield to the jockos?
> Oh, I'm not going to hold back if something comes up I feel strongly
> about, but I'm going to soft-pedal it a bit, at least at the beginning,
> until I'm sure I can make this club. I really believe that if you're a
> marginal player and the manager thinks you're not getting along
> with the guys it can make the difference."[12]

Strategy: Satisfy individual needs by praising and rewarding
members.

> "Joe Schultz stopped by again today to say a kind word. I noticed he
> was making it his business to say something each day to most of the
> guys. He may look like Nikita Khrushchev, but it means a lot anyway.
> I'm sure most of us here feel like leftovers and outcasts and marginal
> players and it doesn't hurt when the manager massages your ego
> a bit."[13]

Strategy: Obtain the assistance of a neutral third party.

> "I got into my uniform and, when the game was over and Cro came
> into the clubhouse, I went over and told him to keep his big nose
> out of my business. . . So he yelled back at me and I yelled back at
> him—bright, clever things that little boys yell at each other, and all of
> a sudden he jumped up and started punching me.
>
> Now, *there's* a dilemma. I don't want to get hit, even by a skinny
> old Cro. At the same time I don't want to hit Frank Crosetti, for
> crissakes. So I sort of covered up and started backing off. Besides, I
> couldn't help it, I was laughing. At that point my friend Elston
> Howard, quickly sizing up the great dangers involved, came running
> over, threw a body block at me and knocked me down. I picked
> myself up, went over to my locker and sat down."[14]

---

[11] Jim Bouton, *Ball Four* (New York: World Publishing Company, 1970), p. 56.
[12] *Ibid.*, p. 83.
[13] *Ibid.*, p. 19.
[14] *Ibid.*, p. 24.

There are other strategies that may be employed to reduce conflict within a small group. If members of a local school board have come to an impass over whether or not to institute a high school sex education program, the chairman might do best to shift the discussion to a less controversial subject such as the allocation of money for textbooks. This shift to a noncontroversial task may provide "cooling off" time and reduce tension among group members. Of course, the chairman might adopt other strategies. He may, for instance, redefine the group's task. Instead of answering the question "Should we institute a sex education program in our high school?" the school board members might address themselves to another question, "Have high school sex education programs in other districts succeeded?" He could then divide the group members into compatible subgroups to reexamine various aspects of this question.

Therapy

In recent years, therapy groups have skyrocketed in popularity. Husbands and wives can join marriage counseling groups to work out problems in their relationship. Drug addicts can seek treatment in a variety of groups such as Daytop and Synanon. Smokers and compulsive eaters can attend group sessions that provide them with emotional support to "quit the habit." Policemen, teachers and business executives can participate in role-playing groups designed to increase their sensitivity to the needs of ghetto dwellers, students and subordinates. Underlining all these purposes are the realizations that it is acceptable for an individual to admit needs and problems to others, and that empathy may increase the effectiveness of communication between people.

A therapy group differs from other small group situations in that there is no group goal; instead the object of the therapy group is to help each individual achieve personal change. Certainly he must interact with other group members in order to benefit, but his main effort is to help himself, not help the group reach consensus, exchange knowledge or spend a socially satisfying evening—although all those things may occur during therapy.

Communication in therapy groups, most typically, involves discussion centered on self-disclosure. In a warm, supportive climate, each member is encouraged to talk openly about his feelings. If conflict arises, it may be encouraged or regulated by the therapist or leader, according to his understanding of each member's ability to cope with it. Feedback helps the individual learn more about the way he responds in certain

Figure 7-3 *Encounter groups often use touch to break down inhibitions, thereby making a person more sensitive to his own needs and the needs of others.*

situations, and helps the therapist see the way the individual behaves with others. The group setting provides an opportunity for interaction that could never occur in a one-to-one relationship in the therapist's office. Thus, emphasis in a therapy group is usually on the communication process rather than on the content of the communication. The question to be answered is not, "Can this group agree that John is a hostile person?" but "How does being in a group influence John's behavior?"

Some therapy groups emphasize total release of inhibitions in intense "encounters" or "marathons," where members are supposed to express feelings with no holds barred except for physical violence. Other groups are more long range and unfocused, such as the therapeutic live-in communities begun in England by R. D. Laing to treat schizophrenics without making them feel institutionalized or cut off from society. And still other groups are highly structured or focused on quite specific personal goals, such as desensitizing phobic people to a particularly fearsome phenomenon—dogs, airplanes, tall buildings and so on.

Although participants in a therapy group often testify to its helpfulness, evidence about the value of such groups is at best tentative. Although authorities may disagree vehemently about the benefits, they concur that any therapy group ought to be run by a person who has proper training and knows the histories of the individuals involved. Groups that undertake such emotionally volatile activities without the guidance of a trained leader may do more harm than good.

Leadership and other group roles

Leadership is not only important in decision-making and therapy groups; it plays a part, however informally, in all group situations. The types and techniques of leadership have been analyzed from many perspectives. Some researchers and observers have been most interested in the traits of known leaders; others have studied the effects that various leadership styles have on group productivity; others have looked at the way leadership evolves and is commmunicated within the group.

The trait approach to leadership attempts to identify the characteristics of a good leader. But numerous studies have failed to come up with a consistent list of traits. The findings most frequently suggest that leaders are more intelligent, better informed and more responsible than nonleaders; that they have achieved more prior to assuming leadership; and that they participate more and have higher status within the group.[15] Leaders also tend to be perceived as self-confident, free from anxiety and strongly driven toward dominance, power and prestige.[16] Unfortunately, lists of such traits are not very useful; they are based on observations of people who have already demonstrated leadership. Perhaps high status and self-confidence are the fruits of leadership rather than the causes of it.

Leadership styles

Another approach to leadership involves examining the effects of various leadership styles on group outcomes. Leadership style refers to the degree of control a leader exercises and his attitudes toward group members. Five distinct styles of leadership have been identified: authoritarian, bureaucratic or supervisory, diplomatic, democratic and laissez-faire or group-centered.[17]

The authoritarian leader is a controller. His word is law and inflexible. His motivation to lead may derive from strong dominance and achievement needs. An authoritarian leader usually relies heavily on rules and order, monopolizes communication and discourages feedback. His group may be well-organized and productive, but at the expense of interpersonal relationships, since group members tend to be tense and antagonistic toward each other. Former FBI Director J. Edgar Hoover is a good example of the authoritarian leader. He ran the FBI like a machine, brooked no interference, resented any criticism and was accountable to no one.

The bureaucratic leader operates as a supervisor, impersonally overseeing and coordinating the group's activity. His god is not himself but The Organization. Rules and agendas make him feel that things are going well. He sees social relationships as unwelcome intrusions into efficiency, so he remains personally aloof and unsympathetic to interpersonal problems among members. He likes to communicate in memos peppered

---

[15] R. Stogdill, "Personal Factors Associated With Leadership: A Survey of the Literature," *Journal of Psychology*, 25 (1948), pp. 35-71.

[16] Michael Burgoon, Judee K. Heston and James C. McCroskey, *Small Group Communication: A Functional Approach* (New York: Holt, Rinehart and Winston, Inc., in press).

[17] *Ibid.*

with officialese; disorderly discussions, however creative they may be, give him a feeling that anarchy lurks around the corner. His group may be productive because it is organized, but members tend to be apathetic and stifled. Factory workers often complain that they are treated this way by foremen whose only concern is the number of items that roll off the assembly line.

The diplomatic leader is a manipulator. Like the authoritarian, he is motivated by recognition and dominance needs, and he uses leadership to put himself in the spotlight. The diplomatic leader tends to exert less control (or is it at least more subtle about it) and to be more flexible than the authoritarian leader. Unlike the authoritarian, the diplomat is not committed to a particular ideology; this provides him with more freedom to adopt strategies to manipulate others. Thus, while he may appear to democratically welcome suggestions and feedback, he secretly tries to direct and control group outcomes. Talk show hosts often use this leadership style to keep control of the discussion without seeming authoritarian to the audience.

The democratic leader exercises much less control than the other three types of leaders. He wants all the members to share responsibility and develop their own leadership potential. He encourages open participation and feedback. He is concerned with both interpersonal and task relationships among group members. Although his group seems less organized and efficient than one that is strong-armed or manipulated into action, it works in a more relaxed atmosphere that tends to breed productivity, originality and creativity because it makes maximum use of each member's abilities.

The laissez-faire or group-centered leader is highly nondirective. Ask him if he is the leader and he may deny it; he is "just one of the group." He wants to get all members to participate without asserting any of his authority. His communication behavior tends to serve as a link or transition that connects the contributions of group members. If no other group member attempts to exert more control than the laissez-faire leader, the group may be disorganized, unproductive and apathetic because members feel the group lacks purpose. However, in certain situations, particularly in therapy groups, laissez-faire leadership is the most appropriate and effective of all five leadership styles.

In examining the effects of various styles of leadership, there is no mention of the way people become leaders, the role communication plays in establishing and maintaining leadership, nor how leadership roles change over time. A consideration of social influence and power recognizes these dynamic aspects of leadership in small groups.

Leadership and social influence

A member may enter a group with externally derived power. For example, a small gourmet cooking class in French cuisine might be headed by a person with well-known credentials, such as Julia Child, or even some lesser known individual who happens to be the chef at a local restaurant. Both teachers, regardless of fame or anonymity, possess externally derived power. It is also possible for a member to build power within the group by establishing his credibility and status and engaging in campaigning behavior. For instance, if Julia Child's pastry is surpassed by that of an unsung member, his ability to influence other group members in this area is likely to be enhanced. As group tasks change and different members emerge as more competent for given tasks, power shifts. However, a person's power at any time also depends on how well he conforms to the group's standards and how well he handles conflict. A potential leader who usually conforms can build up freedom to deviate, if he does so infrequently. The chef who proves himself superior to Julia Child in *haute cuisine* may acquire the authority to promote a few eccentric variations on classic recipes. Sometimes a member who is good at resolving interpersonal conflict becomes the group's socio-emotional leader. A group may have both a socio-emotional leader and a task leader at the same time, although they are unlikely to be the same person.

Communication is received and sent most by those who have the power—that is, the leaders. Also, leaders are more successful at influencing other group members. But if leaders interact primarily with other high status group members, cliques or subgroups may form, low status members may feel threatened and conflict may result. When subgroups form, feedback between them is frequently reduced, thereby diminishing one of the primary advantages of group interaction. Furthermore, competition and conflict among group members can reduce productivity, group cohesion and the satisfaction of individual members.[18]

---

[18] Morton Deutsch, "The Effects of Cooperation and Competition Upon Group Process," in D. Cartwright and A. Zander, eds., *Group Dynamics* (New York: Harper and Row, 1968).

232 | Group membership roles

Group leadership needs to be supplemented by the roles that nonleaders perform. These nonleader roles, in a sense, are very specialized forms of leadership; that is, they involve communication behavior in which leaders usually engage. For example, a group member other than a leader may function as an evaluator-critic who sets standards and evaluates group outcomes according to them. Because of the dynamic nature of a small group, members may engage in a wide variety of role-playing behavior. In fact, if group members share constructive roles, participation and influence within the group are likely to be well-balanced.

Figure 7-4 Leadership plays a part in many group situations. Conferences provide group members with an opportunity to discuss their ideas.

There are three categories of membership or nonleader roles.[19] The first are group-task roles that facilitate completion of

[19] For a complete discussion of all three categories of roles see Kenneth D. Benne and Paul Sheats, "Functional Roles of Group Members," *Journal of Social Issues, 4* (1968), pp. 41-49.

2 | *The structures*

the group's work. In a group studying traffic problems in a congested section of a city, one member may play the role of information-seeker, gathering facts about the precise number of automobiles and trucks in the area at specific times during the day. Another member may function as an initiator-contributor, proposing new goals that the group might consider and offering possible methods to reduce traffic. Someone else in the traffic study group may play the role of orienter, making certain the group remains focused on its goal every time another member complains about the air pollution in the area. And still another group member may function as a procedural technician, making certain that a room is available for each meeting and that there is a chair for each member.

The second set of membership roles are called maintenance roles; they help to keep the group cohesive and maintain good interpersonal relationships among its members. Maintenance roles are especially important in reducing conflict, and people playing them might use the strategies suggested for conflict resolution. Most groups have a harmonizer who makes a joke just at the moment when tempers are about to flare; a follower who listens to and passively accepts the suggestions of other members; a gatekeeper or expediter who regulates communication channels by noting that poor David has not had a chance to talk yet; and a compromiser who is willing to moderate his position when conflict seems likely.

The final category of membership roles are disruptive self-centered roles. Most of us have observed group members who have played these roles; in fact, most of us have played some of these roles ourselves. For example, there is the aggressor who expresses envy and disapproval of other group members and who sometimes attacks the group itself; the recognition seeker who calls attention to himself by telling the group about his latest personal achievements; the help seeker who expresses insecurity in order to gain attention; the self confessor who uses the group as an audience to express his personal feelings about subjects irrelevant to the group; the playboy who makes cynical jokes to let other group members know that he is not involved. Of course, disruptive, self-centered roles divert the group from its function and often do irreparable harm; consequently, they should be avoided by group members.

Group-task, maintenance and disruptive roles are likely to occur in any group, but is unlikely for all the roles within a category to occur. Furthermore, an individual within a group will probably play more than one role. For example, the procedural technician who arranges chairs may also be a follower who passively accepts the suggestion of other group members. Another group member may be a harmonizer who helps to reconcile group differences while also being a compromiser. In other words, many of these roles are not mutually exclusive categories, although certain roles are clearly incompatible for the same individual. We would not, for instance, expect a person to be both a follower and an aggressor.

Role-playing is a complex phenomenon, especially within the small group setting where interactions are many and varied. Nevertheless, an understanding of role-playing can provide helpful insights into the nature of small group communication Some useful questions to ponder are: Which roles are or are not being performed? Which roles should or should not be performed? What effects does the communication behavior of group members have on the group's function? Productive role-playing by members can make the group an evolving, dynamic experience.

1. Small group communication may be defined as the face-to-face interaction by a collection of individuals who share a sense of group identity. Small group communication is more dynamic and spontaneous than public address or mass communication, but it is more structured than dyadic communication.

2. A group may serve some function for the individual, the group itself or the society. Groups may provide members with an opportunity for social relationships, education, persuasion, decision-making and problem-solving or therapy.

3. Sometimes the development of social relationships is the primary function of a group, and to varying degrees, most groups provide social relationships as a secondary function. Small group interaction may satisfy many personal needs such as the desire for affiliation, acceptance, liking, achievement, recognition, dominance and autonomy. The status and power relationships between group members will also affect communication within the group.

4. A group may formally or informally work to obtain and exchange information. Whether or not the small group is successful in educating its members depends on several factors. Three factors unique to the small group situation that may affect learning within it are: the amount of new information, the number of persons in the group and the frequency of interaction between group members.

5. Small groups are common and ideal forums for persuasive attempts. A member of a small group who advocates positions that deviate from the group's norms may be subjected to pressures to conform. To some extent, the amount of information a group member possesses may affect his choice of positions.

6. Small groups are particularly adept at problem-solving and decision-making. Small group interaction seems to produce an assembly-effect bonus, that is, the group's

product is greater than the combined product of the same number of people working individually. The reflective thinking theory suggests that there are six steps in problem-solving and decision-making. These steps are: recognizing the difficulty, defining and clarifying the problem, developing criteria, suggesting solutions, selecting the optimum solution and putting the plan into action. Another approach to group problem-solving and decision-making is Backtrack Programming. This method divides the group's problem into subproblems, each of which is solved according to rigid criteria established for the overall problem.

7. Conflict in a small group may occur for many reasons. Conflict may be the result of unsuccessful attempts at persuasion, problem-solving and decision-making. It may result from a competitive atmosphere within the group, or it may be the product of one member's desire for recognition and dominance. There are several strategies that may be employed to resolve conflict within the group. These strategies include stressing a higher level goal that all members share, reestablishing trust by engaging in some cooperative or compromise behavior, satisfying individual needs by praising and rewarding members, obtaining the assistance of a neutral third party, shifting the discussion to a noncontroversial subject, redefining the group's task or dividing the group into compatible subgroups.

8. Unlike other types of groups, a therapy group usually has no group goal; the object of most therapy groups is to help the members achieve personal change. Therapy groups should be run only by a person who has adequate training and who knows the personal case history of each member.

9. Five styles of leadership have been identified: authoritarian, bureaucratic, diplomatic, democratic and laissez-faire. Each style produces different effects on communication within a small group. Group leadership needs to be supplemented by nonleadership or membership roles. There are three types of group membership roles: group-task roles that facilitate the completion of the group's work, maintenance roles that keep the group cohesive and disruptive roles that damage the smooth operation of a group.

1. Make a list of all the groups you belong to. What functions discussed in this chapter do these different groups serve for you?

2. Apply the "Standard Agenda" for decision-making to the following situation. Establish criteria and make a group decision.

The people in your group represent a panel of doctors. Each of the patients listed below is in need of the services of a kidney machine to do the work of their own failing organs. There are only enough machines available to treat three patients. It is impossible to purchase additional machines. It is the job of your panel to decide, based on the information given, those patients who will receive treatment and those who will not. The patients who do not receive treatment will die.

Professor Tom Swanson: He is 35 years old and a professor of Social Sciences at a major university. Presently he is doing research on the urban poor. He is very active in organizations that help underprivileged children. He is planning to be married in three months.

Mrs. Betty Harlan: She is a 41-year-old divorcee. She has no children but helps to support her bedridden mother. She works as a public health officer, giving seminars in diet and health to various groups. She holds a M.S. degree in social work and is attending school in the evening to complete her Ph.D.

Johnny Bailey: He is an extremely bright 10 year old who has severe emotional problems. He rarely talks with other people and has been removed from the public school system.

Father James O'Donnell: He is a 57-year-old Catholic priest. He has been counseling young people for many years and has established three local missions for alcoholics.

James C. Washington: He is a 19-year-old freshman at a large university. He has been arrested on a number of minor charges, but has never been convicted. He is a member of a black radical group that believes in revolutionary tactics. He works at various jobs to support himself and finish school.

William Zeigler: He is 39 years old, married and the father of four children ranging in age from 2 to 14. He owns and operates a small television repair business.

Jean McBride: She is 23 years old, single and works as an undercover agent in the narcotics division of the city's police department. She gives a large part of her salary to drug-care centers.

Michael Burgoon, Judee K. Heston and James C. McCroskey, *Small Group Communication: A Functional Approach* (New York, Holt, Rinehart and Winston, Inc., in press). This book presents a detailed discussion of the different functions of small group communication.

Robert S. Cathcart and Larry A. Samovar, eds., *Small Group Communication: A Reader* (Dubuque, Iowa: William C. Brown Company, 1970). Some of the classic research in the field of small group communication is included in this collection. Some selections are very technical, but all will be of great value to anyone interested in the subject.

Halbert E. Gulley, *Discussion, Conference, and Group Process*, 2nd ed. (New York: Holt, Rinehart and Winston, Inc., 1969). Designed to help the student better understand the way groups function and the way individuals become effective discussion leaders, this book focuses on the discussion interaction process and leadership. Primary emphasis is on decision-making, although some attention is given to information sharing and other group functions.

Lawrence B. Rosenfeld, *Human Interaction in the Small Group Setting* (Columbus, Ohio: Charles E. Merrill, 1973). This book presents a contemporary behavioral approach to small group communication. Many practical suggestions for increasing the effectiveness of small group communication are offered.

Gerald M. Phillips, *Communication and the Small Group*, 2nd ed. (Indianapolis: Bobbs-Merrill Company, 1973). This is a short, readable introduction to the study of small group communication. The sections on decision-making and problem-solving will be especially useful for interested students.

8 *Public address communication*

At one time or another almost everyone has been bored by a tedious public speaker—at a graduation ceremony, at a political meeting or even in a classroom, where a teacher's droning, sing-song delivery seems likely to put half the class to sleep.

Some people, however, are fortunate enough to find themselves in the presence of a real orator: somone who can amuse, entertain, enlighten or persuade; someone who can move an audience to tears, immerse them in helpless laughter or bring them roaring to their feet with shouts of approval. A really effective speaker can produce an incredible effect upon his audience. In fact, the Athenians of the Golden Age—who thought very highly of the oratorical arts, and who expected every educated man to have some skill in public speaking— also feared the power of a good speaker to sway men's minds and arouse their passions. The Athenians invented a name for a speaker who influenced crowds of people in such a way as to enhance his own power; they called him a demagogue, or a leader of the mob. There have been many demagogues since the Golden Age, among them Adolf Hitler, whose highly emotional speeches at mass rallies in the early 1930s helped the Nazi Party come to power in Germany. American politicians regularly accuse their opponents of varying degrees of demagoguery in their public speeches.

Obviously, most public speakers do not use their skills as means to antisocial ends. Some of the most effective modern orators, such as the Reverend Martin Luther King, Jr. or the Reverend Billy Graham, have used their skills in the service of mankind. However, most public speakers are neither demagogues nor missionaries, and their reasons for speaking are far more prosaic: a government official publicly announces that food prices are still rising; the newly elected president of the P.T.A. makes her first official speech; an executive addresses a business meeting; a father reluctantly lectures a Cub Scout den on the art of tying knots.

Some years ago, schoolchildren were made to memorize long passages of classic oratory, and public speaking was a fairly popular art form. The growth of mass communications has reduced the opportunities for public speaking. However, anyone who aspires to a career in teaching, politics, public relations, or to an executive position in business, a club or any other organization, will almost invariably be called upon to speak before an audience. To people in such professions, a knowledge of the skills and techniques of public speaking is invaluable.

The chief reason for studying public speaking, however, is that public speaking can be fun; there is a little of the ham in all of us, and standing in front of an audience, the center of attention, is something that many people find irresistible. To work hard on a speech, to use one's speaking skills to entertain, persuade or enlighten an audience, offers a special kind of satisfaction, a small sense of power and accomplishment, that is often reward enough for the long hours spent in learning the techniques of public speaking and putting them into practice.

The public speaking situation

Public speaking differs significantly from other forms of verbal communication. Public speaking is a formal communication situation; it is structured and conforms to unwritten rules of behavior for both speaker and audience. It is a constrained situation, lacking the spontaneity and flexibility of face-to-face communication. Feedback is restricted. The public speaking situation is further characterized by both physical and psychological distance between the audience and the speaker. Because of this sense of separation, public speaking generally lacks the intimacy and empathy of face-to-face communication. The fact that the public speaker generally regards his audience as a single entity or body rather than as a group of individuals also tends to depersonalize the situation. This attitude is often necessary, especially with a large audience; it is also true that audiences sometimes respond as one unit. This division between speaker and audience, however, creates some obstacles to good communication.

In a public speaking situation, the speaker generally has complete control over the speech itself. He can prepare and rehearse what he has to say in advance and present it uninterrupted to its conclusion. He thus has control over the content, organization and delivery of his speech.

Yet the speaker has little or no control over other factors in a public speaking situation. One such factor is the environment. The speaker can rarely choose the location in which he speaks; he has no control over the physical appearance of the surroundings, lighting, temperature, insulation against noise and seating arrangements—all of which can influence the effectiveness of his speech. Unpleasant surroundings, glaring or dim lighting, high temperatures, poor soundproofing and uncomfortable seating can all distract listeners and undermine a speech.

Figure 8-1 Seating arrangement and other environmental factors can effect the impact of a speaker on his audience. The gestures and facial expressions that enhance a speaker's effectiveness will be lost to audience members seated on either side of the platform shown in this picture.

A second way in which the speaker lacks control is his inability to adapt to the individual differences among audience members. He is not likely to be familiar with the unique characteristics of the individuals making up his audience. Even if he were, he could hardly adjust his message to appeal simultaneously to every member of his audience. The problem is further compounded by the lack of verbal feedback available in public speaking situations and the often ambiguous nature of the nonverbal feedback. For instance, does a completely silent audience indicate courteous attention or disapproval? Because of these problems, the speaker must treat the audience as a single unit, developing stereotypic conceptions of his audience's characteristics and likely responses. He must also respond to the gross audience feedback he gets rather than to the feedback from individual listeners.

Another aspect of limited control for a speaker is the seating arrangement, which may affect audience interaction. Most public speakers have observed that an audience *creates a contagion:* listeners can emotionally stimulate one another, thus intensifying the effect of the speech. This "social facilitation" was described somewhat cynically by Quintilian:

> The listeners' judgment is often swept away by his preference for a particular speaker, or by the applause of an enthusiastic audience. For we are ashamed to disagree with them, and an unconscious modesty prevents us from ranking our own opinion above theirs, though all the time the taste of the majority is vicious, and the claque may praise even what does not really deserve approval.[1]

Traditional wisdom maintains that close proximity causes this effect. A recent study found, however, that audience members seated in a scattered fashion were more likely to respond favorably to the speech's message than those seated compactly.[2] The explanation offered was that scattered seating is more conducive to logical appeals, and compact seating more conducive to emotional appeals. Although the evidence is inconclusive as to the effects of various seating arrangements, the fact remains that the speaker has little control over the way the audience seats itself. In some instances, he may attempt to arrange the seats or have members of the audience ushered to seats that best serve his purpose; alternately, he may try to adapt his speech's appeals to take advantage of the audience's arrangement. His opportunities to manage the situation will be greater when the audience is small, the rooms have movable chairs and speech topics are extemporaneous.

A final factor that is usually beyond the speaker's control is the audience's influence on him. By their feedback, members of the audience can affect the fluency, utterance rate, voice loudness, anxiety, eye contact and body movement of the

---

[1] Quintilian, *Institutio Oratorica* as cited in Albert L. Furbay, "The Influence of Scattered versus Compact Seating on Audience Response," *Speech Monographs,* 32 (1965), p. 144.

[2] *Ibid.,* pp. 144-148.

speaker. Positive feedback can increase the accuracy of message transmission, reinforce certain message characteristics, strengthen the speaker's self-confidence and reinforce his beliefs. Negative feedback can seriously affect the speaker's delivery and self-confidence and the clarity of his message.[3] Audience feedback can be a powerful force; a restless, bored or obviously disapproving audience can completely demoralize even an experienced speaker.

Because the public speaking situation introduces elements beyond the control of the speaker, he must try to master those elements of the speech over which he does have control. Essentially, this means that the speaker should give great thought to the preparation and delivery of his speech.

Initial planning of the speech

The first steps a speaker must take in planning a speech include deciding the purpose of the speech, analyzing his prospective audience, analyzing the location and occasion of the speech and choosing a speech topic. Carelessness in any of these early planning stages can have drastic consequences on the completed speech; thus, even a technically superb speech could be counted a failure if it is delivered to the wrong audience, at an inappropriate time, or if it introduces unfortunate topics.

Deciding the purpose of the speech

The first question a speaker must ask himself as he prepares his speech is why is he making the speech. Does he intend to entertain his audience? To inform them? To persuade them to some course of action? Sometimes the speaker's overriding goal may be to improve his reputation with the audience. Politicians, for example, may seek to build credibility, selling themselves as honest, sincere, capable people. In other instances, the situation may dictate whether a speaker is to inform, entertain or persuade his audience. An after dinner speech usually involves some entertainment; a freshman orientation speech would probably be mostly informative; a speech at a political rally would be persuasive. The speaker must clarify his purpose in his own mind at the outset, so that he can

---

[3] For an excellent summary of the effects of feedback see James C. Gardiner, "The Effect of Expected and Perceived Receiver Response on Source Attitudes," *Journal of Communication*, 22 (1972), pp. 289-299.

carefully tailor his presentation to meet his goals or the goals of those who invited him to speak.

Analyzing the audience

The second element a speaker must consider is the nature of his audience. The difficulty of identifying the personal characteristics of members of the audience has already been discussed. There are several steps, however, a speaker can take to help him define his audience. He can study the demographic features of his audience: their age, sex, socioeconomic status, occupation and geographic background. He can try to assess their special interests, values, attitudes and beliefs that are relevant to his intended topic. Unfortunately, this preliminary research is often overlooked. The practiced speaker does not ignore such information; he critically analyzes his audience and adapts his speech to take advantage of the information he has obtained. On the basis of what he has learned, he can decide whether he is confronting a friendly, hostile, neutral, apathetic or mixed audience. Such information can determine the types of arguments, evidence and examples he will use, the emphasis he needs to place on establishing his credibility, his choice of language and the delivery style he should employ.

Analyzing the occasion and location

The time and location of a speech are important considerations, for they can impose restraints on a speaker. A special occasion —such as the Fourth of July or a retirement dinner—may dictate the topic for the speech. If he is one of a number of speakers on a given occasion, the speaker will probably want to limit the duration of his speech. A humorous speech would be inappropriate for a solemn occasion, and a solemn one inappropriate for an informal party. A speech before a small indoor gathering and a speech to a large crowd out-of-doors have different requirements in terms of content and delivery. The experienced speaker takes care to ascertain any limitations due to the occasion or location and adapts his speech to take advantage of this knowledge.

A speaker can also effectively utilize the nature of the occasion and location to intensify the impact of his message. A sombre setting can highlight a serious speech; gay surroundings and a festive occasion can make an audience more responsive to an entertaining speech; a crisis can make the audience more susceptible to an emotionally persuasive speech. By adapting his speech to fit the occasion, the speaker can use the physical and psychological circumstances of the situation to enhance the effectiveness of his speech.

Choosing the topic
Even when the speaker is completely free to choose his own speech topic, there are several guidelines he should consider in order to select the best topic.

Suitability to the speaker A common error of beginning public speakers is to select a topic that interests them, but about which they know very little. A speaker may find it difficult to gather authoritative information about an unfamiliar subject; lack of extensive knowledge may make him vulnerable if he should develop a mental block while speaking, or lose his train of thought. If instead he chooses a familiar topic, he will be better able to recover himself under stress; he will also be more prepared to answer any audience questions. A speaker is often asked to speak precisely because of his special knowledge. If the members of a group invite a foreign policy expert to address them, they would probably be disappointed if he delivered a speech on rose gardens.

Relevance to the audience Some topics are simply not suitable for the audience being addressed. No speaker should talk about a technical subject in which his audience has no background—or if he does, he should adapt his explanations to the level of his audience's understanding. The speech should also be adapted to the attitudes and values of the audience. A speech calling for an end to federal support for farm prices would probably not be well received by a group of farmers. The topic chosen should also be adapted so as to make it more meaningful to the audience. A speech on air pollution, for instance, will be more meaningful if it includes information on how pollution affects the lives of the individual members of the audience. The more meaningful and involving a topic is, the more successful a speech is likely to be.

Conciseness Another error speakers often make is to attempt to do too much in the time they have available. The result is either excessively general speeches or excessively long ones. Thomas Jefferson once said, "speeches measured by the hour, die by the hour." The mark of a good speaker is succinctness:

he is clear, specific and brief. A teacher cannot really cover the causes and results of the Civil War in one class; a politician cannot present all of his policies in one speech. The complex topics of drug addiction, growing crime rates or industrial pollution cannot be adequately covered in a five-minute class report. Given time constraints, the speaker must decide how far to narrow a topic, and which aspect of it to emphasize, so that he can sufficiently discuss it and substantiate his position without resorting to broad generalities.

Appropriateness to intermediate and ultimate goals There are times when a speaker cannot achieve his ultimate goal in a single attempt, or when it would not be prudent to direct his speech toward that ultimate goal. For example, a member of the Peace Corps working in an underdeveloped country may find that his first task is to convince his audience that he is trustworthy and that he wants only to help; later speeches can be directed toward persuading his audience to adopt new ideas or techniques. A speaker facing a hostile audience may take a gradual approach to his final goal. Thus, a speaker who advocates socialized medicine before a hostile audience might start by acknowledging his listeners' fears about socialism in general and reassuring them that he is not attacking the whole structure of free enterprise. He might then introduce statistics on the problem of health care, discuss various solutions and, finally, present his arguments for socialized medicine.

Preparing the speech

Once the speaker has decided what his topic will be, he is ready to consider the question of how the topic will be presented. Traditional studies of rhetoric—the art of using language so as to persuade or influence others—prescribes five different concepts to be considered in preparing and presenting a speech. The five concepts are: invention, disposition, style, memory and delivery. *Invention* has been defined as the process of investigating and analyzing the subject of the speech. It is during this stage that arguments or ideas are generated. James McCroskey has said about invention:

> Assuming that thorough investigation has uncovered what is knowable about the subject, invention is the process of discovering what among the knowables are sayable by the particular source to the particular

audience on the particular occasion to accomplish a particular purpose.[4]

The second concept, *disposition*, concerns the selection, apportionment (emphasis) and arrangement of material. These decisions are interrelated with the process of invention and may occur simultaneously. Once the actual content of the speech has been selected and ordered, the third concept, *style*, becomes important. Stylistic decisions involve language choices to express the ideas. The fourth concept, *memory*, is less important today, because most speakers speak from a written text or notes. In times past, however, orators were expected to deliver their speeches entirely from memory. The fifth and final concept, *delivery*, concerns the nonverbal elements of the actual presentation.

Invention

The first step in actual preparation of the speech is generating potential ideas. This step demands of the speaker that he consider all possible aspects of his topic and the beliefs, values and attitudes to which he can appeal.

Generating ideas Several lists of general appeals have been developed that may aid the speaker in discovering all the available lines of argument he may use on a given topic. These classification systems should provoke the speaker to think about his topic from a variety of perspectives. One such list is known as *stock issues*. These are the general arguments pertinent to any message advocating a policy or policies. These stock issues may take the form of six questions that any speech arguing for a policy should answer.

Is there a compelling need? A speech should establish not only that a need for the policy exists, but also that it is a significant, widespread problem. This provides the rationale for adoption of a new policy.

Is the need inherent? This question asks whether the problem can be solved without a major change in the present system, or whether indeed a basic policy change is needed. If the problem will solve itself or can be rectified through minor changes in the present system, then the need is not inherent and the justification for a new policy is minimized. For example, many people have recently called for basic reforms in the financing of political campaigns to reduce corruption in

---

[4] James C. McCroskey, *An Introduction to Rhetorical Communication* (Englewood Cliffs, N.J.: Prentice-Hall, 1972), p. 141.

government. If it could be shown that the trouble lies in the fact that present campaign financing laws are not rigorously enforced, the argument for new laws would be seriously weakened.

Is the plan workable? In advocating a new policy, a speaker should demonstrate that his ideas will actually work. A policy that does not take into account the political, social and economic realities of a given situation is unworkable in that situation. For instance, the idea of establishing a world government is attractive for many reasons, but the proposal is unworkable at present because of differing national goals and international conflicts; very few national governments would consider giving up any of their powers in favor of a single world government.

Is the plan practical? Another issue is whether the proposed plan is practical. Questions of efficiency, time, costs and availability of resources are involved in the issue of practicality. Some people have suggested that colonizing other planets of our solar system might relieve the problem of overpopulation on earth. Given the present stage of human technology, the costs of such an enterprise and the rate of population expansion, however, such a plan is wholly impractical.

Does the plan meet the need? Even if a plan is practical and workable, it may not satisfy the need. Underlying this issue is the question of the true causes of the problem. Harsher laws and stricter law enforcement, for example, have been offered as solutions to growing crime rates. Such policies would probably put more people in jail, but many experts believe that the only real solutions to the problem involve attacking some of the root causes of crime, such as poverty, unemployment and social alienation.

What advantages and/or disadvantages will result? In addition to analyzing the problem that the policy is designed to correct, the speaker should evaluate the side effects that will result from his proposals. For example, locating a new industrial plant in an economically depressed community may bring increased employment and prosperity, but the new plant may also create pollution or harm the quality of life in other ways. In defending a proposal on the basis of its advantages, the speaker must be able to show that the advantages outweigh any disadvantages that might result. Clearly, any proposal that generates more disadvantages than advantages will be indefensible.

Figure 8-2 Regardless of the numerous characteristics that audience members share, each is a unique receiver who will respond to the speaker's message in a unique way.

Assessing effects on the audience To make a successful speech, the speaker must discover arguments that will make the issue relevant to his audience, relating the arguments to the listeners' needs, desires and values. In a persuasive speech, this is important to arouse interest and concern. In an informative speech, an understanding of the audience's needs, beliefs and values is essential, so that the speaker can predict what they will find believable and useful.

Issues that are likely to arouse audience concern include basic physical needs such as food, water and shelter; emotional needs such as affection, security and self-fulfillment; common human desires, such as wealth, material possessions, power, reputation and beauty; abstract virtues, such as courage, honor, generosity and patriotism; and conditions or systems upon which people place greater or lesser value, such as peace, order, justice, equality, freedom, democracy, free enterprise, states' rights and socialism.

Obviously, not all people share the same needs, desires or values, nor do they place them in the same hierarchy of importance. One individual may place great value on job security, a steadily increasing income, the acquisition of material goods and a safe and comfortable life in the suburbs. Another individual might find such a life stultifying, placing a much greater value on the freedom, adventure and variety of a less "stable" existence. Many Americans place a very high value on patriotism, whereas others want no part of what they see as chauvinistic "flag-waving."

The job of the speaker is to assess the needs, desires and values of his particular audience and generate lines of argument that are consistent with or appeal to them. A speech urging people to save money is misdirected if its audience can barely stretch their incomes to cover basic needs of food and shelter; a luxury car salesman's pitch would be wasted on a group of monks whose desires do not include material wealth. A speech on the "wonders of socialism" would have little appeal to a group of small-town businessmen with conservative values; a speech advocating government censorship of newspapers would be inappropriate for a group of civil libertarians.

Arguments that appeal to human fears are often connected with the worst excesses of political demagoguery. Speeches that appeal to racial or ethnic prejudices, speeches that use economic fears to turn one group against another, speeches that promise "instant solutions" to complex problems and offer scapegoats to public wrath can be used by unscrupulous individuals to gain power for themselves. There are, however, more respectable ways of using human fears in constructing the arguments for a speech. A speaker may argue, for instance, that "taxes will inevitably rise," or "basic freedoms will be lost" unless his policies are adopted. He may also claim that following his policies will prevent such evils as war, unemployment, illness or divorce. Mass advertising, incidentally, often uses human fears to sell products or services. The message, whether subtly or unsubtly expressed, seems to be "if you do not use Brand X" (a soap, a deodorant, a beauty aid or a car) "you will be ugly, unloved, professionally unsuccessful or socially unpopular."

In conclusion, the speaker must make sure that his arguments are relevant to the needs, desires, values and fears of his specific audience.

Investigating and analyzing arguments In preparing his message, a speaker often compiles a variety of arguments before he begins to analyze and reject them; without an initially extensive list, the investigation process may be narrow and stunted. The speaker should explore all possible avenues in order to achieve a complete analysis and to make sure he does not neglect arguments that would strengthen his speech.

The investigation of a topic should take advantage of all available resources, including personal experience, books, periodicals, journals, abstracts, pamphlets, unpublished professional papers and persons with special knowledge or related experience. The facts, statistics, opinions, examples, analogies and anecdotes gathered by the speaker will be used as background knowledge in constructing the speech and as supportive material within the speech itself. There are several principles that can be used as guides in collecting material.

The material should be new to the audience. Speeches based on facts that are common knowledge, familiar examples, trite analogies and tired jokes will only bore an audience.

The material should be current. Outdated examples or information may harm the speech. This does not mean that only recent publications should be consulted or that only recent anecdotes and examples should be used. But where conflicting information exists, more credence should generally be given to the more recent findings. Thus, citing 1950s research findings on cancer or 1970 estimates of pollution costs may produce inaccurate conclusions. Failure to use recent evidence may leave the speaker vulnerable to attack or rejection by his more "current" listeners. Moreover, outdated materials may seem uninteresting and irrelevant to an audience.

The materials should be authoritative. Unless the speaker is himself an authority on a given subject, any data he uses to support his subject should be taken from a competent, reputable source and from a source appropriate to the subject. Quoting a history professor on a controversial historical question would be appropriate, but quoting him on a psychological theory would not. The authorities quoted should also be chosen with reference to the nature of the audience. Thus, a certain senator's opinion on international trade might be quite persuasive to one audience, but totally unacceptable to another audience. The important decision is whether the source is competent in the eyes of the audience. The sources of opinions, facts and statistics should usually be documented within the speech (which makes it particularly important that they be accepted authorities). Sources of examples, analogies and comparisons need not be cited, but these should still be taken from reliable sources.

The material should be valid. There are two tests of validity the material should pass: internal and external. Internal validity means that the material is consistent within itself or within the context of the speech. It is also known as face validity. To argue that "all politicians are fools or liars" and then to support your argument with a quote from a politician is an obvious example of an internally inconsistent argument. External validity concerns the consistency of material with other known evidence. A businessman who tries to attract new investors by stressing his efficiency and business sense, when it is well known that he has filed for bankruptcy several times, will have a hard time convincing his audience.

The material should be reliable. In other words, the evidence given by one authority should be confirmed by other authorities. The scientist who reports a miracle cure for cancer that cannot be duplicated by other scientists using the same methods cannot be considered a reliable source. Similarly, the authority who says that world starvation is an impossibility may be regarded as unreliable if five of his colleages have concluded from the same data that it is an imminent danger.

The material should be relevant to the point it is supporting. To cite the charitable act of a businessman as evidence of his honesty would be to present irrelevant material. Similarly, a Presidential candidate who takes credit for lowering crime rates during his administration, or blames rising crime rates on his opponent's administration, is usually indulging in wishful thinking, since policies at the presidential level rarely have any effect on local crime. Unless he can prove a direct connection between his policies and crime rates, his evidence is irrelevant.

Finally, there should be sufficient supporting material. It is not enough to give one example or one statistic to defend an argument. If a communicator is going to be convincing, he should develop his arguments fully in terms of evidence, authoritative opinions, anecdotes and examples.

The speaker must provide enough accurate evidence to support his arguments, but he must also take care not to "overload" his speech with statistics and other evidence, lest he lose audience interest. An in-depth analysis of the subject can be made without sacrificing clarity, conciseness and audience appeal.

Disposition

Concurrently with the invention process, the speaker must consider the dispositional features of his message: the selection, apportionment and arrangement of his materials.

During the investigation stage, the speaker should have uncovered enough information and generated enough arguments that selection is necessary. In addition to the guidelines already offered on choosing content, audience identification should also be considered in the selection process. *Identification* is the process of establishing a common ground, or shared position, with your audience; obviously, this involves consideration of the needs, desires and values of the audience. Where choices exist, the communicator should choose those arguments and materials that have the most meaning and impact for the specific audience to be addressed. A psychologist addressing a parents' club, for example, might use the example of parent-child conflict to illustrate a point he wished to make about human behavior.

Another consideration in selecting arguments is the number to be used, which of course depends partly on the emphasis the speaker wants to give each point. A successful speech usually develops no more than two or three main points, since further arguments can lead to audience confusion and boredom. Just as too much evidence in the form of statistics and examples can harm a speech, too many arguments can lessen the speech's impact.

A final consideration in selection and apportionment is the emphasis the speaker wants to place on *ethos*, *logos* and *pathos*. These are the three traditional forms of proof. Ethos refers to the speaker's credibility; logos refers to logical proof; pathos refers to emotional proof. The emphasis placed on each will be determined primarily by the speaker's goals. If he is most concerned with establishing credibility with his audience, he will use arguments that will show him in his best light, including references to his accomplishments and experience, expressions of praise from others and statements about his own ideals and beliefs that are designed to convince the audience he is trustworthy and competent.

If the communicator wants to stress logos, he will use arguments that appeal to reason and an abundance of evidence. His choice of materials will produce a dispassionate, rational, well-documented message. If his desire is to emphasize pathos, he will select arguments, anecdotes and examples that appeal to the emotions. He will attempt to arouse emotion by playing upon needs, fears, desires and values. Because differing goals necessitate different choices of material and different amounts of emphasis, it is essential that the communicator predetermine his goals.

The next series of decisions a speaker must make concern the organization of the message. One decision he does not have to make: all messages must have an introduction, body and conclusion. Without an adequate introduction and conclusion, a speech would seem incomplete and unpolished. Preparation of the introduction and conclusion is usually left until last, so that they can be properly integrated into the main body of the speech. The speaker's first concern, then, is organization of the body of the speech. In many instances, the nature of the material will suggest the appropriate organizational pattern. A speech on a historical event, for instance, might be organized largely in chronological order.

Where choices exist, though, the speaker should be aware of the possible patterns he can use. The available patterns fall into two categories: logical arrangements and psychological arrangements. The former are those organizational patterns that inherently make sense, that are logical extensions of the material with which they deal. Psychological patterns, on the other hand, are designed to create a psychological effect. These patterns are intended to elicit those audience reactions desired by the speaker.

Deductive organization One of the most fundamental logical patterns is deductive reasoning. From a major premise or general law a specific conclusion is deduced. There are formally three parts to a deductive argument: the major premise (all-inclusive generalization), the minor premise (or specific statement of fact) and the conclusion drawn from the two premises.

Deductive reasoning may be used to organize the arguments of the speech in order to bring the audience to the desired conclusion. Thus, a speaker might argue that since all American children deserve a quality education (major premise), and

Johnny is an American child (minor premise) that Johnny deserves a quality education (conclusion). The speaker might then argue that quality education requires competent teachers (major premise), that Johnny's school lacks competent teachers (minor premise that would require proof), and that therefore Johnny's school does not provide quality education. Continuing this line of argument, the speaker may eventually arrive at the conclusion that taxes must be increased to pay for more competent teachers.

Deductive reasoning

Major premise: All men are mortal.
Minor premise: John is a man.
Conclusion: John is mortal.

In the actual speech, the speaker may easily omit mentioning some of the logical steps because they are obvious (for example, the minor premise that Johnny is an American child). But whether the steps are explicitly stated or only implied, the reasoning is based on the deductive pattern, which moves from general premises to specific conclusions.

Inductive organization In that it moves from the specific to the general, inductive reasoning is the opposite of deductive reasoning. The speaker who uses this pattern presents several examples or pieces of evidence and from these draws a general conclusion. Thus, a speaker might describe local air pollution laws, cite figures showing that air pollution is increasing, give evidence that few industries have been prosecuted under the laws and conclude inductively from those three pieces of evidence that local pollution-control laws are not being adequately enforced.

Inductive reasoning

Evidence: Country X has copper, but no iron.
Evidence: Country Y has iron, but no copper.
Evidence: Country X wants iron; country Y wants copper.
Conclusion: Countries X and Y should trade iron for copper.

Inductive reasoning may be particularly appropriate in a speech before a hostile audience, when the speaker wishes to use a gradual approach to his final argument. Stating the argument at the beginning may make a hostile audience even more resistant; the inductive pattern allows the speaker to present first an abundant amount of evidence which may help soften the resistance of the audience.

Cause-effect organization   Another common reasoning pattern is cause-effect reasoning. This pattern may actually take four forms: cause-effect, effect-cause, cause-cause or effect-effect. In arguments that are ordered from cause to effect, the causes or sources of a given problem are discussed, followed by a discussion of the effects. In the effect-cause pattern, the existing situation is discussed, followed by an analysis of the factors that produced it. Thus, a history professor speaking about World War I might first discuss the causes leading up to the war, and then discuss its effects. For dramatic effect, however, he might prefer to begin with graphic descriptions of the war's effects, and then discuss its causes.

Cause–effect reasoning

Cause: John has five apples.
Cause: Mary has no apples.
Cause: Mary is greedy, aggressive and stronger than John.
Effect: Mary takes John's apples.

Effect–cause reasoning

Effect: Man bites child.
Cause: Child bites man.
Cause: Child laughs at man's lecture on human bites.
Cause: Child bites man again.

If the speaker is dealing with an accepted and understood problem, he may be more interested in the relationship of the causes to one another. For instance, the speaker on World War I may discuss the relationship between nationalism and the European arms race, both causes of the war. Again, he may be more interested in the interrelationship between effects such as war reparations demanded of Germany and bitterness felt by the German people.

Chronological organization Materials frequently require a chronological arrangement. At least parts of a history lecture are most logically presented chronologically, moving either forward or backward in time. Similarly, a speaker may wish to use chronological order in explaining a series of events leading up to some current situation.

Chronological order

Jan. 5:	Independent investigator pinpoints waste in government operations.
Jan. 6:	Newspaper editorials call for action.
Jan. 9:	Congressmen call on President, demand action.
Jan. 10:	5,000 telegrams to White House, demanding action.
Jan. 15:	President appoints commission to study problem.
Feb. 22:	Commission issues preliminary report: situation serious.
Aug. 13:	Commission presents report to President.
Aug. 14:	Newspaper headlines on report; news of multiple murder pushes it off front pages for second editions.
Aug. 17:	President publicly thanks commission; files report without reading.

Chronological order should be used whenever it is important for the audience to understand the time-order relationship of several events.

Hierarchical organization Many arguments or concepts can be explained in a hierarchical pattern; that is, each element builds upon or is intrinsically related to the next.

A speaker may wish to argue from the simple to the complex, from the parts to the whole, from the whole to the parts or from basic needs to higher order needs—all examples of hierarchical organization.

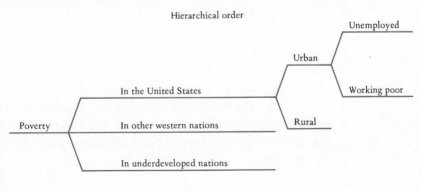

Hierarchical order

Spatial organization Another pattern of organization is based on the spatial relationship between objects, persons or places. The relationships are commonly discussed in an order of left-to-right, front-to-back, top-to-bottom, inside-to-outside or the reverse.

A speaker may wish to include in his speech information on geographical relationships, a description of a room or an account of an accident in terms of relative locations.

Spatial order

A common

form of
business letter

locates

the date at the top right margin,
the address and salutation below
the date and at the left margin,
the body of the letter two spaces
below the salutation, the complimentary close two spaces under
the body either at left margin or
under the date, and the

complimentary close

with the signature
four spaces below.

Process organization In explaining a process or activity, the logical pattern for presentation is according to the process order. Thus, the turning of iron ore into finished steel would be best described by discussing in turn each step of the process. The injunction to "begin at the beginning" is applicable to this pattern.

Process order

1. Bait hook.
2. Cast line.
3. Wait.
4. Land fish.
5. Cook over open fire.
6. Eat.

Structure-function organization   A common organizational pattern is to describe a structure and then explain how it functions. The structure-function method of organization may actually be an elaboration of the process model.

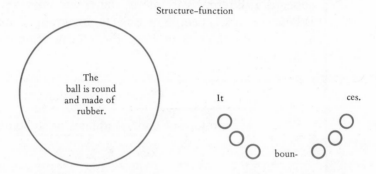

For example, an instructor in auto mechanics would probably first describe each element in the structure of the vehicle, then explain the function or purpose of each part and the interrelationship of parts and finally explain how the parts combine to make the vehicle move.

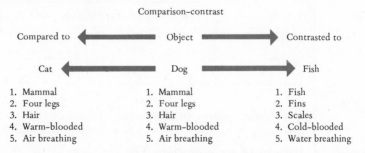

Comparison-contrast organization   Two elements of a speech often need to be compared for similarities and contrasted on dissimilarities. The process of comparing and contrasting may take several forms. All aspects of Element A may be described first, followed by a comparison along the same dimensions for Element B. Or each single dimension of similarity or dissimilarity may be discussed in sequence.

The comparison-contrast organization may also be combined with other patterns. For example, Candidate A may contrast his voting record with Candidate B's voting record and list the votes in chronological order. Or two washing machines may be compared and contrasted by describing their structure and function.

Classification organization Some subjects lend themselves to a topical or classification order: the material is ordered by classes or categories. The arrangement of chapters in this book partially follows this pattern. The first several chapters each concern a different variable in the communication process. Whenever ideas, people or objects are grouped and discussed according to their groupings, the classification pattern is being used.

Classification order			
Opinions of undergraduates on coed dorms			
	Yes	No	Don't know
Men	38%	40%	22%
Women	45%	41%	14%
Freshmen	34%	38%	28%
Sophomores	48%	36%	16%
Juniors	53%	45%	2%
Seniors	67%	30%	3%
Opinions of parents on coed dorms			
	Yes	No	Don't know
	23%	68%	9%

Problem-solution organization \Messages that describe or advocate a solution to some problem generally employ this pattern of organization. The problem is usually presented first, because, unless the audience understands the nature of the problem, they may not be able to grasp the relevance of the solution. For example, unless an audience is made to understand the complex causes of poverty in the United States, they will probably not understand the relevance of the programs advocated as solutions to the problem.

Problem–solution organization	
Problem	Possible solutions
Failing grades	1. Accuse teachers of bias. 2. Quit school. 3. Go to movies to take mind off problem. 4. Study harder.

Reflective thinking organization   This organizational pattern, previously described in the chapter on small group communication, is essentially an expansion of the problem-solution pattern; it is appropriate only for a policy speech. Its advantage is that each stage logically evolves out of the prior stage and criteria are clearly specified, thus guiding the listeners through the decision-making process. The pattern is appropriate both for informative speeches which describe the reasoning behind an existing solution and for persuasive speeches which advocate adoption of a new solution.

Reflective thinking organization

My candidate for mayor is a successful businessman.
Therefore he is efficient and resourceful.
Therefore he would manage city efficiently and resourcefully.
Therefore taxes could be lowered and better services provided.
Therefore my candidate should be elected.

In addition to the twelve logical patterns of organization, there are several organizational patterns which are intended primarily to create favorable psychological reactions.

Degree of familiarity   This organizational pattern begins with familiar arguments and then moves to those that are less familiar. In a persuasive speech, this pattern can be used to establish identification with the audience, since familiar arguments may put the listeners at ease and establish common ground between them and the speaker. In a speech advocating increased federal spending for medical research, a speaker might give the familiar argument that without earlier medical research, such benefits as the polio vaccine might never have been developed. If the audience is given fairly familiar information at the beginning, the familiar material can serve as a structure to which less familiar material can be linked. When the speaker's purpose is to improve his credibility, this pattern can be useful in demonstrating to an audience that he is not ignorant of their knowledge, but that he has more information and newer ideas. In other words, he is highly competent.

Degree of acceptance The degree of acceptance organization is similar to the degree of familiarity organization. The speaker begins with those arguments that are most acceptable to the audience. These should help establish identification and credibility (operating from the same principles as familiarity) before he introduces less acceptable arguments. A lawyer arguing his case before a jury might assure the jurors that he knows "all of you believe in justice" before he tries to convince them of his client's innocence. Presenting extreme arguments first can make an audience highly resistant to any further arguments, no matter how acceptable. Although particularly useful with hostile audiences, this pattern of organization can also be effective in strengthening and expanding the views of friendly audiences.

Monroe's motivated sequence This organizational pattern, developed by Alan Monroe,[5] is designed to motivate the audience to some action advocated by the speaker, although it may be used for informative speeches as well. It is a pattern to be used for an entire speech, from introduction to conclusion. There are five steps: attention, need, satisfaction, visualization and action.

The speech should begin by vividly drawing the attention of the audience to some problem. This is followed by an in-depth analysis of the need or problem. The speaker then offers a solution to the problem and demonstrates its superiority over alternative proposals. In the fourth step, visualization, the speaker tries to make each listener identify with the problem by projecting himself into the future and visualizing what will

---

[5] Alan H. Monroe and Douglas Ehninger, *Principles and Types of Speech*, 6th ed. (Glenview, Ill.: Scott, Foresman and Company, 1967), pp. 264-289.

happen if he does not accept the speaker's proposal. The last step in the sequence is the conclusion, which is a direct appeal to action. A speaker might begin by graphically describing a recent fire in a new skyscraper in which several people died. Then he analyzes the problem: outmoded building codes and fire safety regulations in the construction of new skyscrapers. After reminding his listeners that they or those close to them could easily be trapped in such a fire unless reforms are made, the speaker calls for action: political pressure to change building codes and fire regulations.

Climactic, anticlimactic and pyramidal organization These last three arrangement patterns need to be considered in combination, since only one of the three can be used at a time. In any speech, there is usually one point that is stronger or more interesting than the rest. When this is the last point made, climax order is being used; when it is the first point, anticlimax order is being used; when it appears in the middle, pyramidal order is being used.

The organization used depends partly on the disposition of the audience. When the audience is initially favorable or apathetic, it is acceptable to use the anticlimax order to reinforce and intensify their feelings. The assumption is that if they can be aroused at the beginning, their initial enthusiasm can be sustained during weaker, less interesting arguments. With a hostile audience, it is often advisable to begin with minor points while trying to gain their favor and build toward the strongest point, which comes as the climax. Pyramidal structure is rarely a good choice, since it both opens and closes with weak arguments. The speaker will usually find that some combination of the climax and anticlimax orders is the most effective: opening with a relatively strong, interesting but inoffensive argument and saving the best argument for a strong conclusion. Research results have been conflicting, but do tend to support the preferability of the climax order in gaining more attitude change.

Outlining The process of selecting and arranging the contents of the speech should implicitly generate a speech outline. The effective speaker turns this implicit outline into a complete written outline. Writing an outline forces the communicator to be certain that his speech flows smoothly and includes all the points he wants to cover, and that his arrangement is both logical and effective. This same outline can also serve as notes during the delivery of the speech.

The communicator can determine whether a complete sentence outline or an outline of brief phases only best suits his needs. Some speakers find that a detailed, full sentence outline helps them prepare in advance the best wording for main points and makes specific points easier to recall. Others find such outlines cumbersome.

Basic speech outline

I. Introduction (often written out in full)
II. Body
   A. First Main Point
      1. Supporting argument
         a. Further subpoint or supporting material
            (1) Evidence, examples, etc.
            (2) Evidence, examples, etc.
         b. Further subpoint or supporting material
      2. Supporting argument
      3. Supporting argument
   B. Second main point
      1. Supporting argument
      2. Supporting argument
   C. Third main point
      1. Supporting argument
      2. Supporting argument
      3. Supporting argument
III. Conclusion (usually written out in full)

The general outline for a speech is given above. The number of main points, subpoints and amount of supporting material will of course vary with the chosen topic.

Introductions, conclusions, previews and summaries The last stage in the disposition process is preparing the introduction, conclusion and summaries. The introduction should serve four functions: gaining the listeners' attention; revealing the purpose or topic of the speech; establishing identification; serving as a transition into the body of the speech. The

communicator can gain the audience's attention in a variety
of ways. He may begin, for example, with a startling fact, a
joke, a hypothetical question, an example, an anecdote or a
quotation. The communicator should be able to determine
intuitively what has interest value and what does not. Consider
this introduction to a speech by Four Guns, an Oglala Sioux
Indian judge, at a dinner given for him by a white anthropologist
in 1891:

> I have visited the Great Father in Washington. I have attended dinners
> among white people. Their ways are not our ways. We eat in silence,
> quietly smoke a pipe and depart. Thus is our host honored. This is
> not the way of the white man. After his food has been eaten, one is
> expected to say foolish things. Then the host feels honored. Many of
> the white man's ways are past our understanding, but now that we
> have eaten at the white man's table, it is fitting that we honor our
> host according to the ways of his people.[6]

This introduction immediately captures attention with its
startling and mildly humorous look at the white man's custom
of after-dinner speeches through an Indian's eyes. It is a graceful
and subtle introduction to the body of the speech, which
discusses the difference between white ways and Indian ways
(a subject of particular interest to the anthropologists in his
audience). But Four Guns also has a harsh message for his
white audience. In the body of the speech, he will remind
them that white men put great trust in written words; yet
they have made many treaties with the Indians, and then
broken the treaties. The Indian, he says, has no need of written
promises, for he carries truth in his heart, and acts on it. In
his introduction, however, Four Guns has prepared the way
for his harsh message. By presenting himself initially as the
rather simple Indian (he was not) who finds the ways of
white men strange, he has flattered his listeners as "sophisticated"
white men and encouraged them to feel patronizing and
sympathetic towards him.

At all costs the speaker should avoid the clichés of introductory
material, such as "my speech is about . . ." or "today I'm going
to talk to you about . . ." Such introductions are not only dull,
they are the sure sign of the amateur. If the speaker is going
to try complimenting or flattering his audience, it must be
subtly done. Except on certain occasions, such as college reunions,
reminiscing or telling the audience "how happy you are to be

---

[6] Delivered by Four Guns, Oglala Sioux Indian judge, in 1891. Reprinted in Clark Wissler,
Indian Cavalcade (New York: Sheridan House, 1938), p. 171.

there" should be avoided. Finally, the introduction should flow smoothly into the body of the speech. It should seem an integrated part of the whole rather than a disjointed, discrete element. Speakers who begin with an effective, attention-getting anecdote and then follow it with "my topic is . . . ," have not yet mastered the art of smooth transition.

Like the introduction, the conclusion is intended to serve as a transition, out of the body of the speech into the final statement. It should articulate smoothly with the body, creating a feeling of completion. There are several ways to conclude a speech. Some possible methods are: (1) a summary of the main points; (2) a final quotation; (3) a repetition of the introduction, with a new or more meaningful interpretation; (4) a closing example or anecdote; (5) a projection into the future; (6) a thought-provoking question; and (7) an appeal to action (as in Monroe's Motivated Sequence). The conclusion should receive special attention from the communicator, as it is responsible for the final impression made on the audience.

Nothing has been said yet about previews and internal summaries. These are minor introductions and conclusions which may precede and follow main points or subpoints. For example, after the main point, the communicator might say, "The important things to remember about no fault automobile insurance are first, it costs the insurance buyer less, and second, it lightens the burdensome caseload of the courts." This might then be followed by a preview of the second main point: "No fault automobile insurance is workable as has been demonstrated by other states that have adopted the program." The preview alerts the audience to what to expect next; the internal summary clarifies the speaker's point for the audience, as well as reviews the subpoints in its development so that the audience is more likely to remember them. The combination of internal summaries and previews also makes transitions easier from one main point to the next. Because they serve such useful functions, they need not be used sparingly. In fact, common advice to debaters in their message preparation is to "Tell them what you're going to do, do it, then tell them what you've done."

Style
When the communicator has completed the invention and disposition stages in preparing his speech, he can turn his attention to the style. Style refers to the manner in which we

express our ideas. Style is a deciding factor in whether a potentially good speech has impact. The style of a speech adds embellishment, but it is not just "icing." Different styles can have decidedly different effects on an audience.

Three basic goals of any speech are that the material be perceived accurately, that it gain attention and that it be remembered. These are also the goals of good style. The elements of good style to be discussed below are intended to achieve clarity, interest or better recall. These factors may in turn improve the persuasiveness of a speech.

Conversational speech   An important stylistic consideration is the difference between oral and written communication. Because there are major differences in the way we use language orally and in written form, many of the principles of good writing style are inapplicable to speech. Oral communication is less formal, uses fewer unfamiliar words, shorter words and shorter sentences, more contractions, more superlatives and interjections, more nonstandard words and more self-references. If a speech is to sound natural, therefore, it should resemble normal spoken communication rather than written discourse. This is what is meant by the recommendation that speeches be informal and conversational. Of course, certain situations demand more formal speech, such as inaugural addresses or government policy statements. But in the majority of situations, a more conversational approach is preferable. It is one means of establishing rapport with the audience and conveying an image of poise. Below is part of a politician's speech in which he attempts the conversational approach in a radio and television address. Shortly before the speech, he has been accused of using political funds for his personal use:

> My fellow Americans, I come before you tonight as a candidate for the vice presidency and as a man whose honesty and integrity has been questioned. . .
>
> The taxpayers should not be required to finance items which are not official business but which are primarily political business. . .
>
> Well, then, the question arises, you say, well, how do you pay for these and how can you do it legally? . . .
>
> The first way is to be a rich man. I don't happen to be a rich man. So I couldn't use that.
>
> Another way that is used is to put your wife on the payroll. Let me say incidentally, that my opponent, my opposite number for the vice presidency of the Democratic ticket, does have his wife on

the payroll and has had her on the payroll for the past ten years.

Now just let me say this. That is his business, and I am not critical of him for doing that. You will have to pass judgment on that particular point. . . .

I have found that there are so many deserving stenographers in Washington that needed work that I just didn't feel it was right to put my wife on the payroll. My wife sitting over here.[7]

Vividness Another desirable feature of public speaking style is vivid language. Vividly expressed ideas gain attention and are more easily recalled later. The use of striking words, phrases, comparisons or examples can heighten the impact of a speech. Often metaphors, similes and hyperboles can achieve this effect. Vivid language can be used to create interest and maintain the attention of the audience.

The following example of vivid language is from the inaugural speech of President Lyndon Johnson:

Think of our world as it looks from that rocket that is heading toward Mars. It is like a child's globe, hanging in space, the continents stuck to its side like colored maps. We are all fellow passengers on a dot of earth. And each of us, in the span of time, has really only a moment among our companions. . .

For this is what America is all about. It is the uncrossed desert and the unclimbed ridge. It is the star that is not reached and the harvest that is sleeping in the unplowed ground.

Is our world gone? We say farewell. Is a new world coming? We welcome it—and we bend it to the hopes of man.[8]

Redundancy and brevity Two somewhat conflicting elements of good style are redundancy and brevity. Redundancy refers to repetition of both expressions and ideas. Such repetition can reinforce a particularly strong point, as well as increase clarity. A common practice of experienced speakers is to repeat key phrases so that they become catchwords for the audience. Consider the use of "I have a dream" in this speech by the Reverend Martin Luther King, Jr.:

. . . I still have a dream. It is a dream deeply rooted in the American dream.

I have a dream that one day this nation will rise up and live out the true meaning of its creed: ". . . that all men are created equal."

I have a dream that one day on the red hills of Georgia the sons of

---

[7] Delivered by Richard M. Nixon on September 23, 1952. Reprinted in James C. McCroskey, *Introduction to Rhetorical Communication*, 2nd ed. (Englewood Cliffs, N.J.: Prentice-Hall, 1972), p. 301.

[8] Delivered by Lyndon B. Johnson on January 20, 1965. Reprinted in James A. Frost, Ralph Adams Brown, David M. Ellis and William B. Fink, *A History of the United States* (Chicago: Follett Educational Corp., 1968), p. 659.

former slaves and the sons of former slaveholders will be able to sit down together at the table of brotherhood; I have a dream—. . .

That my four little children will one day live in a nation where they will not be judged by the color of their skin but by the content of their character; I have a dream today.

I have a dream that one day in Alabama . . . little black boys and black girls will be able to join hands with little white boys and white girls as sisters and brothers; I have a dream today.

I have a dream that one day every valley shall be exalted, every hill and mountain shall be made low, and rough places will be made plane and crooked places will be made straight, and the glory of the Lord shall be revealed, and all flesh shall see it together.[9]

When used judiciously, redundancy is a valuable rhetorical device. However, when it is carried to the extreme, it becomes counterproductive. Speakers who are verbose, who use more words and sentences than necessary, bore their audiences. Communicators who can express themselves succinctly are easier to listen to and generally more persuasive. To achieve clarity and interest, the communicator therefore must seek the proper balance between brevity and redundancy.

Parallel structure   An element related to redundancy is parallel structure, which is the use of the same phrasing or sentence structure to express several related ideas. The following speech, a good example of the use of parallel structure, is from the inaugural address of President John F. Kennedy:

Let both sides explore what problems unite us instead of belaboring these problems which divide us.

Let both sides, for the first time, formulate serious and precise proposals for the inspection and control of arms—and bring the absolute power to destroy other nations under the absolute control of all nations.

Let both sides join to invoke the wonders of science instead of its terrors. Together let us explore the stars, conquer the deserts, eradicate disease, tap the ocean depths, and encourage the arts and commerce.

Let both sides unite to heed in all corners of the earth the command of Isaiah—to "undo the heavy burden . . . [and] let the oppressed go free."[10]

This stylistic device not only has aesthetic appeal, it adds organization, clarity and unity; it also improves recall of a message. Parallel structure may be used in expressing main points or subpoints or in paralleling elements of a single idea.

[9] Delivered by Martin Luther King, Jr. on August 28, 1963. Reprinted in McCroskey, op. cit., p. 288.
[10] Delivered by John F. Kennedy on January 20, 1961. Reprinted in McCroskey, op. cit., p. 284.

Variety and originality   The use of varied language and original expressions can add color and distinction to a speech. Clichés and all-too-familiar ideas are the mark of the commonplace speaker. Speeches are more interesting that use fresh and original expressions and vary the language patterns. Consider this excerpt from an 1854 speech by Seattle, a Dwamish Indian chief:

> Every part of this soil is sacred in the estimation of my people. Every hillside, every valley, every plain and grove, has been hallowed by some sad or happy event in days long vanished. The very dust upon which you now stand because it is rich with the blood of our ancestors and our bare feet are conscious of the sympathetic touch. Even the little children who lived here and rejoiced here for a brief season will love these somber solitudes and at even tide they greet shadowy returning spirits. And when the last Red Man shall have perished, and the memory of my tribe shall have become a myth among White Men, these shores will swarm with the invisible dead of my tribe, and when your children's children think themselves alone in the field, the store, the shop, upon the highway, or in the silence of the pathless woods, they will not be alone. At night when the streets of your cities and villages are silent and you think them deserted, they will throng with the returning hosts that once filled and still love this beautiful land. The White Man will never be alone.[11]

Emphasis   An obvious element of a good speech is the effective use of emphasis, which results from the combination of stylistic emphasis and delivery emphasis. An extremely well designed and supported speech can still fail if the speaker fails to focus attention on major points. Striking words or expressions, reversed grammatical structure, redundancy, hypothetical or rhetorical question, imperative statements and explicit references to the importance of a point can all add emphasis.

The use of emphasis is finely demonstrated in the following, from an 1876 speech by Frederick Douglass:

> Had Abraham Lincoln died from any of the numerous ills to which flesh is heir—had he reached that good old age of which his vigorous constitution and his temperate habits gave promise—had he been permitted to see the end of his great work—had the solemn curtain of death come down but gradually, we should still have been smitten with a heavy grief, and treasured his name lovingly. But, dying as he did die, by the red hand of violence, killed, assassinated, taken off without warning, not because of personal hate—for no man who knew Abraham Lincoln could hate him—but because of his fidelity

---

[11] Delivered by Seattle, Dwamish chief, in 1854. Reprinted in Archie Binns, *Northwest Gateway: The Story of the Port of Seattle* (New York: Doubleday and Company, 1941), pp. 103-104.

to union and liberty, he is doubly dear to us, and his memory will
be precious forever.[12]

Personalization   Through the process of personalization a
communicator allows his personality to be revealed. This is
accomplished by abundant use of self-references. Through
expressions of personal beliefs, feelings and experiences, the
communicator may increase his rapport with the audience.
Personalization seems to appeal to our curiosity and sense of
relatedness with others, thus creating interest value.

The speech from which the following was taken was delivered
by Barry Goldwater in accepting the Republican presidential
nomination in July, 1964:

> Our task would be too great for any man, did he not have with him
> the hearts and hands of this great Republican Party. . .
>
> I do not intend to let peace or freedom be torn from our grasp
> because of lack of strength or lack of will. *That* I promise you. . .
>
> I pledge that the America I envision in the years ahead will extend
> its hand in help . . . so that all new nations will at least be *encouraged*
> to go *our* way—so that they will not wander down the dark alleys
> of tyranny, or the dead-end streets of collectivism.
>
> Our Republican cause is not to level out the world or make its
> people conform in computer-regimented sameness.
>
> Our Republican cause is to free our people and light the way for
> liberty throughout the world.
>
> Ours is a very human cause for very *humane* goals.[13]

Humor   Everyone likes to laugh. Although existing research on
humor tends to deny its usefulness as a rhetorical device, few
people would deny that they enjoy a really funny speech or
a touch of humor in even the most serious speech. If it does
nothing else in a speech, humor makes it more enjoyable and
may increase the listeners' sympathetic identification with
the speaker. Humor may take several forms in a speech: a joke,
a humorous anecdote, witticisms, insults or satire. Speakers
considering use of insults or satire should carefully analyze
their audience before they make the attempt; these forms of
humor can easily backfire. Insults delivered in jest may give
real offense; listeners may not recognize that the speaker is
being satiric.

Following the guidelines on speech preparation contained
in this section, the inexperienced speaker can produce an

---

[12] Delivered by Frederick Douglass in 1876. Reprinted in Frederick Douglass, *The Life and Times of Frederick Douglass* (New York: Crowell-Collier, Inc., 1962), p. 492.

[13] Delivered by Barry Goldwater in July, 1964. Reprinted in McCroskey, *op. cit.*, p. 292.

impressively effective speech. The section appropriately concludes with the introduction from a speech made by a college freshman, Charles Schalliol, on the subject of air pollution:

> The strangler struck in Donora, Pennsylvania, in October of 1948. A thick fog bellowed through the streets enveloping everything in thick sheets of dirty moisture and a greasy black coating. As Tuesday faded into Saturday, the fumes from the big steel mills shrouded the outlines of the landscape. One could barely see across the narrow streets. Traffic stopped. Men lost their way returning from the mills. Walking through the streets, even for a few moments caused eyes to water and burn. The thick fumes grabbed at the throat and created a choking sensation. The air acquired a sickening bittersweet smell, nearly a taste. Death was in the air.
>
> Before the clouds of fog lifted from Donora, twenty had died, and 6,000 or half of the population were bedridden. Donora was the site of America's first major air pollution disaster.[14]

Delivery

The final stage in message preparation is rehearsal of the speech. The speech should be rehearsed just as it is going to be presented. Except for formal occasions when a manuscript is necessary, speeches should not be memorized or read from a text. Memorized speeches often sound stilted and monotonous, and the speaker is in danger of drying up if he should forget a key section. Rather, the speech should be extemporaneous.

Extemporaneous speech is fluent, natural and largely spontaneous. It has been rehearsed enough so that the speaker is familiar with it and need not rely heavily on his notes, but not so rehearsed that major portions of it are memorized. To discourage overuse of notes or memorization, speakers use only key-word or key-phrase outlines for notes, with only statistics or quotations written out in full. This forces the communicator to be extemporaneous in his presentation and to be conscious of each point he is about to make. Extemporaneous style does not preclude careful selection of language, and a speech may still incorporate all the stylistic elements discussed above. Repeated rehearsals can insure that these are included, but the speaker should allow enough flexibility in his actual delivery to sound natural and enthusiastic and to adapt to feedback from his audience. A completely memorized speech leaves no room for such adaptation.

Other considerations in the actual delivery of a speech include

---

[14] First place speech delivered by Charles Schalliol in the men's division of the Intercollegiate Indiana Oratorical Association Contest, Hanover College, March 1967. Reprinted in *Winning Orations, 1967* (Detroit: The Interstate Oratorical Association, 1967), pp. 54-57.

the use of the voice, body movement, posture and gestures, facial expression and eye contact. These elements of delivery will be discussed independently. Research findings relative to delivery have already been covered in the chapters on message variables and nonverbal communication. Included here are practical suggestions for good delivery based on traditionally accepted public speaking principles.

Figure 8-3 Brief notes may help to keep a speaker organized. However, excessive reading is likely to bore audience members, thereby reducing the speaker's effectiveness.

Vocalics No matter how excellent a speech he has prepared, the speaker will lose his audience if his listeners cannot hear and understand him. Clear articulation has always been considered one of the primary elements of good delivery. Demosthenes, one of the most famous speakers of ancient time, is said to have overcome a speech defect by long hours of practice at the seashore. Filling his mouth with pebbles, he would deliver his speeches over the roar of the ocean waves. Countless others have used similar exercises to improve the clarity of their speech. It is doubtful, however, that many people beyond childhood years need extensive practice with tongue twisters or other articulation exercises, or that such practice will make noticeable improvements. For those who do have problems with articulation, recognition of the problem and a conscious attempt to solve it will probably produce better results than the practice of artificial exercises. A speaker may be able to pinpoint vocal faults and improve his speech by recording his voice on a tape recorder and playing it back.

Equally as important as vocal clarity is the rate of speech. The rate should be varied, but should not be so fast as to be unintelligible or so slow that it drags. Pauses should be used to vary rate, to draw attention and to add emphasis. Speakers can learn to adjust their rate by listening to themselves on tape and by carefully observing audience feedback.

To be understandable, the volume of a speech must also be adequate. The ability to project one's voice to the back of a large room often requires practice. Again, audience feedback is a good clue as to whether they can hear the speaker adequately. Speakers must learn to adapt their volume to the size of the room they are speaking in. Volume can also be varied to emphasize important points. Sudden loudness can startle; sudden softness can cause the audience to listen more attentively.

Another quality of good vocal delivery is pitch variety. A monotonous pitch can destroy the effectiveness of any speech. Every individual has a characteristic pitch level and a range of pitches he generally uses. To achieve variety, his speech pattern should typically include both high and low pitches that are several steps removed from his normal pitch level. Persons with narrow ranges can increase their vocal variety by practicing speaking at high and low pitch levels. Individuals who have an unpleasant pitch level can also change it through conscious effort, as witnessed by the ability of aspiring radio announcers to develop deep-pitched voices.

Generally, lower pitch levels are more pleasant for both males and females and, as noted earlier, create a better image.

Figures 8-4 One of the most effective speakers in recent years was President John F. Kennedy. His eloquent delivery and spontaneous wit enabled him to captivate audiences at home and abroad.

A pleasant voice quality is also important to good vocal delivery. Persons with irritating, unpleasant voices are stereotyped in negative ways. Like pitch, voice quality can be altered through concerted practice.

The final standard element of good vocal delivery is fluency. Although research demonstrates that lack of fluency does not have a serious negative effect, a fluent speech is easier to listen to and creates the impression of confidence and competence.

Body movement, posture and gestures The most useful advice on body movement, posture and gesture is to avoid distracting behavior. No single pattern of body movement is preferable; it depends on the style that is most comfortable for the speaker. The important consideration is that the speaker not engage in meaningless movements such as nervous pacing, rocking back and fourth on the heels, or shifting weight from one foot to the other. Such behavior draws attention away from the speech itself. Similarly, posture should be whatever is comfortable for the speaker as long as it is not so rigid as to appear unnatural or so relaxed and slouched as to appear disinterested or slovenly. One admonition generally given to beginning speakers is not to drape themselves over the podium or to use it as a crutch.

Much of the traditional advice on gestures is artificial and contradictory. It used to be fashionable for men to place one hand in a pocket; now public speaking teachers advise against it. Some texts recommend keeping one hand on the podium at all times; others recommend moving away from it and even in front of it. The best advice seems to be to make gestures natural, varied, meaningful and large enough to be visible.

Facial expression and eye contact Like gestures, facial expressions can add clarity and interest to a speech. To be effective, facial expressions should be natural, varied, meaningful and visible. Idiosyncratic and repetitive expressions can be distracting. Thus, the overriding consideration becomes one of avoiding distracting behavior.

Eye contact is an important element of good delivery. One of the distinguishing features of effective public speakers is the extensive use of eye contact (A frequent complaint about President Lyndon B. Johnson's speeches was that he seldom looked up from his manuscript, which lowered his audience's attentiveness). By using continuous eye contact and looking at each member of the audience, the communicator secures their attention, appears to be speaking directly to them and can better recognize audience feedback. Moreover, direct eye contact conveys an image of honesty and concern, which can boost the speaker's credibility. The values of direct eye contact are a further argument against manuscript speeches and overreliance on notes.

One final word of advice from one of the earliest rhetoricians, Dionysius the Elder, seems the soundest of all: "Let thy speech be better than silence, or be silent."

1. Public speaking differs significantly from other communication situations. It is more formal than dyadic and small group communication, and feedback is more restricted. The public speaker usually has little control over the context in which he speaks; it is usually not in his power to alter the composition of the audience and the physical environment. However, the speaker does exert significant control over the speech and his own delivery.

2. There are several stages in the initial planning of a speech. It is necessary to consider the purpose of the speech, the particular interests of the audience, and the time and place of delivery. The topic of the speech should be one about which the speaker is knowledgeable and in which the audience is interested.

3. There are five concepts the speaker should consider when preparing and presenting his speech. These concepts are: invention, disposition, style, memory and delivery.

4. Invention is the process of investigating and analyzing the subject of a speech. Invention involves generating ideas for the speech, investigating and analyzing arguments and assessing the needs of the audience members and the effects of the speech's arguments on the audience.

5. Disposition involves the selection, apportionment and arrangement of materials within the speech. All speeches should have an introduction, body and conclusion. However, the speaker may arrange materials in one of two basic organizational patterns: logical and psychological. Logical patterns are those that inherently make sense, those that are natural extensions of the topic of the speech. Deductive, inductive, cause-effect and chronological arrangement of materials are examples of logical patterns. Psychological patterns are intended to elicit from the audience certain reactions that are desired by the speaker. Beginning with familiar or accepted arguments and then moving to unfamiliar or unaccepted ones, and placing materials in a climatic,

anticlimatic or pyramidal order are examples of psychological organizational patterns.

6. Style refers to the way the ideas in a speech are expressed. The requirements for good oral and written communication are different. The careful use of conversational speech; vivid, varied and original language; redundancy and brevity; parallel structure; emphasis; personalization and humor are all stylistic considerations that can enhance the effectiveness of a speaker.

7. A speech should be well-rehearsed; the speaker should be familiar with its content, but he should not need to rely heavily on notes. Speeches which are delivered from memory frequently sound stilted and monotonous.

8. When making his delivery, the speaker's vocal qualities are important. Vocal characteristics include the speaker's articulation, rate of speech, volume, pitch variety and fluency. Distracting gestures and facial expressions should be avoided; however, frequent and direct eye contact with audience members may make a speaker more effective.

1. As a class, choose a campus speaker or news commentator for the entire group to observe. Make a list of all the factors of this person's presentation that made the speech especially effective or ineffective. Compare and contrast your list with those of your classmates.

2. Choose a controversial topic and prepare a short speech outline to be used with a favorable audience. Now revise the outline to adapt the speech to an unfavorable audience. Adapt the outline a third time to an apathetic audience. What changes did you make in your outline? Why?

3. Reexamine the outlines you prepared for Exercise 2. Identify the types of logical and psychological organizational patterns you used in each. Did you change any logical or psychological patterns when adapting your speech to different audiences?

4. Analyze your class as an audience. What changes could your teacher make in adapting lectures to the class? What adaptations might a speaker make in presenting to the class a persuasive speech advocating a program requiring two years of national service for all citizens?

5. Give a series of one minute impromptu speeches to practice direct eye contact, vocal variety, rate control, volume control and use of gestures.

William S. Howell and Ernest G. Bormann, *Presentational Speaking for Business and the Professions* (New York: Harper and Row, 1971). This text discusses techniques for organizing and delivering technical presentations in business and other organizational contexts.

Robert C. King, *Forms of Public Address* (Indianapolis: Bobbs-Merrill Company, 1969). Different types of speeches and public speaking situations are surveyed in this slim volume. Sample speeches and paradigms for analyses of the speeches are included in each chapter.

James C. McCroskey, *Introduction to Rhetorical Communication*, 2nd Edition (Englewood Cliffs, N.J.: Prentice-Hall, 1972). An excellent syntheses, this beginning-level text brings together the findings of both behavioral scientists and rhetorical theoreticians.

Alan H. Monroe and Douglas Ehninger, *Principles and Types of Speech*, 6th Edition (Glenview, Ill.: Scott, Foresman and Company, 1967). One of the classic works on the general principles of speech composition and delivery, this book has been continuously improved over the years. Chapter 16 on the process of adapting speech organization to specific audiences is particularly useful.

Charles Mudd and Malcolm Sillars, *Speech: Context and Communication*, 2nd Edition (Scranton, Pa.: Chandler Publishing Company, 1969). This is a very traditional text, similar to a handbook for speech preparation. The sections dealing with analyses of the issues and outlining may be especially helpful to beginning speakers.

Mass communication

The test of a communication system is not how massive it is but how well it serves its function: providing a medium for expression of ideas and exchange of messages. In some primitive cultures, the drum continues to perform this function, quite to the satisfaction of the tribesmen. In our industrial society, the sophisticated and complex mass media system has grown beyond this basic function and wields power in many secondary roles—but not always to the satisfaction of media critics. Especially in its role as educator, the mass media has stirred controversial opinions.

By the time a child reaches college, he probably will have logged more hours of instruction (if one chooses to call it that) in front of the television set than he will be required to give to his college undergraduate program—and this is only one branch of the media that influences his life. He is exposed to news and entertainment magazines, newspapers, feature films and film documentaries, radio broadcasts and records that can provide him with music, comedy sketches or lessons in a foreign language. If an aborigine on a short-term visit to the United States understood our technical language he might shout "overkill" as he boarded the next plane for the Australian bush. For indeed the barrage of information and other types of messages received through the media before, during and after formal schooling is awesome. One wonders how we are able to process it all without becoming confused—or if in fact we do become more confused than enlightened.

More important, one wonders whether this mass conveyance of information—much of it repetitious borrowings by one medium from another—does not suppress the creativity, individual diversity and desire for self-understanding and awareness that are often the results of more personal forms of communication. To approach it from a somewhat different angle, do the mass media serve to educate us about reality or serve as a substitute for reality and for utilizing our own cognitive and interpretive abilities? Granting that we cannot be all places at once and experience all events firsthand, we must consequently acknowledge the necessity of packaged experience via media channels. But is it not possible for mass communication to facilitate at least some degree of individual participation and expression of personal experience, or must it inevitably reduce its audience to a passive and ineffectual role?

As might be supposed, no absolute responses can be given to such questions. But there is a promising aspect to the media problem: never has there been a time when the media was as self-conscious about its function as it is today. People working in mass communication as well as those outside it have used magazines, newspapers, television, radio and film to explore, evaluate and criticize these very same media channels. The wealth of opinions and research which have resulted from these many probes have provided insights about the nature of mass communications, its daily and long-range functions and its actual and potential effects.

The nature of mass communication

Mass as an adjective has come to characterize much that is representative of modern technological life—mass society, mass production, mass transportation, as well as mass communication. It is the key word to define in discussing such phenomena, and by its nature it is a complex word. Thus it has been the object of extensive studies by scholars and scientists. Some specific definitional guidelines have been established.

Mass generally describes something large in size. It also implies something which is impersonal, and, as in the case of mass society, it connotes a sense of isolation. How many times, for example, have you heard the saying, "all alone in the big city"? One might just as easily say, "all alone with the television set."

The media of mass communication can be defined as the agencies of printed and electronic communication that make information quickly accessible to large and distant audiences through complex organizational systems. In essence, the mass media go back to the fifteenth century and Johannes Gutenberg. In the succeeding five centuries, they have advanced from his simple press with movable type to space satellites capable of sending images and voices around the world.

Characteristics of mass communication
The complexity of modern society and the diversity of interests and aims which motivate its people are reflected and facilitated

by changes in methods of communication. Dynamic interaction between people on a personal level provides opportunities for information exchange and growth in understanding; this can certainly never be wholly replaced by any other form of communication. But it is simply not enough in terms of our present needs. In order to bridge wide geographical separations, in order to integrate as well as convey the numerous kinds of knowledge which are shaping our world, we have had to utilize the more inclusive and efficient techniques of mass communication.

Number of people reached By definition, then, mass communication is impersonal and indirect, aiming to reach large numbers of people, whereas the interpersonal communication of our everyday activities is directed generally toward a very small number of people. If audience number is truly the criterion of media success, broadcasting is easily the most successful, since television alone claims an audience larger than all other media combined.

Television generally attracts heterogeneous audiences because its programs, especially during prime viewing hours, are designed to appeal to some common denominator among different viewer interests. Programs such as *Maude* and *Hawaii Five-O*, for example, respectively capitalize on the general interest in situation-comedy and cops-and-robbers plots. Occasionally, networks introduce special reports or documentaries during prime time which also are designed for broad audience appeal. Yet when these programs present not only the themes but the actual manifestations of violence, poverty and racial tension in our everyday lives, some members of the audience may opt for fictionalized tragedy—switching from NBC's *Murder in America*, for example, to *Marcus Welby*, which had the comparative advantage of a happy ending and therefore enjoyed higher ratings. The more successful special programs in terms of audience viewing may be the made-for-television films which incorporate various quantities of adventure, murder and romance—a little something for everyone.

Much printed material, on the other hand, is aimed at limited special interest groups. This fact is attested to by the growing market for specialty magazines, such as *Organic Gardening, Dog Fancy, Modern Photography* and *High Fidelity*, and the demise of several once popular magazines that catered to heterogeneous audiences, starting with *The Saturday Evening Post*, followed by *Look*, *Life* and *The Saturday Review*. Book publishers have also cashed in on the specialty boom with scores of how-to-do-it, diet, travel and sundry nonfiction offerings. Radio, too, has turned to specialty programming in music and news coverage. Nor is television itself oblivious to the profitability of special interest programs. Soap operas in the afternoon, Saturday morning cartoons, *Sesame Street* and *The French Chef* are cases in point.

Amount of feedback Mass communication, like the communication process in general, requires a sender or source of the message, a channel of transmission and a receiver or audience. But while face-to-face communication travels along a two-way channel—speaker and listener giving instant feedback and taking cues from gestures and expressions—the mass media essentially provide one-way communication in which interaction between the sources of the information and those who receive it is all but impossible. The candidate, the reporter or the actor has no immediate knowledge of his audience's response; the audience has no way to respond immediately to him. Mass communication feedback, therefore, is minimal. What little there is accumulates slowly as the polls, rating surveys and letters to the editor trickle in.

The problem of individual audience member feedback is an especially difficult one in the electronic news media. If readers are dissatisfied with a magazine article, they can directly address themselves to the writer of the article (though feedback is, of necessity, delayed); or if they are consistently opposed to the presentation of news and opinions in a certain magazine or newspaper, they can simply cancel their subscription (though the comparative paucity of news magazines and newspapers leaves the reader with few alternatives). But feedback in response to television news is characteristically indirect as well as delayed. A viewer may address his responses to a particular broadcaster but it may not reach him until several days after the actual broadcast which elicits the response. Furthermore, the broadcaster is often provided with the material for news copy; he does not go to the source or make his own selection of which news he will report. Selection and presentation of the news are subject to behind-the-scenes control, and feedback directed to the broadcaster himself may only indirectly affect the network's news practices.

The fact that broadcasters as well as other media newsmen rely on many of the same sources—wireservices, for example—suggests a more serious feedback problem. Some activists have claimed that if, for example, legislators are discussing an abortion bill, newspeople from all the different mass media will be directed to seek out the commentary and opinions of the legislators themselves or will interview a few nonrepresentative groups. The comments and responses gathered by newsmen in the field are in turn utilized by radio and television people in their own presentation of news. Hence legislators receive their own feedback from the media; and the viewer receives an arbitrarily distilled representation of views and attitudes concerning the news event selected for coverage.

The rather "incestuous" practice by the print and electronic media of picking up the same news event and many of the same feedback sources is well-illustrated by the response to *An American Family*. This television series shown in 1973 was a distillation of seven months' worth of film recording daily events in the life of a middle-class California family. The realities which were exposed—divorce and homosexuality among others—elicited a high degree of audience feedback, partly bcause the family image presented was, to say the least, unflattering and emotionally disconcerting; thus it challenged the values and self-images of many audience members.

Yet even in this case there were feedback problems. For one thing, the series itself focused on only one family. Though the indefinite article used in the title suggested that the family was not necessarily representative, the time devoted to coverage of the family's behavior implied to many people that it was culturally significant. Magazines, newspapers and radio programs—on both sides of the Atlantic—covered this one television series and arbitrarily assigned it prominence among other news items. The degree of feedback from readers and viewers was indeed comparatively high, but most of it was delayed until the end of the total program. Thus a series which had been filmed months prior to its TV release continued to dominate the media (in the form of feedback) months after the completion of its broadcast. And the amount of commentary that glutted the media may have created more confusion than clarity.

Some television stations have been earnestly trying to broaden the base of feedback and to give a more balanced coverage, in terms of the time allotted, to different news topics; yet many problems remain to be worked out. For quite a while now there have been commentaries immediately following important news events such as a Presidential speech. The usual criticism of this immediate feedback is that insufficient time is given to digesting the contents of the speech. But perhaps the more valid criticism is that the analysis and commentary are often the feedback of a single newsman. His point of view is presumably valid and informed, yet it is still only one viewpoint. And even if several newsmen discuss the event, this does not preclude the problem of "media incest"—those on the "inside" are selecting, reporting, as well as providing their own feedback on the news, while the viewer passively sits back. For this reason, certain news media are beginning to provide for audience response on certain vital issues and are seeking ways to reduce the delay in such feedback.

One network, for example, ran a series which explored problem topics such as transportation and pollution. After each aspect of the situation was discussed, the narrator presented the audience with a series of alternative solutions and asked viewers to send in their responses. In order to facilitate gathering these responses, certain newspapers carried the list of alternatives which the public could then fill out and mail to the television network—a type of "media incest" perhaps, but at least used to encourage audience participation. In other instances, television and radio stations have provided telephone numbers for a more direct gathering and collating of feedback, and certain newspapers have themselves initiated public opinion polls on major issues.

Other characteristics Despite such efforts to rectify problems characteristic of mass communication, the drawbacks continue to offset the advantages: mass communication is a large-scale method of reaching people that is rapid and indifferent to geographical separations; yet it is essentially a one-way and impersonal form of communication with a low capacity for feedback. Furthermore, these disadvantages to the audience are matched by problems facing those in control of mass media: the high costs of media production and, as we shall briefly discuss, the limited ability to select audiences.

The problem of audience selection may indeed be considered a blessing by some, but it is a source of concern at least to those who view the mass media in economic terms. They have no means of forcing you to turn to a specific television channel or to read a certain newspaper. Only in the case of events of national consequence are the television channels, for example, given completely over to the use of government—and even then, no one can make you turn on the set. If the targeted audiences are found, what guarantee is there that they will understand the message? What guarantee is there that they will not fall asleep during the program, use the newspaper to housebreak their dogs, break the record on the way home from the store or put the book on the dusty someday-to-be-read pile?

These points should recall the basic question of media effects —of how great an ability the media really have to educate and to shape opinions, especially when compared to interpersonal communication. It is one thing for Howard K. Smith to be actually present in one's living room, discussing some news event, answering our questions, challenging us to analyze and interpret a given reality for ourselves and thus prodding us toward the self-understanding and growth which are natural consequences of interpretative activity. It may be quite another thing to observe and listen to Smith's two-dimensional electronic image delivering an editorial comment on one's television set—an image which we can turn off as soon as we become bored or uncomfortable with what is being said.

Granting that it would be virtually impossible to have Howard K. Smith talk with each of us personally, we may wonder whether a better alternative to watching him on television might not be to discuss a particular news event with those who *are* available to us for interpersonal communication. We might also wonder whether mass communication whets or dulls one's appetite for these "live" interactions. It is not uncommon for human beings to seek the path of least resistance by simply curling up within the security of old thoughts and ideas. The question is whether mass communication has the power to override this natural tendency or whether this remains essentially the function of face-to-face interaction. These and similar problems will be explored in later sections of this chapter.

Functions of the mass communication

What functions mass media ought to serve and how well they do serve these functions is perhaps a matter of perspective. One person may bemoan the dearth of current events programs and praise special news coverage such as the televised Watergate hearings. Another person may angrily turn off the television set when an entertainment program is interrupted by election returns. Some buy the Sunday *New York Times* for the sake of one favorite section. Others avoid the *Times* altogether in favor of tabloids and comic strips. And then, of course, there are the media representatives, sponsors, executives and publishers who test the pulse of media functions and effectiveness by the strength of Nielsen ratings and subscription sales. What all this suggests is that mass communication is validly multifunctional. The essential controversy concerns which function—dissemination of facts, entertainment and profit-making, among others—ought to receive the greatest emphasis.

To inform and to entertain   Primary among the functions of the mass media is the dissemination of information, a job entailing far more than the mere transmission of facts. The media serve in a larger capacity to bridge what is often called "an understanding gap." After seeking out the facts, the media attempt to arrange them in meaningful patterns that encourage informed interpretation. One spectacular example of the media's ability to clarify a wild confusion of data came during the Watergate investigations, with its array of names, committees and contradictory allegations. Besides their general news coverage, *Time, Newsweek* and other printed news media ran periodical summaries of the events. The broadcasting media devoted special programming to discussions, reviews and interpretations as the proceedings unfolded.

Broadcasting is the most effective of the media for increasing immediate general knowledge of information and ideas; and as such it is most valuable for making people aware—through comparatively brief periods of media exposure and with comparatively little personal effort—of what is currently happening in the world. But though there have been attempts at in-depth television and radio coverage of certain events, specific and detailed knowledge is more available, or at least more randomly accessible, in the printed media. A printed report of a government commission, for example, provides far more detail and theory than is commonly offered in general radio and television coverage. Printed matter can also be carried and referred to almost anywhere, since it does not require a specific energy source and does not interfere with the activities and privacy of others. Perhaps most important is the fact that one can reread information and check the accuracy of one's comprehension and retention any time he may wish—an impossibility with broadcasts unless one happens to have his own video tape recorder.

Despite certain advantages and disadvantages peculiar to each, both the printed and electronic media have been rather effective disseminators of factual information in the form of straight news reports, documentaries, interviews and investigative journalism. Yet there is a more subtle, and thus often unrecognized, type of information which is also conveyed through the various media in the form of fiction and entertainment programs: the changing values and norms of the audience which the mass media serve. Previously taboo subject matter such as abortion, marijuana and mental disease are being used as themes not only in sophisticated literature and films (where considerably more outrageous topics have always been explored) but in such unlikely entertainment "genres" as the soap opera and the comic strip. The mass media are rarely avant-garde in their exposure and discussion of cultural trends, but rather they reflect more or less established or widespread conditions. In doing so, however, they legitimize topics for open discussion, broaden the base of cultural change and enhance awareness—one might even say acceptance—of new social conditions.

It is clear that mass communication conveys more information more rapidly than is possible in face-to-face communication. In a half hour, for example, one newsman can inform thousands of people, all at the same time, of major world and local events of the day. His sources are also likely to be more accurately informed than the average citizen, and his presentation is generally given more careful screening for personal and cultural biases than would be the case were he simply communicating with one other person. The very fact that the mass media audience is so vast necessitates quality control, as well as consideration of the quantity or scope of information presented. Indeed, such control is a fundamental responsibility of media officials, as both government and private citizens have frequently emphasized.

Providing entertainment and aesthetic enjoyment are self-explanatory functions of the media. The printed media long ago forfeited the top position in this area to records, radio, film and television, while generally maintaining its status as a primary purveyor of information and education. Lately, however, this function of print has also been challenged by the use of audiovisual techniques and teaching machines in the classroom and the slowly increasing number of educational programs on television. This is not to say that the function of informing and educating has been usurped altogether from the printed media. Print continues to serve this function well and remains, at least to many, a major source of entertainment and enjoyment. But its efficiency as an educational tool has been measurably reduced by the technologically more sophisticated electronic media.

The criteria used to judge the success of both print and electronic media in serving their multiple functions have always been subject to diverse interpretations. It should not be expected, therefore, that any one person or group can devise ultimate standards or assert the right to unilaterally dictate how the media ought to be run. But as the media—especially television—grow in complexity and size, and gain in their power to influence the lives of all people, it is perhaps not too much to expect that at least an *attitude* of responsibility guide those who provide us with our information and entertainment. When we listen to or read the news, for example, we trust that we are receiving a comprehensive, intelligent and, above all, truthful account of the day's events. As members of a society, we rightfully expect that the media try to project a representative picture of all groups which comprise that society and in some way provide for the expression of our diverse comments and criticisms. And by sincerely trying to facilitate two-way communication between people, the media can help us to clarify the goals and values which shape our society.

To earn a profit The media in the United States are for the most part privately owned profit-making agencies, and the continuation of mass communication depends on their earning large profits to cover the enormous costs of media operations. In this respect, earning a profit can be considered an even more primary function of the media than their intrinsic functions of disseminating information and entertainment. Said more simply, there would be no media (other than the publicly sponsored agencies) if there were no profits.

For most of the media, advertising is the major source of income. It follows that the television networks, the magazines and the papers which attract the widest audiences will also attract the biggest advertisers. If a television advertiser is a manufacturer of laundry soap, he looks for programs that reach a large percentage of the housewife audience. He too wants a profit from the money he has invested in the ability of the mass media to encourage mass consumption.

Many arguments focus on the belief that the profit motive inhibits quality production in the media. And indeed several nations—England, Canada and Switzerland among them— have nationalized their mass communication resources in part to prevent commercial exploitation. But for many Americans the idea of a government-operated mass communication system contradicts the principle of free communication. As the arguments rage on, more people are examining both sides of the problem; in fact, much of the discussion is sparked by the fact that the media themselves have given more exposure to it. And the arguments have occasionally exerted healthy pressure on the media to reexamine their policies in terms of their profit-making needs and the public interest. The decision to drop cigarette advertising was one salutary effect of such pressure on the media. Potential competition from community-operated cable television systems may be the next incentive for media reevaluation and reorganization along the lines of public interest.

How mass communication works

Each type of communication situation has unique characteristics that affect the nature of the interaction which takes place within it. Communication researchers have devoted considerable time, energy and money studying the variables operative in the mass communication situation to better understand the nature of audience behavior and to determine the relative value of various mass communication techniques.

One-step vs. two-step flow

"THE NAVY NEEDS YOU! DON'T READ AMERICAN HISTORY—MAKE IT!" So enticed a recruiting poster issued in 1917 when the United States entered World War I. It was one of many such posters, all part of a massive propaganda effort to mobilize the emotional energy of a total nation in support of history's first global and technological war. Newspapers, films, records —all were used in the campaign.

Such propaganda methods paralleled the then current

"hypodermic needle" or stimulus-response theory accepted by most sociologists and psychologists.[1] They assumed that a stimulus caused a direct and immediate response in a person, and communication theorists similary assumed that the media evoked a direct and immediate response from each receiver. Thus they attributed to the media extensive powers to change and mobilize mass opinions, attitudes and values. This "one-step" theory of communication envisioned a society in which individuals were psychologically disconnected and isolated and therefore unlikely to communicate face-to-face on important matters.

The hypodermic theory predominated in communication research until 1944 and the appearance of a book called *The People's Choice*, a study of the 1940 Presidential election by Paul F. Lazarsfeld, Bernard Berelson and Hazel Gaudet.[2] The research behind the book had begun as an attempt to show the direct influence of media campaigning in producing votes; its results were quite different. The authors, in support of their findings, proposed that the one-step theory be discarded because it did not adequately explain the process by which media messages are diffused among the majority of the population. The study stated that "ideas often flow from radio and print to opinion leaders and from them to the less active sections of the population." The flow of information from source to receiver was thus seen as a two-step process: the media affected only certain population groups directly, and these people in turn relayed the messages to others with whom they came in contact. In 1948, a follow-up revision of the original study brought the previous conclusions one step further by stating that interpersonal communication appeared more significant in shaping a voter's decisions than communication received through the mass media.

The two-step theory did much to humanize the concept of mass communication, redirecting toward people the major responsibility for communication flow and attitude change. At the same time, it implicitly showed the mass media to be far less powerful than people had once believed. For these and related reasons the theory appealed to most communication researchers, who have since studied numerous variables that can affect the two-step flow. The research for the most part

---

[1] M. De Fleur, *Theories of Mass Communication*, 2nd Edition (New York: David McKay, Inc., 1970), pp. 112-117.

[2] P. Lazarsfeld, B. Berelson and H. Gaudet, *The People's Choice* (New York: Columbia University Press, 1948).

has concentrated on the opinion leader—who he is and how he functions.

One major revision of the theory suggests that the flow of information is more complex than two-step, that it is a multistep process or chain reaction progressively reaching the different opinion leaders within different population segments.[3] When, for example, a respected diplomat appears on *Face the Nation,* some opinion leaders will hear his views on the Middle East or China. They will pass them on to family, friends and co-workers, each of whom, instead of being just a passive listener, may be an opinion leader in another setting, where the opinions are once more aired, picked up and passed on across various social, economic and cultural barriers.

Opinion leadership

Simplification of the study of opinion leadership divides people into two groups—leaders and followers. Communication interaction, of course, is extraordinarily more intricate and difficult to reduce to neat categories and comprehensive formulas. But, again, certain hypotheses have tested out with consistency and some general characteristics can be described.

Some traits of the opinion leader Opinion leaders exist in all social and economic walks of life. Their followings usually number four or five, but someone can accurately be classified as an opinion leader if he changes the attitude or behavior of just one other person.

Although the influence of an opinion leader is generally concentrated within the major area of his experience, the credibility he establishes in that area may lend at least partial support to his authority in related fields. However, the leader's influence is likely to be sharply attenuated if he ventures too far beyond his established image. The lawyer who is asked about a recent Supreme Court decision might have much to say, but when questioned on the impact of DNA research he would probably defer to the opinion of a physician or scientist.

Opinion leaders are typically the most conforming members of their groups, seemingly to embody or personify the group interests, values and norms. It is just this conformity and personification, in fact, that attract their following. In this

---

[3] H. Menzel and E. Katz, "Social Relationships and Innovations in the Medical Profession: The Epidemiology of a New Drug," *Public Opinion Quarterly, 19* (1955), pp. 337-352.

position, an opinion leader not only transmits information but has the double-edged power either to encourage attitude change or inhibit it. In other words, as Westley and MacLean's model suggests, the opinion leader serves as a gatekeeper, selecting to relay from the media and his other formal information sources the information he considers consistent with his group's interests. He is therefore a group interpreter and opinion maker.

Several studies have shown that opinion leaders often have more exposure to media and other sources of information than those who seek their opinions. One study of influential farmers showed that they read more farm literature, watched more television farm programs and had more contact with agricultural scientists than the less influential farmers.[4] In another classic study it was found that women who were opinion leaders read more magazines and books than did the nonleaders and were also more apt to read material relevant to their area of leadership.[5]

Even in cases where media exposure was not significantly different for opinion leaders and opinion seekers, it was found that the seekers nevertheless looked to the leaders to shape the information and interpret it—that is, to give them their opinions. The broadcasting journalists who analyze news events, political speeches and other such matters serve in this role of opinion shaper. In some cases of heavily unfavorable journalistic analysis, political and other social leaders have censured the media's attempts to shape opinions negatively; not surprisingly, bias in the other direction has not been met with the same disfavor.

Research has established several other characteristics typical of opinion leaders; a summary review will suggest to some degree how opinion leadership affects mass communication and the media. Opinion leaders tend to get their information from sources other than those in their communities or locales. That is, they usually draw on more sophisticated information sources than their followers. In general, these people also belong to several large organizations and have friends and contacts in urban areas.[6] Consequently they may have more experience in diverse social situations and broader knowledge

---

[4] E. Rogers, *Diffusion of Innovations* (New York: The Free Press, 1962).

[5] E. Katz and P.F. Lazarsfeld, *Personal Influence* (Glencoe, Ill.: The Free Press, 1955).

[6] H.F. Lionberger, "Some Characteristics of Farm Operators Sought as Sources of Farm Information in a Missouri County," *Rural Sociology, 19* (1953), pp. 233-243.

of group and interpersonal behavior than the opinion seekers. Perhaps as a further result of their social relationships (or possibly as an explanation of their more cosmopolitan background and experience) opinion leaders characteristically have higher social and economic status than opinion seekers. This status apparently carries with it the suggestion of knowledgeability, at least to those people in lower socioeconomic groups who, according to some researchers, tend to seek opinions on public affairs from those with higher status.[7] The importance of status was corroborated by other studies which showed that opinion seekers look to social peers for advice but to social superiors for information.

One implication of all these studies is that opinion leaders, especially on an interpersonal level, are in a significant position to influence the way in which media information is interpreted and responded to by opinion seekers. The relationship is a dynamic one, and opinion leaders and followers are not mutually exclusive categories. An opinion seeker in one situation may, for example, be a leader under other circumstances. Furthermore, under certain conditions, opinion seekers are directly responsive to media communication.

Opinion leaders and the media   It is known that in times of crisis, the media serve the public directly as a source both of information and of guidance. At such times the opinion leader is bypassed, obviously because there is no need for him. For example, when radio stations and newspapers reported that Pearl Harbor had been bombed by the Japanese, those who heard the news did not need opinion leaders to confirm it as true. Likewise, for those who saw on television the murder of Lee Harvey Oswald or the riots of the 1968 Democratic convention, there was no need for opinion leaders to verify these realities.

Nonetheless, people will soon talk about such events, and opinion leaders, being characteristically more informed, will serve again as gatekeepers, sorting, interpreting and generalizing. Thus, even if the opinion leaders are bypassed when the media information is initially being received by the audience, they are essential to the media's later impact. Thus, they have commanded a great deal of research and respect.

The role of opinion leaders as middlemen between the media

[7] Katz and Lazarsfeld, *op. cit.*

and the population at large has not gone unnoticed—indeed those who plan the scope and presentation of media messages are quite sensitive to the habits and preferences of these middlemen. Perhaps one of the major concerns of the media planners is the role of opinion leaders as catalysts between the advertiser and the consumer. Media advertising, in other words, is not the only, nor necessarily the most important, variable which affects buying behavior:

> . . . Communication about consumption with parents seems to be a particularly important variable intervening between exposure to commercials and actual purchase, especially among older adolescents. This finding indicates clearly that consumption behavior is a "social" process, involving overt communication with others, not simply an individual psychological process triggered by exposure to advertising.[8]

Diffusion of information

How fast do we hear important news? What news do we hear first? Under what circumstances do the media diffuse information directly to a large part of the population? When does opinion leadership dominate the process of diffusion?

Diffusion is the gradual spreading of new information and ideas from source to receivers through the various social and mechanical channels of communication. The channels of diffusion are thus the channels of communication, ranging from word-of-mouth to the complex gadgetry of electronic media. Diffusion research has tried to determine just what news and how much of it is spread at what rate of speed by these different channels.

Special news events   Several studies have dealt with the speed with which special news events, such as the assassination of President Kennedy, reach the public.[9] The Kennedy studies showed that within fifteen to thirty minutes after the shooting was made public by the media, two-thirds of the nation knew about it, and 90 percent knew within the hour.

One group of researchers further proposed that the greater the public significance of an event, the more rapid the diffusion of the news.[10] Certainly the death of the President superseded all other interests at the time, and both media and interpersonal

---

[8] S. Ward and D. Wackman, "Family and Media Influences on Adolescent Consumer Learning," *American Behavioral Scientists, 14* (1971), p. 423.

[9] B. Greenberg, "Diffusion of News of the Kennedy Assassination," *Public Opinion Quarterly, 28* (1964), pp. 225-232 and R. Hill and C. Bonjean, "News Diffusion: A Test of the Regularity Hypothesis," *Journalism Quarterly, 41* (1964), pp. 336-342.

[10] Hill and Bonjean, *op. cit.*

sources were operating at maximum efficiency to spread the news. Another researcher concluded that when a news event is of epic or crisis proportion, interpersonal channels are equally as important as the mass media in disseminating the news; the two types of communication play complementary roles.[11]

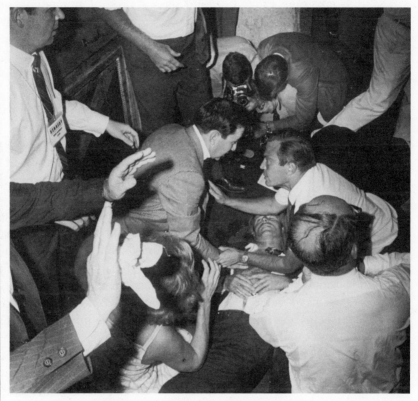

Figure 9-1 Special news events of critical importance such as the assassination of Senator Robert Kennedy reach the public much more quickly than most news stories. The electronic media and interpersonal sources facilitate the rapid diffusion of special news events.

Other research with diffusion of special news events has investigated the part played by each of the media in the process. One study investigated the initial news sources for three events of the period: President Eisenhower's stroke in 1957, the first Sputnik satellite in 1953, and Alaska's statehood in 1959.[12] The first two events were treated as news bulletins by the

---

[11] Greenberg, op. cit.

[12] P. Deutschmann and W. Danielson, "Diffusion of Knowledge of a Major News Story," Journalism Quarterly, 37 (1960), pp. 345-355.

television media and, as such, interrupted the normal programming which had been in progress. The last of the three did not receive this type of coverage. The findings of the study indicate that "extraordinary coverage" in which a special news event is directly and almost immediately transmitted to the public is most often provided through television. Radio coverage ranked second as a source of immediate news information. And newspapers appeared to serve primarily as supplements to broadcast bulletins, since there is usually a comparatively long lapse between the occurrence of a particular event and the newspaper report of it. Newspapers, however, may have been more significant than other media in diffusing nonbulletin news, as in the case of Alaska's statehood.

Media versus personal channels   The media provide the most pervasive and swift channels for the dissemination of general news information. Although face-to-face communication is more effective in producing attitude and behavior change, media and personal information channels are supplementary and complementary in their different tasks of information diffusion.[13] One study suggested that the importance of word-of-mouth as the initial source of information "may be smaller when the story (or information) is of lesser importance or news value."[14] Put more simply, people talk less about what seems less important to them, and some information is spread less quickly than other information.

Personal channels are also instrumental in transmitting information not of interest to the general public but aimed toward specialized groups. This, of course, is the grapevine at work, passing along to those listening the information relevant to their interests and needs. Few would contest the efficacy of this oldest of man's information channels.

Adoption of innovation
The matter of the comparative impact of media and interpersonal communication in effecting opinion and attitude change is related to another learning process called the adoption or innovation process. The adoption process comprises the steps that occur between diffusion of new information and the change that results from that information. What, for example, happens

[13] E. Katz, M. Levin and H. Hamilton, "Traditions of Research on the Diffusion of Innovation," *American Sociological Review*, 28 (1963).
[14] Deutschmann and Danielson, *op. cit.*

between the time someone hears about or becomes aware of a new candidate for public office and the day he votes for that candidate at the polls?

What is the adoption process? According to Everett Rogers, a noted researcher in the field, "the process by which innovations are adopted by individuals is essentially a limited example of how any type of learning takes place."[15] Learning to play the guitar, then, entails much the same steps as the process of switching from one brand of cigarettes to another. Essentially, there are five stages involved in this adoption process.

Before all else, one must, of course, become aware of something new, whether it is information, an idea or a product. However, as we implied in the discussion of opinion leaders and media advertising, awareness is not an automatic result of exposure. People are inclined to selectively perceive, understand and retain that which interests them; and, similarly, they often remain closed even to obvious information if it does not excite their interest.

For example, let us say that you wish to buy a car but do not have (and could not care less about having) an understanding of how a car functions. If, then, a television advertiser for a rotary engine car were simply to list its technical advantages over piston engines, the level of emission, the unique suspension system and so forth, all this new information would probably be deflected from your mind by an impenetrable wall of boredom. The key to drawing your full awareness of the car's features is to sustain your interest. The advertiser, therefore, gives you the basic motivational lesson: a piston engine goes "boing, boing" (a pogo stick is used as the visual complement to make sure that you get the point), while the rotary engine goes "hmmmm" (a very smooth and peaceful humming sound, as though the car were powered by divine inspiration).

At this interest stage, a person develops the motivation for seeking additional information. Perhaps he will talk to a few car dealers or ask for brochures. He may check out *Consumer's Report* and gather other pertinent data that would enable him to proceed to the next stage in his decision-making.

Evaluation, the third step in the adoption process, finds the individual applying the information he has gathered to his own needs and interests. The car buyer, armed with information

---

[15] Rogers, *op. cit.*

about car costs, safety factors and whatever else is of concern to him, attempts what Rogers calls a "mental trial." He tries to determine in his mind whether, for example, a rotary engine station wagon or a foreign sports car is best suited to his needs. Before making the choice, he will find out if service for the foreign car is difficult to get and if the station wagon gets low mileage. In other words, he weighs the advantages and disadvantages of the cars before making his choice. At this point, he also turns more to friends, neighborhood auto mechanics and others trying to find reinforcement for his opinions in their opinions.

In the stage before the actual purchase (or adoption), the car buyer will probably want to take each of the cars for a trial drive. This, of course, is comparable to the trial stage in the adoption process—small-scale adoption on a probationary basis, giving one last chance to reject the innovation. If the results of the trial are favorable, the individual will adopt the innovation for continued use. Or, in the case of the car buyer, if the station wagon drives better, he will put the license plates on the car and drive it home to his garage.

Communication sources in the adoption process   Which of the information sources is most important at the different adoption stages? A general conclusion, based on numerous research projects, is that media sources—impersonal, cosmopolitan, general and informational—are most influential during the awareness stage and continue to be important during the interest stage. Personal interaction, however, is most valuable during the evaluation period. In contrast to the media channels, personal interaction is two-way, generally localized, specific and conducive to opinion sharing. Its importance continues until the adoption is completed.

The impact of personal exchange in the later stages of adoption finds explanation in numerous formal studies. But maybe it is just as easily explained by the old saying, "Birds of a feather flock together." People most often discuss ideas, values and problems with others who share them in common. Thus when election time comes, for example, people talk over voting decisions with others they see in their everyday activities—co-workers with whom they share similar economic concerns or people of the same party with like political leanings. Such exchange opens the way for new ideas and information, and it encourages opinion sharing and evaluation. This is the point in the adoption process where opinion leaders within work or political groups can be most persuasive.

Time required for adoption The factors affecting the length of the adoption period are probably as numerous as the individual instance of adoption, but again the need for operating principles has led to some generalizations. For example, it is usually true that adoption occurs fastest when the innovation is simple and not a radical departure from current practices and beliefs. Another theory proposes that the time between awareness and trial is consistently longer than the time between trial and adoption. Thus it seems safe to surmise that once a person reaches the point of trying an innovation, he will proceed quickly to adopt or reject it.

Extensive research has measured rates of adoption among those who change first (early adopters) and those who change at slower rates (later adopters). Early adopters have been found to pass through the five stages both earlier and faster. Sometimes they are people who simply have a predisposition toward innovations of any sort. Most of us know one person who is always the first on the block to own a new item— be it a color television or a drive-it-yourself lawn mower.

More often, however, the early adopter has a special predisposition toward the innovation in question—perhaps it is an item which seems capable of satisfying a particular need, or a new idea which is consonant with his own thinking; or perhaps it is an innovation which offers hope where there had been none before, as in the case of experimental surgical techniques for those with serious illnesses. The early adopter therefore becomes aware earlier of pertinent information and moves quickly into and through the interest stage, gathering what he needs to make an evaluation.

Interestingly enough, however, early adopters prove to take a relatively longer time to move from trial to adoption than the later adopters. The probable reason is that they are more cautious at this point since they have few or no models to guide them. Later adopters, on the other hand, learn from the experiences of the early adopters. Consequently, they have fewer risks to take and usually move more quickly through the last stages of adoption. Some people, of course, create a series of substages to prolong final adoption. For instance we all know people who will wait until the millennium for color television designers to work out all the "bugs."

Early adopters and opinion leaders share several attributes. Both have wide exposure to information sources, including many beyond local sources. Both groups are also found to be more educated and to hold higher social and economic status than their followers. As the first to learn information and to accept changes, they are of great importance to the mass media. For if the media are to carry on their primary function of dispensing information effectively, they will have to understand the early adopters and opinion leaders and their power to hasten or slow down the process of change.

The effects of mass communication

Gauging the habits and preferences of the audience is a major task of the media planner. But in addition to all he might do toward preparing for a desired audience response, he must also prepare himself for the unexpected. Sometimes, for example, a television program which is expected to flop, surprisingly sustains a high rating for several seasons. Less successful results—especially in news or nonfiction areas—may, however, merely reflect limitations of mass communication which no amount of planning can overcome. The hopes of certain people to encourage social action and change attitudes through the media often founder on the same obstacles which potentially hinder all forms of communication. Perhaps some of these obstacles are built into the design of mass communication— in other words, perhaps mass communication has inherent problems which limit its effect. We turn to available research once again for illustration.

Reinforcement and conversion

A logical consequence of the two-step theory was the need to reassess the powers earlier attributed to the mass media. Did the media, in fact, have the propagandizing effects ascribed to them during World War I? Could they really be utilized to bring about major attitude changes or conversions—a power clearly susceptible to all manner of use and misuse?

Paul Lazarsfeld, one of the authors of *The People's Choice*, participated in later studies that attempted to measure the real power of campaign propaganda in changing voter decisions. Each study produced a remarkably similar consensus: campaign efforts overwhelmingly served to reinforce preexisting voter preferences, and, to a sizable degree, they helped to sway those who were unsure or neutral. But only 3 to 8 percent of the samplings truly converted from one candidate to another.[16]

Perhaps what must be considered in explaining such results is the cumulative effect of social conditioning. By the time a child is capable of reading a newspaper and understanding television and radio news broadcasts, he has already been inculcated with many of the attitudes and values which shape his parents' own responses to media information. And by the time he matures to voting age, he has probably undergone countless experiences which in some minor or significant way have served to shape his political preferences and ideas. This does not mean that he is incapable of changing his mind; but simply that he carries an enormous backlog of conditioning— much of it contributed to by his earlier exposure to media messages—and, therefore, changing his mind may require a subtlety beyond the scope of a single or even a barrage of new media information.

In other words, mass communication is not an effective agent of conversion. Its strength lies in its ability to reinforce and affirm attitudes that were already formed. And its ability to forge new attitudes is usually contingent on the level of previous knowledge and the strength of former opinions concerning the matter at hand. "Fencesitters" are therefore probably most vulnerable to new media suggestion.

Media image

The skeptic who says not to believe everything you read is trying to dispel an attitude common toward all the media. He is inveighing against the mass response to mass information —against people's tendency to credit all the media with being right all the time.

The media are endowed with tremendous prestige as are those associated with the media. Perhaps there is no more vivid example of this than the status bestowed on the stars of Hollywood's glittering years. Think how they were honored and feted and publicized. Remember how their dress styles, hair styles and life-styles irresistably became the nation's styles. Today television satisfies much the same demand for standard-setting.

---

[16] B. Berelson, P.F. Lazarsfeld, and W.N. McPhee, *Voting: A Study of Opinion Formation in a Presidential Campaign* (Chicago: University of Illinois Press, 1954).

The halo that surrounds the media is simply a phenomenon of power—the power to transfigure an obscure face or organization, to reflect the scope and significance of social movements and cultural changes and to provide a nationwide showcase for anything ranging from consumer products to public issues.

> . . . The mass media bestow prestige and enhance the authority of individuals and groups by legitimizing their status. Recognition by the press or radio or magazines or newsreels testifies that one has arrived, that one is important enough to have been singled out from the large anonymous masses, that one's behavior and opinions are significant enough to require public notice.[17]

It has been further proven that when an idea is only vaguely conceived and as yet unarticulated by a person, discussion of that idea by the media will help to clarify and bring it into the open.[18] In this sense, the media undoubtedly possess persuasive powers, which make them especially attractive to advertisers. Assuming that the media are axiomatically prestigious and persuasive in their own right, advertisers long ago assumed that prestigious people plugging a product through the media would be doubly persuasive and bring about increased sales.

Media violence

Any conclusions about the effects of media violence must relate it to man's actual violence. Do the media contribute to the incidence of that violence in ratio to the amount of violence they show? Can the growing rate of crime be curbed by curbing television violence? Some would argue that because the media display so much violence of all types—physical, psychological and verbal—they provide great stimulus for man's violence (be it genetically or environmentally caused). Others would say that because man is violent, he will naturally seek violence as an ingredient of his media fare. In fact, it has been proposed that media violence can relieve the need to perpetrate actual violence, that is, it provides a catharsis or outlet for hostile feelings.[19]

---

[17] P.F. Lazarsfeld and R.K. Merton, "Mass Communication, Popular Taste and Organized Social Action," in L. Bryson, ed., *The Communication of Ideas* (New York: Harper and Brothers, 1969), pp. 95-118.

[18] D. Waples, B. Berelson, and F.R. Bradshaw, *What Reading Does to People* (Chicago: Universtiy of Chicago Press, 1940).

[19] S. Feshbach, "The Stimulating versus Cathartic Effects of a Vicarious Aggressive Activity," *Journal of Abnormal Social Psychology, 13* (1962), pp. 381-385.

Violence has always been a popular condiment for spicing up the media fare. The list of examples is nearly endless in the history of print alone. But violence in print has almost never provoked the quantity nor the emotional quality of criticism directed against violence in the other media. No matter how graphically written a description of violence might be, it rarely has the immediate and overwhelming effect of visual images which require no effort of imagination.

Media violence has, however, been on a continual upswing, following the upswing of technology and the development of electronic media. Radio, records, film and television not only present more violence, but they also give the audiences the sound and sight of violence. They evoke powerful images, and the question of the effects of these images compel researchers.

Early research and findings Television by virtue of its ubiquity has been the prime target of the swelling apprehension about media violence, particularly its impact on children. Data going back to the early 1950s, only a few years after television had become a household word, show that both parental and professional concern over the effects of television violence on children was already high. The attempts to measure those effects continues today. What the research has uncovered to this point, however, might best be classified as insights rather than answers.

The first tests, designed to measure the frequency of violence on television, foundered somewhat on the problems of definition and classification. Was, for example, the violence of pie-throwing on *Truth or Consequences* comparable in effects to the gun-and-fist violence of "cops and robbers" programming? It was supposed by many, for example, that children were similarly affected by observing both types of violence and that they were significantly more damaged by observing fictionalized violence than they were by viewing real-life scenes of it in news and documentary programs. The earliest evidence gathered seemed to indicate that neither supposition was categorically true.

A large minority of the children questioned in an early study did experience fear during and after the viewing of television murder and various forms of gothic horror.[20] The study

---

[20] H. Himmelweit, A. Oppenheim and P. Vince, *Television and the Child* (London: Oxford University Press, 1958).

also found that children were less afraid of the real violence shown, but that they disliked it more. And verbal violence was generally more disturbing to them than physical fighting. However, stories which followed known story patterns, such as was then the case with Westerns, seemed least disturbing of all. The authors of the study concluded by saying that "whether an incident will disturb [be feared or disliked] depends less on whether it is fictional or real than on whether it comes within the child's experience and is one with which he can identify himself."[21]

Next to be considered were the actual effects television violence could have on children's value formation and behavior. By the end of the 1950s, several tests had come up with a consensus that should not surprise us at this point: media violence tends to reinforce existing predispositions toward violence. The media's ability to convert the attitudes and behavior of noninclined viewers and make criminals of them was gauged as very limited.

As would be expected, the tests also showed that media violence was generally most popular among children with deep psychological disturbances and long juvenile delinquency records. Yet even among these groups, the incidence of violence directly traceable to television was estimated as small. Although such a cause-and-effect (stimulus-response) mechanism was decidedly possible, for most of these children the violent television scenes seemed to offer escape and fantasy. Media violence was seen as one very small factor among a complex pattern leading to maladjustment. And its effects were felt to depend largely on the individual child.

The report by the Surgeon General's Committee   The research, the arguments, the parental and professional concern continued through the 1960s. And in 1972, the Surgeon General's Office entered the foray with a long-awaited report of research organized, financed and conducted by a special committee over several years.[22]

The first section of the report offered several insights about media content and control. Especially interesting was one study that characterized violence as the standard method television employs to resolve conflict and show power

---

[21] *Ibid.*, p. 408.

[22] For an excellent summary of this report see Leo Bogart, "Television Violence," *Public Opinion Quarterly, 30* (Winter 1972-1973), pp. 449-521.

relationships. This and other studies explored the assumption that violence is needed to attract audiences. Because audience number is the commercial criterion for success, violence is a large part of American television programming affecting two-thirds of all leading characters in televised dramas.

After examining the relationship between television and social learning, several studies concluded that television violence has some definite measure of affect on social behavior. Unlike earlier studies that looked for hypodermic responses, the emphasis here was on effects over extended periods of time. The findings of the research suggest that television aggression may be perceived by children as a standard against which they can compare their own behavior.

Research dealing with the relationship between television and adolescent aggressiveness primarily confirmed earlier findings that viewers who are predisposed to violence will tend to select television programs featuring violence. In turn, the media will reinforce their violent predispositions.

In focusing on daily viewing habits and patterns of television use, some members of the Surgeon General's Committee found that although television continues to be viewed as much as or more than ever, it does not command the attention it did when first available. Often while the television is on, people walk in and out of the room and talk, they think about other matters as it plays or use it to fill in the background of their day.

The final section of the Surgeon General's Report was utilized to give an overall assessment of the committee's research and to suggest areas for further exploration. The major conclusion echoed much of what had been tentatively proven by earlier studies: not television violence itself but individual reactions to it largely determine its effects. This statement led *The New York Times* to run the following headline: TV Violence Held Unharmful to Youth. It and similar headlines in other newspapers only fired the already hot debate of two decades. The report aroused louder concern among parents and teachers. Was violence, then, to continue running rampant across the millions of television screens in the United States?

In response to this concern, the Surgeon General, appearing before a Senate Subcommittee, attempted to redirect popular understanding of the report. He emphasized that evidence compiled on televised violence and its relationship to negative social behavior was sufficiently damning to justify immediate corrective measures. No data, he explained, which deals with the variables shaping social behavior will ever be conclusive enough to satisfy all social scientists or to supply a neat formulation of cause-and-effect. "But," he said, "there comes a time when the data are sufficient to justify action. That time has come."

Effects of mass media on society

Because the mass media are by nature prestigious and because they reach out to many or, as in the case of television, to most segments of the public, they have been able to contribute heavily to changing social standards and practices, while at the same time effecting a degree of stabilization and homogeneity among the disparate elements of society.

Without the mass media, it would be virtually impossible to keep all members of society simultaneously informed of national and world events which are affecting, or will affect, their lives. And it would thus be impossible to rally national or multinational support in times of political, social or environmental crisis. It is true that the media have been periodically remiss in serving this function. Certain aspects of our social and political reality have been unduly magnified in importance by media coverage while other aspects have been allowed to work insidiously beneath a facade of benign appearances. The Watergate affair, for example, might have been exposed much sooner—when it would have had even more immediate political consequences—had it not been for a certain degree of journalistic complacency. On the other hand, the public might have drifted indefinitely in its own unrealistic complacency had it not been for superb investigative efforts and detailed coverage of the scandal by the various media. The point is that the media carries within its scope at least the potential for significantly influencing the public through its informational function.

The social impact of the mass media, especially in terms of its informational function, can also be observed on a cultural level. If there were no means of introducing and updating social and cultural norms and values on a mass scale, the rifts that already divide people might very well deepen. Whether or not a white collar worker in Manhattan agrees with the life-style of a radical student living in San Francisco is, in one sense, beside the point. That both these people know of, and to an extent understand, one another is the essential factor,

Figure 9-2 Communication satellites and other technological advances have created an instantaneous worldwide communication system, making the planet, in the words of Marshall McLuhan, a "global village."

since it creates a sense of community and provides for cultural integration. The mass media further contribute to the creation and maintenance of these cultural ties between the subgroups of our society by serving as a force for the standardization of basic speech patterns and other language habits.

By speeding the process of cultural diffusion in ways we have suggested, mass communication has beneficially served as an agent of social change. However, a substantial number of people have claimed that this expansion of cultural consciousness has also brought about the expansion of "thing" consciousness, placing a disproportionate emphasis on material values. Indeed, our nation's mass media—especially television—are for the most part intimately connected with big business, and big business is intimately concerned with selling—both the products and the images that supposedly come with their purchase. Which toothpaste will really enhance sex appeal? Which car will bring the most prestige? Which clothes will create the most powerful identity? Media advertising seems to invest these and similar questions with more significance than is perhaps warranted. Some critics contend that such questions imply that a person's individual worth is based on his ability to give the right answers.

Whether the mass media will give its fullest efforts and ingenuity to such meaningless content or will strive to utilize its enormous potential for benefiting our society is the real question; and it cannot be answered by anyone but the individual people living in this society.

1. Mass media are those organizationally complex systems of printed and electronic communications that make information rapidly accessible to large and distant audiences in an impersonal fashion.

2. Mass communication is characterized by three traits. The audience is large and heterogeneous. The information flow is rapid and one way with a minimal amount of feedback. The mass media are also unable to select or coerce their audience.

3. The explicit functions of mass media are to disseminate information, entertain, distract and provide aesthetic enjoyment. Implicitly, as economic entities, the primary function of the media is to earn a profit through the sale of advertising directed at the audience.

4. The concept of society as a group of isolated individuals was the basis for the one-step, stimulus-response theory of mass communication. The one-step theory has been replaced by a more sociological, two-step flow theory. This newer theory sees the mass communication process as indirect, involving leaders and followers.

5. An opinion leader differs from his followers in various ways. He tends to have influence only in the area of his competence, although some influence may transfer to related areas. Typically, the opinion leader personifies many of the group's values. His greater exposure to media permits the opinion leader to serve as a gatekeeper, shaping and interpreting information for others. Opinion leaders tend to belong to several large organizations, be more cosmopolitan in their contacts, draw on a wider range of information sources, and enjoy higher economic and social status than their followers. Except in times of crisis, opinion leaders act as middlemen between the general public and the media.

7. The adoption of innovations involves five stages: awareness,

interest, evaluation or mental testing, trial and adoption. Impersonal, informational and cosmopolitan media sources are apparently most influential in the first two stages, whereas personal interactions are more likely to affect the later stages of adoption. Early adopters are similar to opinion leaders in some ways: they are more widely exposed to information sources and possess higher social status than late adopters.

8. Mass communication seems more effective in reinforcing already existing attitudes than in changing attitudes. The selective processes of exposure, attention, perception and retention may explain the mass media's inability to effect major attitude change.

9. Television's image-evoking powers have made media violence a public issue. Early research findings suggested that children react differently to different forms of violence and that the observation of real violence is as harmful as the observation of fictional violence. The 1972 Surgeon General's Report concluded that violence is an essential aspect of American television programming, that it has some effects on children's aggressive behavior over time, that viewers predisposed to violence will select such programming and that individual reactions generally determine the effects of media violence.

10. Mass communication has had a tremendous impact on society in general. The mass media have created new forms of social activity focused on the manipulation of media symbols. They have vastly expanded the potential range of man's awareness of the world. Mass communication has helped to homogenize and standardize speech patterns. The media are arbiters of social status; they are able to confer enormous prestige to products, ideas and persons. Family life has been altered as new role models and sources of information become available through the media. Mass communication may be partially responsible for making consumerism an essential aspect of American life.

1. Discuss the relative strengths and weaknesses of the different media (radio, television, magazines and newspapers) as to accuracy, bias, choice of topics and completeness of coverage.

2. For three days keep a diary of your contacts with all forms of mass media. Itemize and compare your exposure time to each medium. Do the results surprise you?

3. Discuss the controversy concerning bias and the reporting of news. Is objectivity of news reporting possible? Do you think it is desirable?

4. Make a list of five advertisements you consider to be "good" and five you consider "bad." What criteria did you use to distinguish good from bad advertising?

5. What evidence is there that violence viewed on television increases the level of violence in everyday life? Do you think the content of television programming should be regulated to control violence?

6. A former Federal Communications Commissioner referred to television programming as a "vast wasteland." Do you agree? In view of the monopolistic nature of the television channels, what are some of the responsibilities of a television station? In your view, how well are these responsibilities fulfilled?

7. What arguments can you make for and against the financial support of television by government on the federal and/or local level? Do you think educational television should be supported by giant private corporations? Discuss your responses with those of your classmates.

8. Studies in mass communication have revealed that people are not necessarily persuaded and influenced by the media. If that is the case, why are vast sums spent on advertising? What justification is there for the ban on cigarettes and hard liquor on television? Discuss with your classmates.

Lee Bogart, "Television Violence," *Public Opinion Quarterly*, 30 (Winter 1972-1973), pp. 499-521. This is a critical summary of the technical reports on television violence and its effects on viewers prepared for the Surgeon General's Committee. Bogart discusses the five categories of research in order to argue against the unsophisticated interpretations of the general press regarding the innocuousness of television violence.

Melvin L. De Fleur, *Theories of Mass Communications*, 2nd Edition (New York: David McKay Company, Inc., 1970). This book is an effort to provide a theoretical framework for the study of mass communication. Although not a summary of empirical studies of the impact of mass communication, this work pays considerable attention to the historical development of the media in the United States.

Elihu Katz, "The Two-Step Flow of Communications: An Up-To-Date Report on a Hypothesis," *Public Opinion Quarterly*, 30 (Spring 1957), pp. 61-78. This article presents a detailed discussion of the two-step flow theory and various modifications that have been made to it.

Joseph T. Klapper, *The Effects of Mass Communication* (New York: The Free Press, 1960). This classic work attempts to collate and integrate research findings regarding the social and psychological effects of mass communication.

Everett M. Rogers and F. Floyd Shoemaker, *Communication of Innovations: A Cross Cultural Approach* (New York: The Free Press, 1971). Drawing on studies in anthropology, sociology, education and related areas, this summary of more than five hundred studies of the diffusion process also includes an extensive bibliography on the subject. The author offers a number of hypotheses for further investigation of the process of diffusing innovations.

part 3

The functions
of the communication process

Persuasion

It is not uncommon for a television viewer to listen to a celebrity advertise a product (aftershave cologne, for example); to accept the celebrity's suggestion that the product will enhance one's effectiveness with the opposite sex; and to subsequently purchase the product—with little or no conscious realization of the fact that he has become one more statistic attesting to the power of persuasive communication. Not all successful attempts at persuasion are as easily analyzed. The viewer, in this case, was simply emulating a person with status, wealth and a publicized reputation in the field of romance. And not all attempts at persuasion achieve their objective with the same ease and rapidity, a frustrating fact of life for everyone from the media advertiser, to the politician, to the child who exasperatedly tells his parents, "I can't change your minds about anything!"

An unwillingness to be persuaded is not an isolated phenomenon in the communication process. Many of the same personal factors which obstruct other forms of communication similarly shape our resistance to the overt or implicit influence of others. As we mature, certain of our ideas about the nature of reality tend toward becoming absolute convictions; our affective behavior follows more or less fixed patterns; and our cognitive processes—that is, the way in which we think, analyze and interpret—become less open to change. Thus communicators who seek to change our attitudes, emotions and perceptual framework often must deal with rather ingrained tendencies and predispositions.

The tenacity of our past ways of thinking, feeling and perceiving probably accounts for the fact that persuasive communication sometimes fails to be effective when most logically and directly planned and most heavily substantiated by reasons for change. Two years ago, for example, a radical activist might have made a reasonable case for recognition of Red China. Yet many people, clinging to preconceptions about America's "enemies" and fearfully reacting to the stereotype image of the radical, would have as naturally resisted being persuaded on basis of facts as they now have naturally accepted the present relationship between these two nations.

ite:
ight © 1960
ul Steinberg.
The Labyrinth,
r & Row, Publishers.
ally published
New Yorker.

This example is matched by numerous other curiosities in the area of persuasive communication. Why, how and in what ways people are persuaded to change—anything from their brand of toothpaste to their political party—is the interesting subject of several communication theories.

Defining the persuasion process

The various theories of persuasion radiate from some central ideas about the nature of persuasion. To understand the theories, one needs to begin with a workable definition of persuasion. A common definition says that persuasive communication is "a conscious attempt by one individual to modify the attitudes, beliefs or behavior of another individual or group of individuals through the transmission of some message."[1] Another definition maintains that persuasion is "the act of manipulating symbols so as to produce changes in the evaluative or approach-avoidance behavior of those who interpret the symbols."[2] That is, persuasion may simply change your opinion about pornographic bookstores, or it may change your behavior by causing you to act for or against them—for example, patronize them or picket them. Like most others, both of these definitions stress three elements in persuasion: conscious intent, message transmission and behavioral influence.

Definitions such as these raise some problems, since they eliminate certain kinds of activity that one would tend to classify as persuasion. For example, the criterion of conscious intent eliminates a situation in which persuasion occurs without an intent to influence. A company president might unintentionally persuade junior executives to live in his neighborhood or join his country club because he is perceived as a success model to be emulated by them. A movie star who says he believes in astrology may influence millions of fans to adopt his position. People continually influence others inadvertently, through both verbal and nonverbal communication. However, unintentional persuasion is almost impossible to study systematically. Therefore, students of persuasion are limited to the context of intentional persuasion—while acknowledging that people also exert considerable influence in

---

[1] E. P. Bettinghaus, *Persuasive Communication*, 2nd ed. (New York: Holt, Rinehart and Winston, Inc., 1973), p. 10.
[2] G. Cronkhite, *Persuasion: Speech and Behavioral Change* (Indianapolis: Bobbs-Merrill Company, 1969), p. 15.

unintentional and not always understandable ways.

In many instances, common sense provides the necessary guidelines to assess the persuasive intent of a communicator. Most people would probably agree that the company president who lives in a luxurious suburb is not necessarily exerting conscious pressure on his employees to do the same; in fact, he might prefer to enhance his status by remaining the only company member who can afford to live there. On the other hand, most people would agree that a political candidate who spends millions of dollars on his campaign displays clear intent to persuade citizens to vote for him. In some instances, it may be difficult to discern a communicator's intent because he is consciously attempting to conceal it. A guest on a radio talk show may just "happen" to mention an enjoyable meal at one of a chain of taco stands—in which he owns a controlling interest.

A second problem raised by most definitions of persuasion centers on the nature of change necessary to so label a communicative attempt as persuasive. Has an educational television station's fund-raising effort succeeded in persuading a viewer to contribute at the point when the viewer phones in his pledge for fifty dollars? Would you remain convinced that persuasion had occurred if the viewer never sent in his fifty-dollar check? Essentially this problem focuses on the differences between attitude and behavior. Most people assume that attitude and behavior are related; in fact, a common definition of *attitude* is "a predisposition to behave in certain ways." However, research indicates that a person's attitude and behavior are often inconsistent. The educational television viewer may be persuaded to hold the attitude that if he watches public television without supporting the station financially, he is a parasite. But he might still fail to send in his check— no matter how guilty he feels.

One classic study demonstrated this inconsistency between a person's attitude and behavior.[3] On the West Coast, at a time when many people held anti-Oriental attitudes, 92 percent of a group of hotel and restaurant clerks told researchers that they would not serve Chinese people. However, when a well-dressed Chinese couple arrived at the hotels and restaurants, in only one case were they refused service. Unfortunately, the attitude-behavior discrepancy also works the other way; many people express positive attitudes toward minority group

[3] R. T. LaPiere, "Attitudes vs. Actions," *Social Forces*, 13 (1934), pp. 230-237.

members, yet behave or treat them in negative ways.

Furthermore, changed behavior does not always indicate changed attitudes. This fact is reflected in a currently popular poster that says, "Just because you have silenced a man does not mean that you have converted him." A persuader who achieves conformity without attitude change is not much of a persuader, unless he is merely concerned with behavior. A politician who gets votes because he is viewed as "the lesser of two evils" might be content with that type of victory. A persuader must decide whether he wants to influence behavior, attitudes or both.

In determining the kind of persuasion that has occurred, the communicator can only infer attitude change from behavior. We only know another person's attitudes by what he does and what he says. However, making these inferences is easier if one understands the variety of forms that change can take. Persuasive communication can lead to changes in opinions, beliefs or values; and these changes in turn lead to changes in perception, affect, cognition or overt action.

Opinions are verbalized evaluations of people, things or ideas. An opinion may be favorable, neutral or unfavorable. If you read a drama review that persuaded you to say, "I think it is impossible for American actors to perform Shakespeare well," you would have undergone an opinion change.

A *belief* is a conviction about truth or falsity. If you believe that the earth is flat, and you are then shown pictures of the earth taken by the astronauts and these photographs change your mind, you have undergone a change in belief. Unlike an opinion, a belief is not evaluative. For example, "Many people smoke marijuana" is a belief; "Marijuana smoking is good" is an opinion.

A *value* is similar to an opinion, but is more deeply held and more resistant to change. Values exert an enduring influence on a person's thinking and behavior. A good example of the difference between a value and an opinion was provided by a recent Supreme Court decision, which held that a man could qualify as a conscientious objector if he could demonstrate that he held value-based objections to war. In this decision the court was recognizing that values other than religious ones might exempt a man from the draft. However, the justices made it quite clear that a mere opinion against a specific war was not a basis for deferment. In short, an opinion that the war in Vietnam was immoral was legally differentiated from deeper religious, philosophical or ethical values.

These three internal states—the holding of opinions, beliefs and values—are the first targets of persuasive communication. Changes in these states can lead to changes in perception. For example, a change in belief may lead to a change in perception. A student who becomes convinced that a professor is discriminating against him is likely to perceive everything that happens in the classroom from this point of view. Changes in beliefs, opinions and values can also lead to affective, or emotional, change. By appealing to emotions, persuasion can alter a person's mood, self-concept and state of mind. Many messages try to produce affective change by inducing guilt and fear. For instance, a person who goes through a profound change in religious values may become fearful of "fire and brimstone." Sometimes affective change is the only goal of a persuader. For instance, a man may try to persuade a woman to love him. At other times affective change is sought so that further change will result; a man may attempt to persuade a woman to love him so that she will marry him.

Cognitive change influences a person's rational thought processes. People change their behavior partly by considering alternatives and revising their ideas to adapt to new information. A parent who wishes his child to give up smoking might begin by presenting factual evidence supporting the health risks associated with smoking. Cognitive change may also be desirable for its own sake. For example, a history teacher is (he hopes) helping his students achieve cognitive change as they move through the course. Changes in beliefs, opinions or values can aid cognitive change, as in the case of a student who has to be convinced that a black studies course is valuable before he enrolls in it.

Overt action is observable behavior. Although overt action can be influenced by changes in a person's beliefs, opinions or values, this is not always the case. For example, a person can use coercion to induce overt behavior that is unrelated to the beliefs, opinions or values of another person. A teacher may induce a student to study by threatening a failing grade, but he may not necessarily change the student's opinion about the value of the subject matter. Of course, attitude changes are not always reflected in overt behavior. A man may be convinced that the Republican candidate would make the best governor for his state, but still not go to the polls on Election Day. If a person changes both his internal state (beliefs, opinion or values) and his behavior, then optimally effective persuasion has taken place. The most enduring change of this sort occurs when a person alters his behavior to conform with new values. A woman who becomes convinced that feminism gives her a way to understand pervasive political and personal grievances, and who changes her way of life and her relationships with men and other women to reflect her new values, will be relatively resistant to persuasive attempts that argue counter to those values.

Figure 10-1 summarizes the effects of persuasive communication. The persuader must decide what he wants to change, how to construct his appeal, and whether or not he has achieved the desired change. To a great extent, the persuader's goals determine the kind of change he needs to seek. One situation may warrant an attempt to change behavior; another situation may call for attitude change.

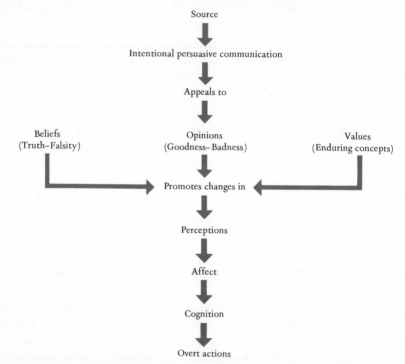

Figure 10-1   Model of persuasion

Theories of persuasion

Several schools of thought attempt to explain the psychological processes that take place during a change in attitudes—

that is, opinions, beliefs and values. Each theoretical position makes different assumptions about the nature of man, the way he processes information and deals with his environment. But they can all be helpful to a persuader, who needs to know the way attitudes are formed and changed.

Learning theories

An infant is born without any opinions, beliefs or values. Through the socialization process, he learns to respond to his environment, to behave acceptably and yet in his own self-interest, to accept certain ideas as true or false, good or bad. In fact, learning can be defined as the process of acquiring or changing behavior in response to individual encounters with people, events and things.

Yet much that is said about persuasion, and about communication in general, implies that the person being persuaded already holds an opinion, belief or value, and that the communicator is simply trying to induce a switch—from Jones to Smith, from pro to anti, from Ultra-Brite to Gleem. However, in many cases the person being persuaded doesn't care any more about Jones, pro, or Ultra-Brite than he does about Smith, anti, or Gleem. In other words he may have no feelings at all on the matter. The Esso company spent an enormous sum of money on an advertising campaign to familiarize people with its new corporate name, Exxon. The goal was clearly factual learning rather than attitude change. In such cases, the persuader needs to be aware of general principles of learning, so he can structure his message effectively.

All theories of learning center on the relationship between stimuli and responses.[4] A stimulus, in this context, is anything that occurs in the communication transaction and is perceived by the receiver; a response is what the receiver does as a result of the stimulus. For example, a speech advocating a high tariff on foreign-made televisions might be a stimulus; an attitude change in the direction of the advocated position or a vote for a bill establishing such a tariff might be the response. A speaker's choice of words and delivery may function as stimuli. If the receiver perceives them as offensive, the response might be dislike for the speaker and resistance to his message. A pleasant spring day, the speaker's bow tie, the

---

[4] See for example Winfred F. Hill, *Learning: A Survey of Psychological Interpretation* (Scranton: Chandler Publishing Company, 1971) and M. D. Smith, *Theoretical Foundations of Learning and Teaching* (Waltham, Mass.: Xerox College Publishing, 1971).

grinding of a garbage truck, the receiver's own emotional state and other nonverbal or psychological factors may serve as stimuli that elicit responses.

The stimulus-response relationship can be manipulated in order to enhance learning. For instance, most learning theories assume that reinforcement is necessary to induce learning. There are two kinds of reinforcement: positive and negative. Suppose a man came to your door and asked you to allow your name to be listed in an advertisement supporting a political candidate. If the man told you that you would be listed as a "prominent" citizen along with the mayor, several movie stars and other celebrities, that your participation would make you a patriotic person, and that you would be paid five dollars for allowing your name to be used, he would be offering you positive reinforcement or rewards. If he told you that anyone who does not allow his name to be used will be considered unpatriotic and furthermore might find himself under investigation by the Internal Revenue Service, he would be offering negative reinforcement; that is, he would be offering you an opportunity to escape from an undesirable situation. Negative reinforcement is not the same as punishment. Negative reinforcement leaves open the door to the desired behavior; punishment takes place only after the receiver has behaved in an undesired way. If you rejected the offer to be listed in the ad, and the next day found that you had been fired from your job because FBI agents had made some unsavory suggestions to your boss, that would be punishment.

Advertisers often use positive reinforcement to link products (stimuli) to increased sexuality, likeability and other supposedly desirable states in order to increase sales (desired response). They also use negative reinforcement—for example, by linking a mouthwash to escape from the supposedly undesirable state of having "bad breath." Both positive and negative reinforcers are likely to have impact on the receiver's behavior. If the communicator can demonstrate to a person the way he will be rewarded or will escape an undesirable state by complying with the communicator's request, behavior will probably change. However, punishment does not usually work so well. People who do not escape the undesirable state and are punished tend to withdraw from the situation.

Most learning theories also assume that the time between response and reinforcement affects the speed of learning. If you know that by signing the political advertisement, you will be paid five dollars in cash on the spot, you might be more willing to sign than if you learned you would get a five-dollar tax rebate the following year. Negative reinforcement is also more effective if escape from the undesired state will be immediate. For instance, telling a young person that he will live to be seventy instead of sixty-eight if he stops smoking is not likely to be as effective as telling him that smokers are automatically disqualified from an athletic group he wishes to join.

Furthermore, specific reinforcements tied to specific desired responses are more effective than vague ones. A speaker who tells you that your life will be better if you support the police is likely to be less persuasive than one who says you will not be mugged if you sign a petition to add 5000 more policemen to the force. Therefore, learning theory suggests that a persuader design his message to state the exact behavior desired and the exact reinforcement that will result.

Because people differ in their abilities and readiness to learn, repetition can induce learning. A persuader cannot be sure that everyone has understood his message; repetition helps him reach as many receivers as possible, and helps solidify the learning of those who understood the first time. Probably everyone is familiar with the kind of organizational foul-up in which a manager claims to have told all his subordinates what was expected of them but somehow did not get through. The importance of repetition is consistent with the idea that persuasion is most successful when it is part of a campaign. That is, one-shot attempts at persuasion often do not work; follow-up communication is needed. Repetition is especially important if the receivers are people with differing backgrounds, information and abilities. However, even people with similar capacities to handle communication differ in their willingness to respond at a given time. Within a group of receivers, some may be distracted by personal problems, noise, other messages they have recently received and any number of additional physical and psychological factors. Repetition can help overcome these barriers to receptivity. It can also help the persuader overcome such obstacles as selective attention, distortion and forgetfulness. Anyone who uses repetition to persuade must be careful not to hammer away with a message that is never going to be accepted. The speaker who assumes that anyone who does not agree with him has simply not understood him is a familiar irritant. "You don't seem to get my point" can only alienate someone who has already gotten the point and rejected it.

Learning theory also indicates that simple elements are more easily learned than complex ones. For instance, in early advertisements, aspirin was advertised as a way to relieve headaches. Each company claimed that its brand did the best job. As the campaigns progressed, each company presented more complex information about its product. Language teaching proceeds in a similar way. A beginning student first learns some basic words, then strings them together into simple sentences, and finally moves on to writing paragraphs or holding conversations. Mastering simple elements strengthens the receiver's willingness to respond to more difficult material. Persuasion should begin on a simple level; once the receiver understands and is rewarded, he can respond to more complex messages.

Another assumption of most learning theories is that people generalize their responses from one situation to another. The "coattails" of a victorious political candidate, for instance, may sweep into office some more obscure members of his party. Institutional advertising, which popularizes the name of a company that makes many products, is also aimed at the generalization response: "If you like our company's green beans, you'll love our ketchup." It is fortunate that generalization occurs as often as it does, because it is economical. Without generalization, a persuader might have to repeat his message in every situation. However, learning in one situation does not always transfer to others. People may love a company's green beans but take a dislike to the shape of its ketchup bottle; and in that case, two separate communication efforts will have to be made. One cannot assume that generalization will always occur.

Learning theory emphasizes the importance of feedback. Positive feedback can work as a form of reinforcement, rewarding the receiver and helping to insure that he will continue to respond in the desired way. For example, a press agent whose job is to persuade writers and reporters to do stories about his client—say, the blue-jeans industry—may reward the authors of favorable stories with praise for their fine abilities or with "freebees"—a new pair of jeans, or tickets to a rock concert. Similarly, negative feedback can facilitate learning if it is perceived as constructive. The press agent might suggest that a writer whose story on the apparel industry failed to mention blue jeans now has an excellent opportunity to sell a follow-up story that does talk about jeans. However, if negative feedback is merely critical or does not give specific suggestions for improvement, it can be perceived as punishment and have undesirable results.

Learning theory does not offer the only explanation for human change. In fact, much learning theory has been criticized for its stimulus-response model, which critics believe is a simplistic view of the nature of man. A good deal of such criticism has been focused on radical behaviorists, such as B. F. Skinner, who maintains that "attitudes" are only conditioned behavior, that a man is the sum of his conditioning —no more. According to this school of behaviorism, all social problems could be solved if people were conditioned in desirable ways. In addition to raising questions about who would control the conditioning process, this theory also raises questions about the nature of man. Other theories about human change assume that man makes decisions and engages in behavior that does not depend on the stimulus-response relationship. These theories deny that man merely responds to stimuli in his environment; in fact, some of them suggest that a person does not always respond in the way that would bring him the best reward.

Consistency theories

While most learning theorists prefer to ignore variables within the receiver's mind that might interfere with the stimulus-response relationship, other persuasion theorists have focused on the mind as a "middle-man" between the stimulus and the response. For example, cognitive theory sees the mind as a complex mechanism that organizes past learning and present stimuli into meaningful units. Thus, the mind is not simply being bombarded with unrelated stimuli; it is always organizing information into a pattern.

A mind operating in this fashion evaluates persuasive communication in terms of the way it fits into an organizational pattern. If the new communication fits into the pattern, the receiver's internal state remains balanced. For instance, if a man recently lost several thousand dollars because of shady and irresponsible dealings by his stock broker, and he then hears a speech proposing stricter regulation of brokerage firms, he can fit the speaker's proposals into the pattern of his experience and feel comfortable with the conclusions. He does not need to be persuaded. If the communication does not fit into a pattern that the receiver's mind is familiar with, it creates internal inconsistency. For instance, if a stock broker heard the same speech, he might have trouble resolving the speaker's proposals with his own opinions, no matter how logical the speaker was. The stock broker must be persuaded.

Internal inconsistency makes people feel uncomfortable; it might happen when a person disagrees with another whom he admires, when he is asked to behave at odds with his opinions, beliefs or values, or when he holds two attitudes that are incompatible. *Balance theories* assume that a man is a comfort-seeking animal who will strive to reduce internal inconsistency, and that he is a rationalizing animal who will find ways to justify changing his attitudes or behavior.

The earliest balance theories dealt with relationships between two persons and some object or idea.[5] The relationships, or linkages, can be either favorable or unfavorable. When they cause internal inconsistency, one or more of the linkages can be changed to restore the balance. Figure 10-2 shows the basic patterns of linkage in balance theory.

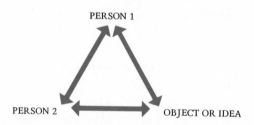

Figure 10-2   Balance theory/Linkage patterns

Linkages between the people are favorable or unfavorable, depending upon credibility, attraction, interpersonal experience or power relationships. Linkages between each person and the object or idea—that is the topic of communication—can also be favorable or unfavorable, depending on each person's opinions, beliefs and values. When the combinations of favorable-unfavorable linkages that appear in Figure 10-3 occur, a state of balance exists, and no persuasion takes place.

In Situation A of Figure 10-3, Person 1 likes Person 2, is favorable toward the topic of communication, and knows

[5] F. Heider, "Attitudes and Cognitive Organization," *Journal of Psychology,* 21 (1946), pp. 107-112.

that Person 2 agrees. For example, the cheated stockholder likes and agrees with the speaker advocating stricter control of brokerages. This combination of variables creates a state of balance, and persuasion is not needed. In Situation B, Person 1 is unfavorable toward both Person 2 and the topic, and knows that Person 2 disagrees. In this case, to pursue the stock market example, Person 1 might be a broker who has grown rich by questionable methods and who also dislikes the reformer's personality and politics. He would remain unpersuaded by Person 2, perhaps rationalizing that only a self-righteous and politically biased man would favor reforms. Again, balance remains secure. Similarly, balance is maintained in Situation C in which Person 2 is disliked and takes an opposing position on the topic, and in situation D in which both parties like each other and oppose the topic.

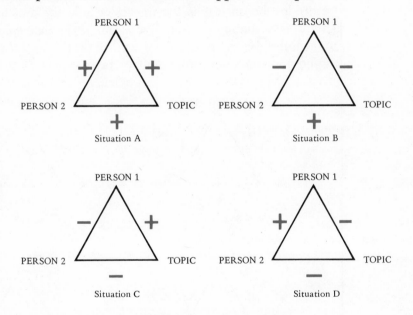

Figure 10-3   Balance theory/Balanced situations

In all the balance models shown in Figure 10-3, persuasion is not likely to occur because there is no internal inconsistency for either party—and internal inconsistency is the motive for change. Without such imbalance, the two people remain comfortable with the linkages between themselves and the issue and will seek to maintain that comfort. However, in the situations illustrated in Figure 10-4, the linkages are unbalanced and some type of change must occur.

In Situation E of Figure 10-4, Person 1, the cheated stockholder, dislikes the reformer but agrees with him on the need for reform. The stockholder will probably change his opinion of the speaker, because people tend to like others who agree with them. However, if the feelings of dislike are very strong, the stockholder might change his attitude toward the topic, deciding that someone he dislikes so intensely must be wrong and that the shady firm he bought his stocks from must have been an exception to widespread integrity in the financial world. Yet another alternative would be for the stockholder to change his perception of the reformer's position. He might decide that the reformer proposes only superficial changes that will not really work. Whatever the actual shift in the stockholder's position, the situation illustrated in Situation E must cause some alteration in his attitudes, because it is too uncomfortable for him to remain as he is. Situations F and G are similar in that we feel uncomfortable when someone we like favors something we oppose, or opposes something we favor.

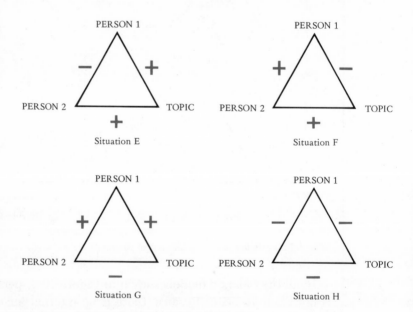

Figure 10-4 Balance theory/Unbalanced situations

In Situation H it is difficult to predict the change that will occur. We do not feel comfortable when people we dislike oppose what we oppose. We want to agree with our friends and disagree with our enemies. The receiver of persuasive communication in this situation might reevaluate the source and use the agreement as a basis for increased liking, or he might change his own opinion to disagree with the disliked source, or he might change his perception of the source by denying the honesty of the communication. For instance, if a leading conservative suddenly made a speech favoring the Allende government in Chile, a socialist listener might decide to like the conservative, decide he himself must have been wrong about Allende's government, or decide that the conservative has some devious reason for making this statement.

There is a handy rule of thumb for determining whether or not a communication situation is balanced or unbalanced. Any time there are an odd number of negative signs on the triangle, the linkages are unbalanced and change must occur. When there are an even number of negative signs (or no negative signs), the linkages are balanced and change does not occur.

Several principles allow one to predict the kind of change that will occur in an unbalanced situation.[6] If there is a contradiction between a receiver's feelings toward the source of the communication and the content of the communication, the attitude toward the content is more likely to change. In other words, it is more difficult to change one's view about a person than about an idea. This fact helps explain why a highly credible source is often so successful at persuasion; people prefer to alter their opinions on the subject rather than to alter their opinions of the man's credibility. In preferring to change that way, people are altering negative linkages rather than positive ones. ("I like the man, so I'll change my dislike of his views.") However, if the receiver feels very negatively toward the issue, he will resist changing his attitude toward it; more likely, he will change his attitude toward the source. Thus, highly involving issues about which people are polarized are less likely to follow the negative sign-changing tendency.

Symmetry theory elaborates on the balance model and shows the way communication affects internal consistency.[7] According to symmetry theory, communication leads to more interpersonal similarity. That is, if you like another person, you desire to

---

[6] W.J. McQuire, "The Current Status of Cognitive Consistency Theories," in S. Feld, ed., Cognitive Consistency (New York: Academic Press, 1966).
[7] See T.M. Newcomb, "An Approach to the Study of Communicative Acts," Psychological Review, 60 (1953), pp. 304-404 and "The Prediction of Interpersonal Attraction," American Psychologist, 11 (1956), pp. 575-586.

be similar to him, and will therefore try to resolve disagreements. When you and someone you like disagree, you feel internal inconsistency and a pull toward symmetry. The strength of the pull depends on how much you like the person, and how intensely you feel about the issue. The more these two factors conflict, the more pull you feel to resolve the conflict. This pull increases the likelihood that you and the other person will communicate about the issue. And as research shows, communication leads to increased similarity in views. Perhaps you and a close friend, for instance, will find ways to compromise on an issue, or perhaps one of you will change his view after learning about the other's arguments and feelings. Symmetry theory differs from balance theory in that it helps explain the reasons attitude shifts occur.

Congruity theory is a refinement of balance and symmetry theories.[8] It predicts mathematically both the amount and the direction of change that will occur in an unbalanced communication situation. One of the failings of balance theory is that it allows for only one change in a situation. For instance, in Situation E of Figure 10-4, if Person 1 changes his opinion of Person 2, balance is restored. Congruity theory allows for more subtle changes. For example, suppose Figure 10-5 reflects your attitudes toward the source of a communication (a respected friend) and toward his position (favoring amnesty for draft resisters).

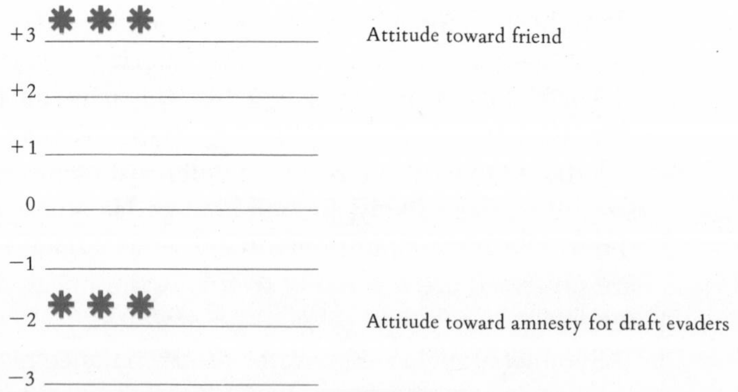

+3 *** ———————— Attitude toward friend

+2 ————————

+1 ————————

0 ————————

−1 ————————

−2 *** ———————— Attitude toward amnesty for draft evaders

−3 ————————

Figure 10-5 Congruity theory/Attitude scale

Your respected friend is rated very favorably on the scale (+3), and you moderately oppose (−2) his statement that

[8] C. E. Osgood and P. H. Tannenbaum, "The Principle of Congruity in the Prediction of Attitude Change," *Psychological Review*, 62 (1955), pp. 42-55.

draft resisters should receive amnesty. According to congruity theory, you would probably change this unbalanced situation in two ways. First, you would become more favorable toward amnesty, because someone you respect is in favor of it. At the same time, you will become less favorable toward the friend, because he spoke for an issue you opposed. However, you will not change in an equal amount toward both source and issue; you will change most whichever attitude is least strongly held. Assuming that your attitude toward amnesty changed more than your attitude toward your friend, balance (with both attitudes occupying the same line on the scale) would be achieved in the way shown in Figure 10-6.

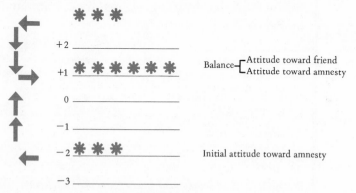

Figure 10-6   Congruity theory/Attitude scale

   Congruity theory claims that attitudes toward both the source and the content of a message change as a result of communication. Through relatively complex mathematical formulae, congruity theory can predict the magnitude and the direction of attitude change after communication. Congruity theory is valuable for its precision and for its assumption that multiple changes can occur.

   All of three types of consistency theory—balance, symmetry and congruity—assume that man strives for internal consistency among his opinions, beliefs and values, and that he is able to rationalize and justify the changes he must make to maintain or restore that balance.

Social judgment theory

Social judgment theory differs from learning theory and consistency theories in several ways.[9] First, it views attitude

---

[9] See C. W. Sherif, M. Sherif and R. E. Nebeigall, *Attitude and Attitude Change: The Social Judgment-Involvement Approach* (Philadelphia: W.B. Saunders, 1965).

change as a two-stage process. In the first stage, the receiver judges the relationship of a communication to his own attitude. For instance, if Susan X believes that amnesty for draft resisters is a good idea, and she hears someone argue that it is tantamount to condoning treason, she will judge the communication to be widely discrepant from her view. In the second stage of attitude change, Susan X makes changes in her opinions, beliefs or values. How much change she makes will depend on how much discrepancy she feels between her view and the source's view.

Social judgment theory treats attitudes as more complex than favorable-unfavorable or positive-negative reactions. It claims that attitudes are best represented by a continuum as shown in Figure 10-7.

Latitude of acceptance	Latitude of noncommitment	Latitude of rejection
1. Unconditional amnesty. 2. Amnesty when all POWs return home. 3. Amnesty if draft evaders work in some national effort for two years.	4. Amnesty if draft evaders fulfill their military commitment.	5. Make draft evaders publicly apologize. 6. Bar draft evaders from forever returning. 7. Make draft evaders serve jail sentences.

Figure 10-7   Social judgment theory/Acceptance-rejection continuum

The receiever has his own position on an issue; this is called his *prime attitude*. In the example above, the receiver believes that unconditional amnesty should be granted. In addition to his prime attitude, he has a *latitude of acceptance*—a range of positions that he is willing to accept (1, 2 and 3). The *latitude of noncommitment* is a range of positions on which the receiver is neutral or has divided feelings (4). Finally, the range of positions that the receiver finds unacceptable (5, 6 and 7) form the *latitude of rejection*.

The receiver's attitude continuum for this example is shown in Figure 10-8.

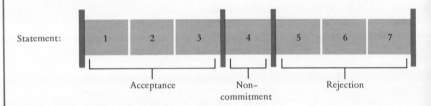

Figure 10-8   Acceptance-rejection continuum

According to social judgment theory, a persuasive message that falls within or slightly out of the latitude of acceptance is perceived by the receiver as closer to his prime attitude than it really is.[10] Suppose a source argued, in a well-prepared persuasive speech, for statement 4: "Draft evaders should be given amnesty if they fulfill their military commitment." The receiver would tend to assimilate this position into his own latitude of acceptance. Then his attitude continuum would look like Figure 10-9.

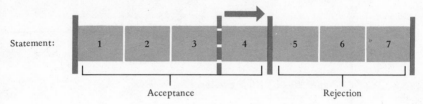

Figure 10-9   Acceptance-rejection continuum

With this new continuum, Statement 5 ("Make draft evaders publicly apologize.") is now close to the latitude of acceptance, and might be assimilated into it after more persuasive communication.

On the other hand, if a source argues for a position that is in the receiver's latitude of rejection, it is seen as more discrepant than it actually is. If a source argued, for instance, that all draft resisters should be imprisoned, the receiver would contrast the source's statements with his own, and remain unpersuaded. This contrast effect may lead in some instances to a "boomerang" effect. The receiver in the amnesty example, for instance, might be so repelled by the suggestion of imprisonment for draft resisters that he would shrink his latitude of acceptance, and decide that all positions except for his prime attitude are unacceptable. This situation is illustrated in Figure 10-10.

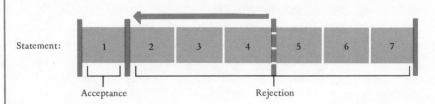

Figure 10-10   Acceptance-rejection continuum

10 Sherif, Sherif and Nebeigall, *op. cit.*

Social judgment theory also predicts the ways in which the receiver's ego-involvement affects his attitude change. High ego-involvement corresponds to a wide latitude of rejection; low ego-involvement corresponds to a wide latitude of noncommitment. For example, a draft resister would be highly ego-involved on the subject of amnesty. His latitudes might appear as they do in Figure 10-11.

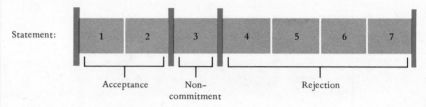

Figure 10-11   High ego-involved receiver

A person who does not even know any draft resisters, and who has nothing personal at stake in the issue might have latitudes such as those shown in Figure 10-12. (Note that ego-involvement does not affect the latitude of acceptance.)

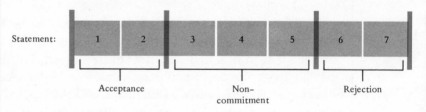

Figure 10-12   Low ego-involved receiver

Because an ego-involved person has a wide latitude of rejection, persuasive messages are more likely to fall into that range and be contrasted with his prime attitude. Thus, attitude change is difficult. A receiver who lacks ego-involvement, on the other hand, has a wide latitude of noncommitment into which persuasive messages are likely to fall. Such messages can then be assimilated into the acceptable range, and persuasion is more successful. Common sense certainly supports this conclusion that a person is more reluctant to change his attitudes on issues that are directly important to him.

1. Most definitions of persuasion stress three elements: conscious intent, message transmission and behavioral influence. Although people may persuade others unintentionally, the criterion of conscious intent facilitates the formal study of persuasion. A persuasive message may lead to changes in a person's attitude (beliefs, opinions and values) which in turn may lead to changes in a person's perception, emotions, cognition or overt action. An opinion is a favorable, unfavorable or neutral evaluation of a person, thing or idea. A belief is a nonevaluative conviction about the truth or falsity of something. A value is a deeply held opinion that exerts influence on a person's thinking or behavior.

2. Learning theory centers on the relationship between stimuli and responses. A stimulus is anything in the communication situation that is seen by the receiver; a response is the receiver's reaction to the stimulus. According to learning theory, the effectiveness of communication can be enhanced through the use of positive or negative reinforcement. Positive reinforcement involves rewarding the receiver for making the appropriate or desired response. Negative reinforcement involves threatening the receiver with an undesirable situation for making the wrong response. But negative reinforcement is not punishment. Punishment occurs after the receiver has responded in an undesired way; negative reinforcement provides the receiver with an opportunity to behave in the desired way. Learning theories stress the following concepts: The time between the response and the reinforcement may affect the speed of learning. Specific reinforcement tied to specific desired responses are more effective than vague ones. People generalize their responses from one situation to another. Feedback may function as positive or negative reinforcement.

3. There are three types of consistency theories: cognitive balance, symmetry and congruity. Cognitive balance theory views the mind as a complex system that organizes past

experiences and present stimuli into meaningful patterns. People tend to evaluate a persuasive message according to the way it fits into the pattern. If the message fits, the receiver's internal state remains balanced. If the message does not fit, the receiver is in a state of internal inconsistency. To establish balance, the receiver must change his attitude toward either the source or the message. Other things being equal, if there is a contradiction between the receiver's attitude toward the source and the message, the receiver's attitude toward the message is more likely to change. However, if the receiver feels very strongly about the topic, he is likely to change his attitude about the source. Symmetry theory modifies the balance theory by trying to explain the way communication affects internal inconsistency. Congruity theory claims that when internal inconsistency exists, attitudes toward both the source and the message change.

4. Social judgment theory views attitude change as a two-step process. First the receiver judges the relationship of a communication to his own attitudes and then he makes changes in his attitudes. According to this theory, a person's attitudes about a topic are best represented by a continuum, ranging from the most acceptable to the most unacceptable. The position a receiver finds most acceptable is called his prime attitude. A receiver also has a latitude of acceptance (positions he finds acceptable), a latitude of noncommitment (positions about which he is neutral or divided), and a latitude of rejection (positions he finds unacceptable). A persuasive message that falls within or slightly out of the latitude of acceptance is perceived by the receiver as closer to his prime attitude than it really is. Thus, the receiver tends to assimilate this position into his latitude of acceptance. A position that falls within the receiver's latitude of rejection is seen as more discrepant than it actually is. A receiver who is very ego-involved in the topic has a wide latitude of rejection into which a persuasive message may fall, whereas a receiver who is not ego-involved has a wide range of noncommitment. Since a receiver perceives messages as more similar and more discrepant than they actually are, persuasion is likely to be more successful with the receiver who is not ego-involved than the one who is very ego-involved.

1. The class should select a topic of interest to all its members, and then it should divide into groups of 4 to 6 persons. Each group should select one of the three theories of persuasion discussed in this chapter. Using the principles of the theory selected, each group should design a persuasive campaign to change attitudes about the subject. Each group should then make a persuasive presentation to the remaining class members. How do the assumptions of each group differ? How are their assumptions similar? Which approach does the class as a whole find most useful? Can the theories of persuasion be combined to make a better presentation?

2. Evaluate the other courses in which you are enrolled. Determine the way each professor is trying to change your beliefs, opinions or values. Which theory of persuasion does each professor seem to use? In which course does the most learning occur? Can you explain the reasons more learning takes place in this course than in the others?

3. Write an anecdotal description of a situation in which you experienced cognitive imbalance. Make certain you specify the different variables operative in the situation. Now repeat the exercise, writing descriptions of situations in which you received positive reinforcement, negative reinforcement and punishment. Which type of situation do you think is most likely to change your attitudes?

4. Write an anecdotal description of a situation in which your attitude about an object or idea become more similar to the attitude of another person. What variables were important in your interaction? What communication factors might cause two persons' attitudes to become more discrepant? Write an anecdotal description of such a situation.

Thomas D. Beisecker and Donn W. Parson, eds., *The Process of Social Influence: Readings in Persuasion* (Englewood Cliffs, N.J.: Prentice-Hall, 1972). This collection of readings contains a number of classic articles in the areas of speech communication and psychology. The initial section includes essays that present a thorough review of the theories of attitude change discussed in this chapter. Variables affecting persuasion and the impact of persuasive communication are covered in the remaining sections.

Erwin P. Bettinghaus, *Persuasive Communication*, 2nd Edition (New York: Holt, Rinehart and Winston, 1973). This introductory text presents a general overview of the persuasive process. The beginning student interested in factors affecting attitude change will find it particularly useful.

Gary Cronkhite, *Persuasion: Speech and Behavioral Change* (Indianapolis: Bobbs-Merrill, 1969). An excellent analysis of persuasion from a historical and scientific viewpoint, this work provides a sound treatment of persuasion from a variety of divergent perspectives.

Charles A. Kiesler, Barry E. Collins and Norman Miller, *Attitude Change* (New York: John Wiley and Sons, 1969). Perhaps the best single critical study of the different theoretical approaches to the psychology of attitude change, this volume presents an excellent comparative treatment of the various theories and associated research. The material is fairly technical, but nevertheless readable, even for beginning students.

Gerald R. Miller and Michael Burgoon, *New Techniques of Persuasion* (New York: Harper and Row, 1973). The effects of role-playing and counterattitudinal advocacy as persuasive techniques are discussed here, together with a thorough analysis of consistency theories. Techniques for inducing resistance to persuasion are also considered by the authors.

Edgar Schein with Inge Schneider and Curtis H. Baker, *Coercive Persuasion* (New York: W. W. Norton and Company, 1961). An in-depth analysis of brainwashing techniques used on American prisoners-of-war in Korea, this book examines the way theories of persuasion operate in the extreme situation of a prison camp.

Information exchange

Information exchange may take place in any type of communication situation. Devoting a separate chapter to it might be an unnecessary redundancy if the results of information exchange (and the repercussions of misinformation or a lack of information) were not central concerns in the lives of all people. For information can increase understanding and serve as a basis for action, just as the lack or misconception of it can hinder and confuse understanding and lead to actions that are inconsonant with reality.

For example, citizens have available to them many public services that may help to solve individual medical, economic, social and psychological problems. But without information about these services (either interpersonally or mass communicated) they may as well be nonexistent. Likewise social, economic and political grievances of more general significance, such as those which are voiced by feminist leaders, cannot be serviced unless the base of orientation and understanding is broadened through information exchange. Information concerning rallies, meetings, public events and demonstrations, pertinent legislative efforts, and the results of all these actions must be easily available to all people if the issues raised and changes sought are to filter into the consciousness of the entire population.

Of considerable concern to businessmen and to people in government is the quality and scope of information and the methods used to avoid distortion in the process of information exchange. In business and industry, the wrong data can often result in very costly financial losses. A chewing gum manufacturer, for example, once advised executives of a network television company that it wished to change the time slot for one of its lengthy commercials. The proper information never reached the traffic department (where programming is organized), the commercial was run and the network was obliged to absorb the loss of a very impressive fee. Apparently little was done to improve information exchange, for the very same commercial was incorrectly programmed on two subsequent occasions!

More massive and less easily reconcilable losses may result from inaccurate or misused information gathered by governments.

For example, one analysis of the Vietnam war suggests that the spirit and determination of the North Vietnamese were never computed into the assessment of their military strength. In other words, vital information was either not available to those in charge or was seriously misinterpreted. Subsequent to large-scale involvement in the war, there were many other occasions when information was inaccurate or inaccurately transmitted. The actions which resulted—for example, the bombing of nonmilitary targets—represent the more tragic consequences of inaccuracy in the exchange of information.

Accuracy of information exchange

Information is sometimes deliberately distorted or deceptively worded so that its actual meaning will be bypassed, and sometimes people consciously misinterpret information to suit their own purposes. In most cases, however, people want to be understood and to understand others correctly; but they can not effect a high quality of information exchange if they fail to control the accuracy of their messages—an especially difficult, yet important, procedure when a chain of communication is involved. It is therefore worthwhile to examine certain variables associated with information accuracy and ways to avoid or rectify problems and errors that may arise.

Interpersonal factors affecting accuracy

When a programmer encodes information for a computer, he knows beforehand the machine's capacity for data processing and its limitations of design. And when he decodes the information received from the computer, he does not have to correct for personal biases and emotional pre-sets—for the computer has none. In other words, barring malfunctions of the computer, information accuracy is contingent only on the programmer's knowledge and skills. In human communication, each interactant brings with him a *set* of variables—for example, his knowledge, cognitive ability, past experiences and perceptual framework—each of which may affect message accuracy.

Sometimes cultural dissimilarities between the interactants cause problems in the exchange of information. Scientists from different countries may have few accuracy problems in communication, because their information is based on principles and procedures governing all experiments, whether they are conducted in Moscow or Madison. But information that is defined by unique cultural experience is susceptible to misinterpretation by those who have matured within a different economic, social and political milieu. For example, a Zuni would not be able to accurately understand information about ballistic missiles and atomic stockpiles not simply because his own cultural subgroup has no knowledge of sophisticated weaponry and no language of technology but, more importantly, because there is no equivalent in his cultural experience for aggression and hostility—he would not be able to comprehend the *purpose* of a weapons arsenal.

Even when people do share similar cultural backgrounds, they almost invariably exhibit differences in intellectual capacity and emotional perspective. A person of average intelligence may grasp the overall significance of a complicated piece of information but not be able to comprehend its more subtle aspects. The cognitive skills and ability of this person would therefore set the limit on the accuracy of information exchange with a person of higher intelligence, assuming it were possible to equalize all other interpersonal variables.[1] Or a person may be intellectually capable of processing any data presented to him, but his selective processes may block out certain kinds of information. For example, if a person does not wish to believe that he has been negligent or unwise in his choice of friends and associates, he may filter out any information that disparages these people or implicates them in wrongdoing. Similarly, the person actually conveying the information about these associates may modify its accuracy (whether or not he does it consciously) because he wishes to tell the other person "what he wants to hear."

In terms of interpersonal communication, then, information accuracy is contingent upon the efforts of both parties to overcome personal limitations. In striving for accuracy, both in transmitting and receiving information, a communicator necessarily must strive for an understanding of the other person's perceptual framework and for an awareness of any preconceptions and prejudices of his own which may affect information exchange. He must try to determine whether his or the other person's past experience predispose them to certain

---

[1] Albert Mehrabian and Henry Reed, "Some Determinants of Communication Accuracy," *Psychological Bulletin*, 70 (September 1968), p. 370.

interpretations of data or if information will be perceived and interpreted in the actual context of its presentation. In other words, both parties must be willing to go beyond what once seemed to be true (or what they wish were true) if they are to accurately perceive and judge new information; and both parties must be willing therefore to listen fully to the information that is being conveyed to them.

Sometimes failure to do so can have rather humorous consequences. The plot of many a situation comedy, for example, has utilized "the rumor"—the progressive distortion of a single fact or event as it is conveyed from husband to wife to neighbor to grocer and on down the grapevine. More formal situations, however, may warrant painstaking attention to those interpersonal variables which limit the accuracy of information exchange.

In Tombstone, Arizona there is a simple, flat gravestone which reads "George Johnson—hanged by mistake." The epitaph evokes at least a wry smile from the visitors to Tombstone, although its irony is lost to George Johnson. Perhaps lawyers are motivated by similar testaments to inaccuracy when they subject potential jurists to severe and intense questioning. Personal prejudices, low intelligence, the inability or unwillingness to examine the feedback of other jurists concerning the information presented at trial—all these factors may seriously affect the accuracy of the jurist's perceptions when he receives and considers the evidence of the defense and prosecution.

Language usage and clarity
Closely related to differences in personal background are the differences in the way people understand and use language. The same words may be learned under a variety of conditions and therefore accumulate a variety of connotative and affective meanings. A communicator must therefore realize that the words he uses to codify information may not be interpreted as he intended them to be, but according to the receiver's experience with those words.

Whether or not special terms, complicated grammatical constructions and a high-level or technical vocabulary will be a boon or a hindrance to comprehension must also be considered by the communicator. People in government and the sciences, for example, often use a "technicalese" even when they are discussing information that could be as easily conveyed in everyday terms. Their vocabulary would undoubtedly boggle the layman's mind (perhaps it is sometimes intended to) and obscure the information being conveyed to him. But one may question the efficacy of using technical terms even among those who are accustomed to them. It is true that since there are only a finite number of language symbols to describe an infinite number of "things," the scientist is obliged to create new words to accommodate newly discovered phenomena. But terminology such as "overkill," and "defoliation" tend to neutralize the emotional impact of information and abstract the human beings who would be affected if such words became reality. Despite their sophistication and apparent precision—or because of these deceptive qualities—certain technical terms may comprise a major obstacle to accuracy of information exchange.

The "things" actually being described may also modify the level of accuracy. Certain objects or situations, for example, display ambiguous and complex qualities that cannot be conveyed in direct and simple terms. A high degree of accuracy is therefore difficult to achieve, because there is no clearly defined way of codifying the information. If one is dealing with information content that manifests simple and comparatively unambiguous qualities—for example, a round and red rubber ball—the degree of accuracy in conveying such information is significantly greater.[2]

A communicator must also consider language differences that influence the way things are perceived, and hence, the way they are described. There is the obvious difficulty of individual word differences, but there is also the more subtle problem of different styles of speech. An interpreter would distort the accuracy of information if he were simply to give a literal translation. In fact, there are many words and expressions for which there are no equivalents in the English language. As part of his training, therefore, the interpreter must study the culture that shaped, and was shaped by, the language. He can then accurately convey, among other things, the "meaning" of a certain tone of voice, the inflection given to various words and the significance of idiomatic expressions.

Even those people who conduct business and government transactions in countries where the second language spoken is English must be tuned to the nonverbal behavioral patterns of each culture. In Japan, for example, business negotiations

[2] *Ibid.*, p. 378.

are almost ritualistically complex, with certain gestures and mannerisms a necessary part of any transaction. If an American businessman were to ignore such formalities, he might be perceived as a man of bad faith, and subsequent information exchanges would be distorted by the negative personal image he had created. The more general significance of this point is that in any country, even one's own, communication accuracy suffers if a person's intentions are suspect or his attitude is negatively perceived, no matter how impressive or effective his use of language.

Organization, presentation and feedback

Unless there is agreement about the meaning of language symbols used within a particular context—that is, unless certain rules of language are consensually observed by all those involved in a communication setting—only the simplest information could be exchanged with any degree of accuracy. But language clarity alone will not insure that a person is understood. He must organize and present his information in such a way that it is comprehensible to the particular person or audience he is communicating with. Even the computer programmer, utilizing a highly formal and precise "language," must consider how he should program data if he expects to receive accurate feedback.

If information is detailed or lengthy it may be advisable to break it down into manageable message units that can be discussed in a straightforward manner. The different size headings in each chapter of this text serve this function. In regard to rate of message delivery, one study reported that comprehension increased from 175-275 words per minute (perhaps because people were obliged to pay greater attention at the higher rate) but then decreased between 275-375 words per minute.[3] In judging how rapidly he should speak, the communicator should consider the receiver's listening skills, cognitive ability and previous experience with similar information.

Unfortunately this information is sometimes unavailable to the speaker before he actually initiates the information exchange, and feedback therefore becomes an important guide in judging the effectiveness of his approach. Let us say that a person is speaking too rapidly or that his presentation is

---

[3] Ronald H. Reid, "Grammatical Complexity and Comprehension of Compressed Speech," *Journal of Communication, 18* (September 1968), p. 242.

extremely disorganized. He may blissfully continue in this way unless he is provided with evidence that his message is not getting through or that there is a discrepancy between the message he wishes to express and the message the receiver perceives. Perhaps the receiver will simply tell him to slow down or to repeat the information. Or perhaps a puzzled look will suffice to modify the communicator's method of delivery. Sometimes, however, feedback is delayed and thus can only serve as a guide for future information exchanges. In response to negative feedback—or as a procedure when immediate and diversified feedback is unavailable—the communicator can employ a variety of techniques to clarify, emphasize or reinforce his message and thus facilitate the accuracy of comprehension.

Figure 11-1 The receiver's nonverbal behavior may help the source to evaluate the effectiveness of his verbal communicative attempt.

Research indicates that the accuracy of message reception may be affected by the number of channels through which information is exchanged.[4] The more channels, the more accurate the information exchange. For instance, suppose the executive of a food company tells his plant manager that he wants a new quality control program instituted at the plant

[4] For a more detailed discussion see D. Faules, "The Relation of Communicator Skills to the Ability to Elicit and Interpret Feedback Under Four Conditions," *Journal of Communication*, 17 (1967), pp. 362-371 and H. J. Leavitt and Ronald A. H. Mueller, "Some Effects of Feedback on Communication," *Human Relations*, 4 (1951), pp. 401-410.

and then specifies complicated guidelines for each department. The executive would probably do best if he followed up his oral presentation with a written memorandum repeating the information. By increasing the number of channels in this example, the executive is increasing the redundancy of his message, and redundancy enhances the accuracy of message reception.

Figure 11-2 By increasing the number of communication channels, models and other visual aids may enhance the accuracy of message reception and retention.

Likewise, the use of multiple channels may facilitate accuracy when physical or psychological noise distracts the attention of the receiver. One study showed that visual cues from the lips of the communicator (lip-reading) may increase understanding of his message when noise or other interfering stimuli are present.[5] If possible, then, the communicator should try to be close enough to the receiver so that visual cues can be received. In the event that this is not possible, or even as a way of enhancing visual cues, the speaker can modulate his voice to emphasize important points. This will aid

[5] Mehrabian and Reed, op. cit., p. 375.

not only in the accuracy of the initial perception but also in the accuracy of retention.

Another form of emphasis that may increase accuracy involves the repetition of key points or concepts. A speaker may, for example, integrate brief summary statements after each section of his presentation. In this way, if at any time during the information exchange, the receiver becomes confused or forgets certain points, he has another opportunity to refocus his understanding. Accuracy may also be enhanced by an introductory statement that focuses the receiver's attention on the major points to come. All these techniques increase redundancy and thus facilitate accurate message reception.

Information exchange within an organization

We have discussed general ways to improve accuracy and to avoid, or correct for, inaccurate communication. But there is one information setting which requires a specialized knowledge and approach to accuracy: the formal business organization. Information exchange within an organization serves a specific purpose—to facilitate the production of goods or services. The vital importance of this function necessitates a comparatively higher degree of accuracy than one might need or expect in more casual communication settings. Inaccurately communicated information would not merely inconvenience or hinder the efforts of one person but could effect the total efficiency of an organization, especially if the inaccuracy is perpetuated along a chain of people.

Those who plan organizations therefore try to anticipate communication problems that could result from the sheer complexity of an organizational structure. Less easily controlled or anticipated is the human factor; that is, the motivation, skill and performance of organization employees and their ability and willingness to observe procedures that would ensure effective communication.

The supply of research based on this specialized communication setting is rather scanty. Theorists cannot always explain the reasons communication dysfunctions occur, nor can they always predict the effect of a number of variables on overall communication accuracy. It is possible, however, to trace the flow of communication within different organizational structures and suggest certain factors that may directly or indirectly relate to the quality of information exchange.

Communication in formal organizations

The formal structure of an organization incorporates all the designated functions of the various company subunits and all the planned procedures for information exchange within and among these units. The formal structure defines production goals for the people working within the organization; it divides the numerous duties and responsibilities of each department among the personnel; and it coordinates individual worker activities by providing leadership at the various levels of organization. This last feature—coordination of activities— may be facilitated by any one of several formal systems of communication that links each unit of the organization to a central information point. In this way, problems in production may be perceived, analyzed and resolved without halting the flow of production.

Scope of the communication network

One variable of a formal communication system is its size. The system employed may consist of individual circuits, each of which functions within a single company department or section of a department. Or it may be an all-inclusive network of communication that is designed to service the entire organization. Communication problems related to this variable often occur when company executives misjudge the scope of the communication system being used—that is, when they believe that information is reaching a larger number of people than is actually the case.

Pattern of transmission

Information that is formulated at the upper echelons of the company structure may be transmitted in exactly the same form to each of the subunits. This repetitive transmission is probably the most efficient way of conveying simple and direct messages throughout the organization. For example, the list of holidays which are observed by an organization can simply be typed up and duplicated for mass distribution since this information has the same meaning for all employees and departments.

However, in dealing with more complex material, repetitive transmission may actually confuse or hinder organization activities. In such cases, it is necessary to modify the information being transmitted so that its relevance to a particular subunit is made clear.

Communication links Within a single communication network (which might include, for example, only top level personnel or one department or subunit) there may be two or more communication links—that is, information can be exchanged between two or more people within a given network. Some empirical evidence suggests that the performance of a group of people working on a task may be more efficient if communication links are kept to a minimum.[6] But even without the benefit of research, one can easily surmise the complications that could result from a multi-link method of information exchange.

Let us say that in a particular organization two departments, each comprised of five employees and a supervisor, are working on a joint project. Let us also suppose that the method of communicating information about that project is to have one of the departmental supervisors give instructions to one of his employees, who in turn conveys the information to a second employee, and so on, down to the fifth departmental worker. This last person would then introduce the information into the second department where it subsequently would be communicated from one employee to another.

In other words, ten communication links would punctuate the flow of a single piece of information! Obviously, the time required to exchange the information would in itself impair production efficiency. But, more important, the odds against accuracy would be unquestionably high. Some of the information is bound to be omitted, misrepresented or modified, especially if at each link the source or receiver of the information adds his own digressive comments or interpretation to the original message.

Suppose each departmental supervisor were to call a meeting and communicate the new information to all of his employees at once. In effect, this would be two-link communication— the supervisor being one party and the *group* of employees being the second party—and the exchange would be more rapid and accurate than in the ten-link situation. If confusion did arise, the employees could receive immediate clarification

---

[6] For a complete discussion see R. Dubin, "Stability of Human Organizations" in M. Haire, ed., *Modern Organization Theory* (New York: John Wiley and Sons, 1959), pp. 218-253 and H. Guetzkow and W. R. Dill, "Factors in the Organizational Development of Task-Oriented Groups," *Sociometry*, 20 (1957), pp. 175-204.

during the meeting. And if the employees did forget or become confused about the information after they actually began work on the project, they could draw on their "collective" memory of the information exchange, since they all received the information from the same source.

Pattern of feedback In terms of organizational structure the flow of communication is predominantly channeled in one direction. But whatever directional system is employed, there must be provision for feedback, even if it is only in the form of a confirmation that certain messages have been received. Information that is complex and of vital importance to the quality of output from the organizational units should elicit feedback. For example, the feedback could include a report on the specific ways that messages were implemented by the various subunits, the adequacy (or inadequacy) of the information provided in facilitating production efficiency and any changes that it may have been necessary to make on the information received.

Difficulties arise when feedback is not proportional to the amount or type of information received. Top executives, for example, may only receive a response to their communication from those who are directly subordinate to them. Feedback from lower levels of the organization may be distorted by the time it is received by the initiator of the message, or it may not be received by him at all. Organizational efficiency could be severely impaired, therefore, if feedback is not consistently available and accurately processed.

1. Successful information exchange is crucial to effective action in social, political, business and governmental organizations.

2. The accuracy of information can be affected by interpersonal factors (knowledge, cognitive ability, past experience and perceptual framework), cultural dissimilarities, language usage, message organization and presentation, and feedback. On an interpersonal level, information accuracy depends upon the willingness of both parties to understand each other's frame of reference, overcome prejudice and emotional bias and revise their preconceptions.

3. The way a language is used or understood by people may alter the character of the information conveyed. Technical terms used by specialists sometimes obscure meaning. The genuine complexity of certain subjects makes simple, unambiguous statements difficult. Finally, the subtleties of grammar, syntax and linguistic style, as well as associated nonverbal behavior, influence the process of information exchange.

4. Message reception is determined in part by the organization and presentation of the information. Feedback opportunities, the size of message units and the speed of their delivery may significantly affect message reception. Visual cues, repetition of key points, and the use of multiple channels may help to make information exchange more effective.

5. The accuracy of information exchange in the formal organization is vital to the effective coordination of departmental activities and the efficient production of goods and services. There are four variables characteristic of a formal communication system that can affect the accuracy of information exchange. The size refers to the inclusiveness of a given communication network. The pattern of transmission refers to the repetition of messages and techniques used to clarify information for individual departments. Communication links are the number of people involved in information exchange within a given network.

As the number of communication links increases, the probability of message distortion increases. Feedback is the formal provision for message response at all managerial levels. Organizational efficiency may be hampered if adequate feedback is not available.

1. Select four students from the class and designate them Person 1, Person 2, Person 3 and Person 4, respectively. Have all four students leave the room. The professor or a student should then relate a brief but detailed anecdote to the other members of the class. Call Person 1 back into the room. One student who heard the message should then relate it to Person 1. Call Person 2 back and have Person 1 relate the story to him. Repeat the procedure with Persons 3 and 4. In all instances, no verbal feedback should be permitted. Was the message accurately transmitted? What was added, deleted or altered? What was accurately transmitted? What were the effects of increasing the number of links in the chain of communication?

2. Repeat the exercise above, but this time allow the person(s) listening to ask questions or take notes. Was this message more or less accurately received than the message in exercise 1? Why? What other things can be done to improve accuracy?

3. Think of a situation in which a message you transmitted was inaccurately received? What factors caused the message to be inaccurately received? What could have been done to correct the situation?

4. Identify the organizational communication pattern of your college or university. What barriers to upward and downward communication exist? How can they be removed? How do these barriers affect students, faculty and other staff members.

M. F. Hall, "Communication Within Organizations," in W. A. Hill and D. Egan, eds., *Readings in Organization Theory: A Behavioral Approach* (Boston: Allyn and Bacon, 1966), pp. 403-415. This article discusses communication and decision-making in organizations. The author offers communication strategies to promote organizational change.

William V. Haney, "Serial Communication of Information in Organizations," in S. Malick and E. H. Van Ness, eds., *Concepts and Issues in Administrative Behavior* (Englewood Cliffs, N.J.: Prentice-Hall, 1962), pp. 150-165. This is a very readable article which focuses on the reasons that the message sent is often not the message received. The author presents specific guidelines to improve the accuracy of message transmission in a variety of settings.

Daniel Katz and Robert L. Kahn, "Communication: The Flow of Information" in *The Social Psychology of Organizations* (New York: John Wiley and Sons, 1966), pp. 223-229. Organizations as communication systems and the problems of information flow within complex organizations are the subject matter of this excellent chapter.

James C. McCroskey, Carl E. Larson and Mark L. Knapp, "Accuracy and Understanding," in *An Introduction to Interpersonal Communication* (Englewood Cliffs, N.J.: Prentice-Hall, 1971), pp. 16-36. In this chapter, the authors provide a comprehensive review of the research on variables affecting the accuracy of message transmission.

Ralph G. Nichols, "Do We Know How to Listen? Practical Help in a Modern Age," in *The Speech Teacher, 10* (1961), pp. 118-164. In a convincing argument, the author claims that the primary cause of inaccurately received messages is our inability to effectively listen. He offers ten guidelines to achieve effective listening.

12 Social relations and conflict resolution

According to Japanese tradition, when two people meet they engage in a bowing ceremony. Status distinctions dictate the depth of each person's bow to the fraction of an inch—with the more humble person bowing deeper. Little children are excused from this ritual because the information needed to determine such precise status distinctions—based on wealth, power, age, sex and other factors—takes so long to learn and is so complicated.

To a Western observer, such interactions seem to be rigidly controlled by the society's standards. Yet that same observer's own behavior often follows similar, if less conscious, patterns. For instance, if the observer is a professor, he is likely to converse with a student in one way and with the head of his department in another. His tone of voice, choice of words, subject matter and even his posture are controlled to some extent by his status relationship with the person to whom he is talking. In other words, he is behaving according to a pecking order, the subliminal equivalent of the Japanese bowing ceremony.

Many people assume that in social interactions where status difference is less clear, or less observable, they behave with unfettered freedom. Certainly in the company of your friends, you may feel that you can talk about any subject, in any language, while positioning your body in any ways that feel comfortable. Yet even in these intimate interpersonal relationships, behavior is not exclusively random or idiosyncratic. Certain patterns can be observed.

Most people are probably aware of some of the patterns that indicate the nature of an established relationship. Whether you are a student of kinesics or simply supplied with folk wisdom, you can probably guess the attitudes of two persons who sit with their backs turned slightly toward each other, or two persons whose eyes keep interlocking. But fewer people realize that there are also patterns indicating whether or not relationships will develop, the way they develop and the way they are maintained. Various communication factors can make it more or less likely that you and another person will become, or remain, friends.

Like and dislike are among the most basic factors in communication. People associate with each other on the basis of these feelings, and even in groups, like and dislike can affect the patterns of communication and influence. It is widely believed that such feelings are fundamentally irrational. Indeed, they often seem that way, as in the case of two friends who have nothing in common but the fact that they "feel good" around each other.

However, sociologists have developed methods to measure interpersonal attraction, and it is more patterned than one might first suppose. The sociometric test is one way to test interpersonal attraction. It was devised to determine the preferences of group members for each other by establishing a procedure and setting up a criterion for choices of liking. For example, in an elementary school classroom, each child might be asked to choose those classmates with whom he would prefer to work on a project. The choices might be unlimited in number; or the child might be asked to pick his first three choices in order of preference; or he might be asked to rank the entire class. The criterion of preference might vary: The child might be asked to choose on the basis of work ability, simple social attraction or any other basis. When the data from a sociometric test are analyzed, one gets information about the individual most frequently chosen, those not chosen at all and (if the choosers are identified) a picture of the patterns of attraction in the group. For instance, everyone picks John as his first choice, indicating that John is a key member of the group. Likewise four people might all choose each other, indicating a clique or subgroup.

Researchers have also studied nonverbal ways to measure attraction. Eye contact, changes in the size of the pupil in the eye and the distance between two standing persons have all been used to measure interpersonal attraction. These and other measurement techniques have enabled researchers to determine some of the variables involved in the interpersonal attraction process.

Physical determinants of attraction

Some variables of the attraction process are based on physical presence. People are, in one sense, objects that occupy space. How often they are present, and how pleasing their appearance is perceived to be when they are present, play an important part in determining attraction and provide the opportunity for the development of further, nonphysical attraction.

Proximity   One obvious, though easily overlooked, variable that determines attraction is proximity. Clearly, it is difficult to like someone unless you know him, and difficult to know him unless you have contact with him. It follows, then, that the more contact there is between persons, the more opportunity they have for liking each other and the greater the probability that they will like each other. A considerable amount of research has validated this conclusion. Proximity has been called the "almost sufficient condition" for attraction. Although proximity does not insure attraction (close neighbors can be worst enemies), the process of attraction is highly dependent on this variable.

Several studies on friendship choices have corroborated this theory. For example, students who lived together in the same residence halls or apartment buildings, or who sat next to each other in classrooms tended to develop stronger friendships among themselves than with students from whom they were geographically separated, even by small distances.[1]

In line with these findings were the results of studies of married couples living in a new housing project. Once again, friendships were found to increase in proportion to the degree of geographical proximity: couples who were next-door neighbors developed friendships with much greater frequency than those who were separated by one or several houses. Even more interesting was the effect of architectural design. For example, those couples who inhabited the few project houses which faced the street were, in effect, socially isolated from couples who lived in homes facing the inner courtyard.[2] Less prominent architectural features, such as the position of stairways and mailboxes, also had an effect on friendship formation: if residents lived near stairways—and thus the major flow of traffic through the apartments—or if their mailboxes were clustered with those of other residents, they generally developed a greater number of friendships. The interesting implication of all these related observations is that the social

[1] L. Festinger, "Group Attraction and Membership" in D. Cartwright and A. Zander, eds., *Group Dynamics: Research and Theory* (Evanston, Ill.: Row, Peterson, 1952) and D. Byrne, "The Influence of Propinquity and Opportunities for Interaction on Classroom Relationships," *Human Relations, 14* (1961), pp. 63-70.
[2] L. Festinger, S. Schachter and K. Back, *Social Pressure in Informal Groups: A Study of Human Factors in Housing* (New York: Harper, 1950).

relationships of people living within a given housing project or complex can be virtually *planned* in terms of architectural design.[3]

Even mate selection may, in some cases, depend upon those same factors that facilitate the formation of friendships. In apparent confirmation of the boy- or girl-next-door "theory" of romance, one study found that of 5,000 applicants who had registered for marriage licenses in one city, 12 percent of the couples lived on the same block, and one-third of them lived no more than five blocks away from each other.[4] Comparable studies have supported the positive effect of proximity on mate selection.

In apparent contradiction of these findings would be the idea that people are apt to dislike each other as the physical distance between them decreases. Yet there is considerable evidence to support this hypothesis, implausible as it might seem upon first consideration. For example, police records of a major city in the United States reveal that victims in a majority of robbery cases were either related to or acquainted with the thief. It was similarly found that victims of aggravated assault and homicide had lived in close proximity to the perpetrators of these crimes. In fact, almost one-third of all murders occurred within the family unit.[5]

Reconciling these contrary groups of studies based on proximity may not be an impossible task if we understand the underlying factor in all of them. The closer together people live or work, the greater their opportunity for sharing experiences and gathering information about one another; and it is primarily through interpersonal knowledge that people develop strong mutual sentiments. Whether they be those of hostility and aggression or the more positive sentiments of friendship and love is, for purposes of understanding the suggested hypotheses, beside the point. It can be assumed that since people need each other for a variety of personal reasons, they will utilize their knowledge of one another to promote a mutually supportive relationship. But this fact does not preclude exploitative needs that can be easily satisfied through close proximity with others.[6]

---

[3] L. Festinger, "Architecture and Group Membership," *Journal of Social Issues*, 1 (1951), pp. 152-163.

[4] J. H. S. Bossard, "Residential Propinquity as a Factor in Mate Selection," *American Journal of Sociology*, 38 (1932), pp. 219-224.

[5] E. Berscheid and E. H. Walster, *Interpersonal Attraction* (Reading, Mass.: Addison-Wesley, 1969), p. 48.

[6] *Ibid.*, p. 49.

Physical attractiveness The perceived physical attractiveness of another person is especially important in the early phases of a relationship. Given limited information about a new acquaintance, one tends to perceive him as something of an "object," and to evaluate him on the basis of how pleasing he looks. In one study, 89 people evaluated their own attraction to strangers of both sexes, and this attraction was greater toward those who were seen as physically appealing.

Physical attraction naturally varies from person to person; one man's Monroe is another man's Medusa. But certain cultural stereotypes do exist, and most research indicates that within a society there are high levels of agreement about those characteristics that constitute physical beauty. From childhood on, one is bombarded with photographs of movie stars, fashion models, brilliant young men and women stepping out of limousines and other standards of attractiveness. One is told that fat is ugly, that women should have smooth, small features, that men should have broad shoulders and rugged chins. It is difficult to escape such conditioning, especially since it plays an important role in determining attraction between members of opposite sexes. Recently, women's liberation advocates have criticized the "objectifying" of men and women that is the source of such stereotypes, but that process is more likely to subside very slowly as a result of sex-role changes than it is to vanish as a result of direct attack.

Physical objects may also send messages that may be perceived as attractive. Clothing, hair style, even the newspaper or book under the arm, all help others to perceive you as you wish to be perceived. Such accoutrements are often used to convey a message about one's values, political stance or life-style in order to attract people who share those attitudes.

Interpersonal liking and similarity

Although it would be inaccurate to suggest that physical proximity, attraction and liking occur in certain fixed or formal patterns, we can, for the sake of discussion, examine possible modes of behavior that incorporate these interpersonal variables. For example, if one is physically attracted to someone, he may try to be in close proximity with that person as often as possible. Both physical attraction and proximity thus pave the way for interpersonal communication. And through such communication, interpersonal liking may be perpetuated and reinforced.

Sometimes physical attraction and liking are generated as a result of being liked. In other words, reciprocal liking may occur simply because you hear that someone likes you. If that person happens to be someone whom you had previously admired, the esteem conferred by his attraction and liking for you may be sufficient motivation for use to seek his company and to initiate communication. In the course of that communication you will both gain knowledge about one another that will either create a foundation for the initial liking or will convince you that you have no basis for building a relationship.[7]

Perhaps circumstances may warrant communication with someone to whom you are not especially attracted and for whom you feel no particular liking. Let us say, for example, that you are conducting negotiations with someone who just happens to be the representative of the business firm with which you are dealing. In other words, expedience rather than choice have brought the two of you together. It is nevertheless quite possible that in the course of communicating with this person you will grow to like him. Perhaps certain appealing qualities or quirks of personality will manifest themselves even though the actual content of the communication may be formal and impersonal. Or perhaps the other person's friendly tone of voice and relaxed manner will invite more casual conversation that can serve as a basis for attraction. Liking in this case follows communication and then may be reinforced by further interactions.

The cycle of attraction, liking and communication can occur in any order and with each variable reinforcing (either positively or negatively) the previous variable in a given cycle. But affecting the cycle at any or all of its steps is the factor of perceived similarity. People are often attracted to one another because they share beliefs, attitudes or values. For instance, a group of college students was tested at the beginning of the freshman year to determine attitudes on specific topics. Predictions were then made about the friendship choices that would be likely to occur. By the end of the term, those choices were validated. The students created friendships on the basis of shared attitudes, though it should be noted that it took them a full term to discover actual rather than assumed similarities.[8]

---

[7] *Ibid.*, pp. 52-54.

[8] T. M. Newcomb, *The Acquaintance Process* (New York: Holt, Rinehart and Winston, Inc., 1961).

Sometimes liking or any sort of positive feelings toward another will lead us to perceive similarities in our attitudes, whether or not they actually exist. On the other hand, being favorably disposed toward someone (even someone with whom we have had no personal interaction) may lead us to believe that our attitudes would be dissimilar. In one study, subjects were asked to estimate the similarity of their own attitudes with those of a white man and a black man, both strangers to the subjects. Those subjects who were prejudiced against blacks claimed that they would probably be in greater and more consistent agreement with any attitudes that might be expressed by the white man. Unprejudiced subjects assumed that attitudinal similarity to both men probably would be equal.[9]

Other evidence indicates that if people are forced to communicate they often discover attitude similarities and subsequently develop a positive mutual attraction—despite obvious or assumed differences of religion, race, social class and other factors of background. For example, union leaders and management may assume that their attitudes are irreconcilable and may therefore approach contract negotiations with feelings of suspicion and hostility. Nevertheless, if communication channels remain open, both parties may discover that their goals and attitudes regarding company policy intersect at many levels. Once these similarities have been perceived, there is a chance for mutually beneficial bargaining in areas in which real disagreement exists.

Often when a cycle of perceived similarity, attraction and liking are created between two people, they begin to modify their communication so that it deliberately reinforces these other variables. For example, if we have grown very close to another person and share a deep mutual liking with him, we might tend to gloss over his dissimilar attitudes if they seem to flaw the desired perfection of the relationship. Or if we are fearful of losing our attraction or causing him to dislike us, we may gradually begin to suppress any attitudes of our own that we think might disrupt the harmony of our interactions. Our communication therefore becomes increasingly more supportive of one another's attitudes and may gradually effect a merging or negation of differences that actually had existed. Husbands and wives who grow in their love and affection for one another often follow this pattern of interaction that

[9] D. Byrne and T. J. Wong, "Racial Prejudice, Interpersonal Attraction and Assumed Dissimilarity of Attitudes," *Journal of Abnormal Social Psychology*, 65 (1962), pp. 246-252.

leads from perceived similarities to real similarities in the way they express themselves, in the way they respond to the same situations—and even in their personal habits and clothing preferences.

Figure 12-1 To some extent, similarities of age and race can help to develop attraction between persons. This attraction, in turn, may facilitate more interaction, more attitude similarity and more interpersonal liking.

Social gratification

Perhaps the most basic purpose of communication is satisfying the need to socialize with others. The greatest torment of being locked in solitary confinement is not the lack of physical comforts or the strict regimentation of one's habits; rather it is the lack of companionship, the absence of someone whom one can talk to and who will respond in turn. Even if a person is free to travel and explore the entire world, his sensations, experiences and observations will, in a sense, be unreal to him—that is they will simply accumulate as isolated fragments in his mind—unless at some point he can relate them to another human being. In the process of communicating with another, a person begins to understand the full meaning of his experiences, how they fit in with the continuum of all human life and how they integrate into the pattern of his own life.

It is not enough simply to receive communication; nor is there sufficient gratification in communicating on a level that does not utilize one's social and cognitive capacities. Otherwise, for example, a housewife would be satisfied by watching and listening to television or talking to her young children about topics that they understand and that interest them. What her weary husband, home from a day at the office, may construe as a deliberate drain on his remaining energy and patience is simply his wife's real and important need to relate to another through communication. She prods him about his experiences during the day and, perhaps more importantly, she expresses all her own pent-up thoughts and feelings. It is not enough, in other words, for her to be affected by events and by the thoughts and experiences of others; she must also be able to affect others with her own life and experiences, even if it is only through inconsequential or nonpurposive conversation.

Affecting others and being affected by them can, of course, be satisfied through more impersonal forms of communication. Setting up a street stand to distribute pamphlets is undoubtedly gratifying to the social needs of some people. Through pamphleteering and talking about their political or religious philosophies with passersby, they can break through the isolation of their own particular ideas and perspectives and establish some sort of rapport with the impressions and experiences of others. As transitory and superficial as this type of communication may be, it serves as a connecting link between the individual and his social environment.

Therapeutic results of communication

Through communication we receive positive and negative feedback, both of which provide us with reference points for assessing and evaluating our own behavior. Positive reactions from others instill within us a feeling of confidence and the sense of belonging in the world. Negative feedback—if properly perceived and utilized—can motivate us to reexamine, and possibly change, our behavior and values in order to elicit more supportive responses in the future. But if improperly perceived or misinterpreted, negative feedback may create or intensify conflicts between people and thus fail to serve its therapeutic function.

Because communication is a process through which individuals largely confirm each other's assumptions, the rejection of a person's beliefs or values may be construed as hostility. The person who feels he has been rejected or ridiculed by his friend may become increasingly cautious about what he says and what he discloses about himself. Instead of responding openly, he begins to communicate defensively—he behaves under the assumption that he is being threatened, or will be, by what the other person is saying.

Paranoia is an extreme and pathological condition that can lead from defensive behavior and communication. But almost all people, even those who consider themselves "normal," behave paranoically from time to time. If one expects criticism and hostility, he, in effect, creates these negative responses for himself. Even from the most casual, everyday sort of interaction he may infer hostile, critical and exploitative meanings. His increasing lack of spontaneity is not confined to his speech —even his facial and bodily gestures may reflect a stiff and defensive attitude. And in order to compensate for the feeling of inadequacy which an overly negative perception of feedback can produce, he may become overly assertive and dogmatic about his own values and beliefs.

This defensive and paranoid behavior isolates the individual from those he thinks have rejected him. All attempts to persuade him that his behavior is unjustified may be futile; in fact, persuasion itself may be interpreted as a hostile, manipulative act. The broader tragedy is that nations themselves often become locked into defensive postures. On the personal level, the defensive individual is primarily the one who suffers from failed communication. But on the international and political level, whole populations may suffer from disturbed relations between leaders—and they may suffer in irreversible ways, if one believes that atomic warfare is a real and not simply a tactical threat. Thus when differences between parties build to dangerous levels of conflict, therapeutic solutions must be sought and utilized.

Conflicts in one form or another seem to be an inescapable part of the human condition. Nations go to war; ethnic groups within nations settle their differences in blood; a bar-room quarrel ends in a knife-fight; an individual is driven by internal conflicts to commit suicide. On a less serious level, manufacturing nations compete for markets; a high school debating team competes for national honors; two men go after the same job; and Joe Consumer agonizes over the choice between a Sony and a Zenith portable radio.

Communication—or lack of communication—can be a significant factor in the development of conflicts. A brawl may start over an imagined insult, where no insult was intended. The conflicting sides may issue statements of principle or "non-negotiable" demands; each group may reinforce its behavior patterns by propaganda about the justice of its own cause or the heinous behavior of the other side. Communication is even more important to the process of resolving conflicts; most conflicts are reduced or eliminated only when both sides learn to trust one another and to cooperate.

The types of conflict

No reasonable person would claim that all conflict is the same. The individual who "fights" with himself about which television set to purchase, the parent and child who argue about allowance money and the two gangs that "rumble" in the park are clearly not engaging in the same activity. One way to view the different types of conflict is to categorize them as intrapersonal, interpersonal or intergroup.

Intrapersonal conflict As long as human beings are faced with choices, there is the potential for conflict: shall I vote for Candidate A or Candidate B? shall I stick to my well-paid but hateful job, or give it up for a simpler life in the country? shall I be honest and tell my family that I am homosexual, or would the knowledge shatter them? Judson Brown, a psychologist, proposes the following model of internal conflicts: S represents a stimulus, and T_1 and T_2 represent two incompatible tendencies leading to two different responses, R_1 and R_2.[10]

---

[10] Judson Brown, "Principles of Intrapersonal Conflict," *Journal of Conflict Resolution*, 1 (1957), pp. 135-154.

In Brown's model, the resolution of the conflict depends on the relative strength of T_1 and T_2, or the conflicting tendencies. In other words, when one tendency is much stronger than the other, the choice is relatively easy to make. Given the opportunity to go sailing or horseback riding, a man who prefers water sports will have little trouble deciding; besides, he may go riding another day. Some choices, however, involve serious conflicts, especially those choices that involve deeply held ethical values, overall life goals and societal pressures. A prisoner of war may be faced with the alternative of being tortured or of giving his captors secret military information. The idea of torture may horrify him; but if he talks, he may forever after be considered a coward and a traitor by his countrymen and by himself. He may consider the second alternative worse than the first. The strength of the two tendencies may increase or decrease in the course of the decision-making process. Thus, increased torture may force the prisoner to reevaluate his choices.

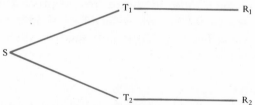

Figure 12-2 Model of intrapersonal conflict.

Internal conflicts may be classified as approach-approach, avoidance-avoidance and approach-avoidance.[11] An *approach-approach* conflict occurs when an individual is presented with two positive but incompatible goals: going to a World Series baseball game or seeing a close friend off on a long trip; or accepting one of two job offers, both of them attractive for different reasons. An *avoidance-avoidance* conflict occurs when an individual faces two choices neither of which is pleasing to him; in effect, he must choose the lesser of two evils. It is of course sometimes possible to reject both choices and withdraw from the situation, as when two friends issue party invitations for the same night, and both parties are likely to be boring. But it is not always possible to withdraw. The prisoner of war who must talk or be tortured faces an avoidance-avoidance conflict from which he cannot withdraw. An *approach-avoidance* conflict involves a positive goal which

11 *Ibid.*

carries with it intrinsic unpleasant consequences. A man might wish to marry a woman, but with the marriage he would also acquire some unpleasant and unavoidable in-laws, and two obstreperous children from a former marriage. A politician may find that he can win an election, but only by making underhanded political deals that might haunt his future career and torment his conscience.

Many psychiatrists believe that the ability to handle internal conflicts rationally and with relative ease is the mark of the well-adjusted personality. The neurotic, on the other hand, may be too rigid to change his goals with changing circumstances, or too lacking in self-confidence to make a decision in the first place. A country's leader who possessed these qualities might bring disaster to his country by refusing to reconsider his policy choices when present policies are seen to be failing, and hesitating endlessly between possible courses of action where the situation demands action. However, it is not clear that choices made with great facility are the best for the individual or his society. The individual who changes goals or desires at every turn may have no solid core of character or values; he is shaped by events instead of shaping his own life. The politician whose decisions are all based on expedience, who shapes his policies to fit the popular whims of the moment, can be a serious danger to his society.

Interpersonal and intergroup conflict   Interpersonal and intergroup conflicts are the most familiar and dangerous of all conflicts: a father and son quarrel, two football teams compete, nations jockey for political advantage or fight over scarce resources, superpowers armed with nuclear weapons threaten to destroy one another and take the rest of the world with them.

The three types of intrapersonal conflict may also occur on interpersonal or intergroup level. Approach-avoidance type conflicts may exist within a group; a society may choose to devote its productive capacity to creating consumer goods or expensive armaments, and the people of a nation losing a war may greatly desire peace, but be very slow in surrendering because the psychic cost of losing is also very great. Approach-approach conflict may occur when people share the same interpersonal goals but manifest them in contradictory patterns during a given interaction. For example, two people may wish to impress each other with their accomplishments and project an image of self-confidence and self-reliance; at the same time they genuinely wish to disclose their fears and problems openly and freely express their need for mutual support and reassurance. Two desirable, yet conflicting, goals are thus sought in the same interpersonal encounter. If both people are able to integrate these goals at the same time, there will be no conflict and the interaction will serve its purpose (no matter which of the goals dominates the communication). But, for example, if one person confesses certain weakness only to have the other person counter with claims of his strength and superiority, conflicting and defensive behavior will mar the communicative effort.

In considering interpersonal and intergroup conflicts, it is useful to distinguish between the less serious and more serious forms. Simple confrontations between individuals or groups may have positive benefits in the form of opening up dialogues and producing changes in the behavior patterns that produce tension. During the 1960s, civil rights groups confronted the larger society of the United States with the contradictions and brutal conseqences of racism. As a result, many laws were passed, some of the attitudes and behavior patterns of white people were changed and American society evolved toward a more humane society.

So long as a confrontation does not develop into an exercise in "brinksmanship," it can serve as a unifying force and release the creative energies of the opponents. Two ethnic groups that confront one another in an inner-city neighborhood may learn through the very process of confrontation to trust and respect one another. They may also learn that in order to avert greater conflict in the future they must cooperate to reduce tensions. Finally, they may join together to solve common problems—perhaps in the process confronting a third group, such as the city administration. Confrontations can thus help reduce tensions and keep a society open and flexible. A society that is too rigid, due to poor communication and lack of confrontation is ripe for more serious forms of conflict.

Certain other forms of conflict, no matter how fierce, still take place in controlled situations. An incumbent President may want very badly to be reelected, but failing that, no American President has yet sought to stay in power through military force or other extralegal means. Even violent conflicts may be limited and controlled. In eighteenth-century Europe, both duels between individuals and wars between nations were governed by strict codes of conduct that were carefully observed. The important point is that in controlled conflicts the opponents generally maintain some mutual respect and trust. It is often in the interest of both parties to keep conflict within limits and reach a settlement; maneuvering may be directed mostly toward obtaining relative advantages at the end of the conflict instead of toward complete victory. A labor strike is such a situation; neither side wants the factory closed down completely, and both sides would like the strike to end and normal work resume. There is some degree of mutual trust and respect between labor and management, and the conflict is restricted to hammering out the terms on which the strike will be ended.

The really dangerous conflicts are win-lose situations in which each opponent becomes to the other a depersonalized enemy who must be crushed or eliminated by any means possible. Irrationality and emotionalism play a large part in such a conflict. During the Cold War of the 1950s, the United States and the Soviet Union adopted an "us or them" mentality toward one another. Hysterical fears and cold mistrust were encouraged on both sides. Billions were spent on nuclear weapons, and each time there was a minor skirmish between the two superpowers at one of the world's trouble spots, the world held its breath for fear that the next day or the next hour might bring World War III.

Communication and conflict Almost every form of conflict is affected by communication. Even internal conflicts result in many cases from a disparity between individual desires and societal expectations, or from a disparity between the values of the society at large and the values of a subgroup of that society. Thus, a woman might want to become an auto mechanic, but may fear ridicule and discrimination from customers who are not ready to accept a woman mechanic. Her dilemma might be complicated by her academically-oriented family and their attitude toward a career choice that involved manual labor.

In the most serious conflict situations, the opponents may believe they really understand each other's position: the conflict resulted because "the other side" refused all reasonable solutions and will continue to do so. In fact, communication of either position is so highly distorted that it is more accurate to call it propaganda. During the United States involvement in the Vietnam War, both the United States and North Vietnam branded the other the aggressor nation, a brutal and untrustworthy enemy that must be stopped in order to bring peace to Vietnam. Neither side would admit faults or uncertainties on its own side, or virtues on the other; this would be a sign of "weakness" which might result in a subsequent loss of bargaining power. Internal dissidence over the war was ignored or suppressed as much as possible— this might give aid and comfort to the enemy. Rather than dealing flexibly with one another, both sides tended to harden their demands, issue threats and escalate aggressive behavior which only tended to make things worse.

In such an atmosphere of intransigence, mistrust and distorted communication, neither party is likely to back down. The threat of loss—even loss of face—acts as a continued deterrent to open channels of communication. When trust is absent, the lack of trust is more negative in its effect than the presence of trust is positive when it is present.[12] Thus, *no* negotiations can take place when each side believes that the statements and intentions of the other side are completely untrustworthy. One of the first steps in resolving conflicts, then, is the creation of an atmosphere in which both parties can begin to perceive the other as at least partially rational and trustworthy. They must be brought to perceive that continued conflict will not yield the desired results, and that cooperation will provide increased rewards. Though basic values and goals may not have to be abandoned, it must become clear to the parties that some degree of compromise is necessary.

Strategies to reduce conflict

In an age of nuclear weapons and increasing violence, the processes of conflict resolution have become an important concern of social scientists and communication experts—and indeed of every thinking individual. Although there are no easy solutions to the varieties of human conflict, some processes tested in laboratories and in real-life situations offer promise in reducing or eliminating conflict.

Creating a nondefensive environment The most direct method of reducing hostility is for one side simply to abandon the competitive and aggressive posture. An argument in a local tavern will end abruptly if one of the antagonists suddenly

---

[12] M. Deutsch, "Trust and Suspicion," *Journal of Conflict Resolution*, 1 (1958), pp. 265-279.

smiles and says. "You're absolutely right! Let's be friends."
This strategy is known as the Gandhian model of conflict
resolution, after Mohandas Gandhi who led the people of
India to independence from British rule.[13] Gandhi believed
that the means of conflict resolution cannot be separated from
the ends; the means not only determine the ends, they are
the ends. If one party was morally right, the only victory
possible lay in convincing, not defeating, the opposing side.

He believed, moreover, that the adoption of nonviolent
tactics automatically gave his side a moral advantage over
the opposition. The opponent in turn is encouraged to foresake
the hostile stance—and indeed in the face of nonviolent
resistance, the opponent's aggressions can become a serious
embarrassment to the opponent's side. With the cessation of
hostilities, dialogue can begin again, and both sides can start to
work together to resolve the causes of the conflict. In its
high-mindedness and orientation toward cooperation, the
Gandhian model is an attractive one. It does not, however,
work in all cases. Where it has worked—in Gandhi's time in
India, and in the 1960s nonviolent civil rights movement
led by Martin Luther King in the United States—certain special
conditions were present. Gandhi and King were able to
persuade their followers to adopt nonviolence as a tactic;
Britain and the United States were essentially humane societies
and sensitive to world public opinion; finally, both Britain
and the United States were willing to concede most of the
changes advocated by Gandhi and King. Obviously, these
conditions are not met in many conflict situations. Nonviolent
resistance would have been of little use, for instance, under
the rule of the Nazis in Germany.

Cooperation versus competition   One of the ways social
scientists predict attitudinal adaptability is to test people's
reactions in games. Some of the games thus developed are
useful in showing that people do learn through games that
cooperation can be as rewarding as competition.[14] It must be
remembered, however, that a laboratory game, with its limited
structure and artificial nature, cannot be equated entirely with
real-life situations.

[13] For a complete discussion see Arne Naess, "A Systematization of Gandhian Ethics of
Conflict Resolution," *Journal of Conflict Resolution*, 2 (1958), pp. 140-155.
[14] For support see M. Deutsch, *op. cit.* and P. S. Gallo, Jr. and C. G. McClintock, "Cooperative
and Competitive Behavior in Mixed-Motive Games," *Journal of Conflict Resolution*, 9
(1965), pp. 68-78.

One laboratory game is called *Prisoner's Dilemma.* In this game two volunteer subjects, or prisoners, are interviewed separately by the prosecutor, or person running the experiment. Each prisoner wants the same thing: freedom. Each has a choice of remaining silent or confessing to the prosecutor. Only one prisoner can be granted complete freedom, and that happens only if one prisoner confesses while the other maintains silence. The one who confesses goes free, the other gets a ten-year sentence. If each prisoner confesses, however, thus trying to stick the other with the long sentence, both prisoners get five-year sentences. Finally, if neither confesses, both prisoners are convicted and will spend one year jail.

Faced with the decision whether or not to confess, each prisoner must consider that if he does not confess, he has a 50 percent chance of receiving a ten-year sentence and a 50 percent chance of receiving a one-year sentence. If he does confess, he has a 50 percent chance of serving five years and a 50 percent chance of freedom. Thus, to each individual prisoner, competition or confession seems a more rational choice than cooperation or silence. However, since each prisoner faces the same decision, it is likely that both will make the same seemingly rational choice—to confess. Of course, this results in a five-year sentence for both, an outcome that is less preferable than a one-year sentence for both. Studies using the *Prisoner's Dilemma* game have demonstrated that at first participants do compete. However, with repeated playing, they learn to change their behavior pattern from competitive to cooperative. Moreover, when the "prisoners" had a chance to confer with one another before announcing their choices, trust tended to increase because the prisoners reconfirmed a sense that their behavior would be rationally plotted and that cooperation would produce the desired result.

1. Interpersonal attraction, which can affect the patterns and effectiveness of both interpersonal and intergroup communication, is partly based on factors of physical presence. Proximity allows people the opportunity to gain knowledge about one another upon which to base mutual sentiments of liking and disliking; and the physical appearance of a person may inspire, enhance or decrease his physical attractiveness to another.

2. Proximity, physical attractiveness, perceived similarities, liking and communication are variables that can occur in any sequence in a mutually reinforcing cycle. Physical attractiveness and liking may lead to proximity and communication, or may be generated as a result of being liked by another person. Sharing similar attitudes and beliefs may also initiate the cycle and then lead to communication and liking. Or liking in itself may cause us to perceive similarities, whether or not they exist; and we may subsequently modify our communication so that it reinforces the positive attraction and perception of similarity with another.

3. Communication can satisfy the need for social gratification. It enables us to share our experiences and to affect and be affected by others in our social environment.

4. The therapeutic function of communication can be served through the positive and negative feedback we receive from others. Properly utilized such feedback can enhance one's self-esteem and guide him in changing behavior and attitudes that impair the effectiveness of his interactions with others.

5. Intrapersonal conflicts may be classified as approach-approach (two positive but incompatible choices), avoidance-avoidance (two equally unattractive choices), and approach-avoidance (an attractive choice modified by concomitant circumstances that are unpleasant). These same conflicts may also occur on an interpersonal and

intergroup level and lead to mutually beneficial dialogue and behavioral changes, or deadlock situations. Distortions in communication may create or intensify such conflicts.

6. Conflict resolution requires trust, open communication and a willingness to compromise. Hostility and violence may be supplanted by a nondefensive and trusting atmosphere if one opponent simply abandons his aggressiveness (the Gandhian model of conflict resolution). Both parties must strive to cooperate rather than compete and to bargain and negotiate over differences rather than emphasize the intransigence of their positions.

1. Make separate lists of adjectives that describe a person you would find attractive and one you would find unattractive. Do these lists correspond with the variables of the attraction process discussed in this chapter? Compare your lists with those of your classmates. In what ways are your lists similar to those of your classmates? In what ways are they different?

2. Think about a person whom you did not like at first. What factors lead to your initial dislike? Describe the role that communication played in changing your feelings about this person. Did finding out about the other person affect your feelings? Repeat the exercise this time describing a person you first liked and then came to dislike. What factors caused this change?

3. Think of an important internal conflict that you experienced. Using Judson Brown's model of intrapersonal conflict, identify the incompatible tendencies and possible responses. Identify a variable that if introduced to the situation might have changed your response.

4. Write an anecdotal description of an approach-approach, approach-avoidance and avoidance-avoidance conflict that you have experienced with another person. Have three other students read your anecdotes to determine if they would classify the situation in the same way. How may intrapersonal differences lead to interpersonal conflict?

Ellen Berscheid and Elaine H. Walster, *Interpersonal Attraction* (Reading, Mass.: Addison-Wesley Publishing Co., 1969). This brief book presents a comprehensive discussion of the variables affecting the interpersonal attraction process.

Fred E. Jandt, ed., *Conflict Resolution Through Communication* (New York: Harper and Row, 1973). The author has brought together one of the finest collections of readings about conflict and communication. His two original articles are important contributions to understanding conflict resolution.

Robert D. Dye, *Conflict Among Humans* (New York: Springer Publishing Company, 1973). The last three chapters of this very readable text focus on the types of communication patterns that lead to conflict and modes of conflict resolution.

Paul Watzlawick, Janet H. Beavin and Don D. Jackson, *Pragmatics of Human Communication: A Study of Interactional Patterns, Pathologies and Paradoxes* (New York: W. W. Norton and Co., 1967). The authors take a clinical approach to understanding communication and conflict. Their analysis of *Who's Afraid of Virginia Woolf?* is both entertaining and insightful.

K. L. Kahn, D. M. Wolfe, R. P. Quinn, J. D. Snoek and R. A. Rosenthal *Organizational Stress: Studies in Role Conflicts and Ambiguity* (New York: John Wiley and Sons, 1964). Although somewhat technical for the beginning student, this is a particularly valuable study of the ways organizations produce conflict among persons.

Epilogue:
Communication and the future

Although this book discusses human communication and the way
it functions in contemporary society, no book can do more
than begin to explain such a complex phenomenon.
Communication is a process, with no identifiable beginning
or end; the information contained within these covers can
be useful only if it is understood and applied by the reader
—and even so, it probably raises more questions than it answers.
For these reasons, this section of the book emphasizes the
notion of continuation rather than conclusion.

Much of that continuation is up to you, the reader, as you
consider the kind of communicator—or for that matter, the
kind of person—you desire to become. The decisions you
make will be personal. The material in this book is as potentially
valuable to the would-be huckster as to the sincere and truthful
individual, and no number of prescriptive statements could
prevent a reader from behaving in ways he considers appropriate.
Despite individual differences, there are some questions about
communication in the future that must concern society as
a whole.

The way man adapts to change is a matter of paramount
importance, with many implications for communication.
Anticipating change and planning for it are not new challenges,
but the rate of change is constantly accelerating as technology
expands. And as Leo Bogart, a mass media specialist, has
noted, what is radical change today will look moderate to
people in the near future:

> It is hard to think seriously about the future because we take the
> present so much for granted. We hardly think twice about the fact that
> throughout the world music is a commonplace feature of daily life,
> at leisure and at work. We think of it as a part of mankind's heritage,
> like sun, air, and water. Yet this has only come about in the few years
> since the invention of the phonograph and the radio.[1]

Man is quickly becoming simultaneously liberated and
imprisoned by his technology. He is less and less faced with
the task of ensuring his physical survival, yet more and more
faced with unprecedented leisure time and other technological
by-products to which it is difficult for him to adjust. Although

[1] L. Bogart, "Mass Media in the year 2000," *Gazette,* *13* (March 1967), p. 24.

it is no longer necessary for people in this culture to live
by a work ethic, with a job at the center of their lives, no
new ethic has surfaced to take its place. People feel estranged
from old values, but have not found suitable replacements
that will help them make decisions about their lives.

These circumstances also estrange people from each other
and make communication more difficult. The telephone, the
747 and the interstate highway seem to make distance
meaningless with their ability to bring far-flung people close
together; but they are also manifestations of a way of life in
which it is not unusual to "pick up and go," to separate
ourselves from others on a moment's notice. Each year, Detroit
manufactures millions of automobiles that allow people to
travel at high speeds in their own private bubble. The mass
media provide ways to spend leisure time that can be called
"communication" only in the loosest sense, and a good many
parents have turned over the task of socializing children to
ABC, CBS and NBC.

At the same time, the problems created by advancing
technology demand that people communicate in order to solve
them. Unless crucial decisions about overpopulation, pollution,
the depletion of our natural resources and other side effects
of progress are to be left solely to those in positions of power,
people must communicate in order to participate in
decision-making. They must know the way to persuade
and the way to be the critical consumers of persuasion. They
must know the way to seek more reasonable ways of resolving
conflict. Without communication, decisions are likely to be made
by the powerful few, persuasion is likely to remain the weapon
of special interest groups and conflict is likely to be resolved
with the technological capacity to annihilate.

The very complexity of the technology often hampers the
communication process, since specialization raises barriers
to effective communication. The ability to communicate, one
of the principle characteristics of man's humanness, is blocked
by a lack of common ground or agreement on first principles.
In the past there was a generally agreed-upon common store
of knowledge on which to base day-to-day decisions; and
when there were doubts on how to proceed, there were always
experts—the wise men, the priests, the human repositories
of accumulated knowledge—on whom one could rely. Most
men did the same work, faced the same problems and availed
themselves of the same solutions.

Epilogue: Communication and the future

Today, far more complicated problems afflict almost every citizen. The store of information is immense, but access to it, for particular problems with a source that is trustworthy, is another problem all in itself. Daily life is saturated with information: society appears obsessed with techniques for gathering, storing and transmitting all kinds of data. Furthermore, the amount and variety of information that people have to process has changed their lives as drastically as the growth of cities or the invention of the automobile.

Indeed many contemporary occupations are devoted to information processing. Managers, lawyers, teachers, clerks, accountants, advertising and publishing workers, secretaries, employment and real-estate agents and many others are engaged in the business of processing information. Other groups are engaged in generating ever more and more data. High-speed computers, satellites, television, telephone transmission of everything from voices to photographs, and numerous other technologies collect and transmit more information than anyone can evaluate or absorb. Information grows at a geometric rate, while man's ability to use the information remains relatively constant, and is funneled into more miniscule areas of specialization. Whether or not information overload is possible and what happens if it is are questions yet to be answered.

The information explosion has challenged many assumptions. Marshall McLuhan has noted that the Vietnam War was the first twentieth-century war fought on American soil. People were able to witness the events of the conflict as they occurred —via television coverage—and had more information about it than any other war in history. When the information people received from the government did not conform to what they saw, the credibility of the government was undermined and assumptions about both the government and the war were challenged in new ways.

Similarly, the information explosion raises questions about education. For centuries, educational institutions have trained "information storers"—students who could amass data and keep it in mind long enough to spew it back on an examination paper. The highly educated person was one who knew many facts. Even today, some classrooms still put a premium on the content of the subject, but students and many teachers have begun to object and to demand new methods. They have the uneasy feeling that the old methods are not relevant to present and future needs, and they are probably correct.

Epilogue: Communication and the future

Education will have to change if people are going to meet the challenges of the information explosion. The emphasis must shift from information storage to information retrieval and processing. Healthy trends in this direction are beginning to emerge. Students are learning how to ask meaningful questions, rather than how to memorize answers. Speech communication courses center more on interpersonal communication and decision-making in a variety of situations, with emphasis on the individual's growth and development as a communicator rather than on correct or proper ways to communicate. Under these changing circumstances, students are being asked to assume responsibility and risks that require more commitment than a "right answer." This new alternative is, for some students, more difficult, but the rewards—the ability to handle information confidently and develop criteria for decisions—make the additional effort worthwhile.

Because information is power, man's ability to understand and use new technology is a critical skill for effective communication both now and, moreso, in the future. Much of people's knowledge about their society is acquired through the media and this knowledge affects even their relationships with others. In past generations, people relied on interpersonal communication for most of their information: friends and neighbors told each other not only what society expected of them, but what was going on in the world outside their own community. This mode of communication had certain drawbacks —among them local distortions and ignorance—but there are also drawbacks to the present system, under which the media have become the dominant sources of data about the world. One scholar claims that "little of what we think we know of the social realities of the world have we found out first-hand. Most of the 'pictures' in our heads we have gained from these media. . . ."[2]

Another study concludes that "Television, by its very nature, brainwashes children in that it shapes the way they view the world and the kind of people they will be."[3] There is no longer any doubt about the media's pervasive influence. However, there remain many questions about those things (if anything) that should be done to mitigate that influence.

The television industry as well as the daily newspapers are

---

[2] C. W. Mills, "Some Effects of Mass Media," in Alan Casty, ed., *Mass Media and Mass Man* (New York: Holt, Rinehart and Winston, 1968), p. 32.
[3] R. M. Liebert and R. Paules, "TV for Kiddies: Truth, Goodness, Beauty—and a Little Bit of Brainwash," *Psychology Today*, 6 (June 1972), p. 128.

Epilogue: Communication and the future

under constant attack both from those who would like to
see greater control and those who feel that news coverage is
insufficient. High government officials in administrations as
unlike in their ideologies as those of Kennedy and Nixon have
objected to the treatment they received from the media.
Vice-President Agnew in an address at Des Moines, Iowa has
even gone so far as to say that:

> One federal communications commissioner considers the power of the
> networks to equal that of local, state, and federal governments
> combined. Certainly, it represents a concentration of power over
> American public opinion unknown in history. . . We would never trust
> such power over public opinion in the hands of an elected government—
> it is time we questioned it in the hands of a small and un-elected
> elite.[4]

Spokesmen for the television industry were quick to answer
Agnew's criticism with the response that a free press and
free airways serve fundamental functions in a free society
by operating as a source of information and as a watch dog of
government. On the other hand, minority groups as well as
those with nonconformist views criticize the media because they
fail to get any coverage. They claim the mass media is too
sensitive to pressure from the large advertisers who fear to
offend the consumers of their products. Thus in a certain
sense, the pressure circulates from the public, to the advertiser,
to the press, to the government, and back again, with space
for leverage at each point.

For these reasons many people are beginning to emphasize
the importance of "alternate media"—small, local or special
interest media—that provide information and opinions unsuitable
for the mass media. Local radio and television stations have
commercial, government or university sponsers, and the
great variety of magazines each have their special clientele.
Nevertheless, questions of bias, fairness and the selection of
coverage remain critical and require careful consideration.

Another area of potential control arises out of the question
of man's right to communicate. The United States Constitution
guarantees freedom of speech, assembly and the press.
Defining the limits to these freedoms has been in process
from the founding of the republic. Freedom of speech does
not include the right to yell "fire" in a crowded theatre. But
at what point does a speech critical of the government become

---

[4] Delivered by Vice President Spiro Agnew on November 13, 1969 in Des Moines, Iowa at
the Midwest Regional Republican Committee.

Epilogue: Communication and the future

a speech inciting riot? Does the First Amendment include the right to publish pornography or show "dirty" movies and is it the police who are to define it by closing a theatre, or the post office by refusing to deliver books and pictures, or the courts by criminally prosecuting a publisher? Does freedom of the press include the right to publish information that might endanger international negotiations? Does freedom of the press protect a reporter from government officials seeking his sources of information concerning the possible commitment of crime?

The idea of a right to communicate raises another question: Is there a right not to communicate? The information explosion and its accompanying technology raise some problems about human privacy. Credit bureaus are able to use computers to amass databanks containing information about the economic status of individuals; government agencies have been given broad information-gathering powers to collect data about many aspects of the lives of citizens. Because such activities tend to be secret, people are not given the chance to correct errors in the data; careers, reputations and lives have been ruined as a result. Even if people can correct databank information about themselves, does anyone have the right to collect, store and use information about another person? Should the right to collect information be protected in the same way as the right to disseminate information? If not, who is to decide the ground rules? Although all of these questions may sound like a depressing catalogue of potential national crises, it is encouraging that so many can be mediated through communication. In a free society, anyone who is willing to engage himself with other people and with the decision-making process can participate in the dialogue of communication.

Photo and illustration credits

Fig. 1: Berk Uzzle/Magnum; Fig. 2: Carew/Monkmeyer; Fig. 3: Adapted
from H. H. Martin and K. E. Anderson, eds., *Speech Communication:
Analysis and Readings* (Boston: Allyn and Bacon, 1968), p. 9; Fig. 4:
Adapted from C. E. Shannon and W. Weaver, *The Mathematical Theory
of Communication* (Urbana, Ill.: University of Illinois Press, 1949),
p. 98; Figs. 5 and 6: Adapted from B. H. Westley and M. S. MacLean, Jr.,
"A Conceptual Model for Communication Research," *Journalism Quarterly,
34* (1957), pp. 31–38; Fig. 7: Adapted from D. K. Berlo, *The Process of
Communication* (New York: Holt, Rinehart and Winston, Inc., 1960),
p. 72; Fig. 1–1: World Wide Photos; Fig. 1–3: Mark Godfrey/Magnum;
Fig. 1–5: Inge Morath/Magnum and Zimbel/Monkmeyer; Fig. 2–1: Bruce
Davidson/Magnum; Fig. 2–2: Leonard Freed/Magnum; Fig. 2–3: Mark
Godfrey/Magnum; Fig. 3–1: Hugh Rogers/Monkmeyer; Fig. 3–2: Cornell
Coyea/Magnum; Fig. 4–1: Magnum; Fig. 4–2: Silberstein/Monkmeyer
and Leonard Freed/Magnum; Fig. 4–3: Charles Harbutt/Magnum; Fig.
4–4: Bettman Archives; Fig. 4–5: Magnum and Elizabeth Burpee/DPI;
Fig. 4–6: Henri Cartier-Bresson/Magnum; Figs. 4–7 and 4–8: Adapted
from A. E. Scheflen, "The Significance of Posture in Communicative
Systems," *Psychiatry, 27* (1964), p. 323; Fig. 5–1: Merrim/Monkmeyer;
Fig. 5–3: Adapted from L. Carmichael, H. P. Hogan, and A. A. Walter, "An
Experimental Study of the Effect of Language on the Reproduction of
Visually Perceived Form," *Journal of Experimental Psychology, 15* (1932),
pp. 73–86; Fig. 5–4: Maro Ribaud/Monkmeyer; Fig. 6–1: Charles
Harbutt/Magnum; Fig. 6–2: Erich Hartman/Magnum; Fig. 7–2: Dungan
Allen/Black Star; Fig. 7–3: Ian Berry/Magnum; Fig. 7–4: Hiroji Kubota/
Magnum; Fig. 8–1: Bruce Davidson/Magnum; Fig. 8–2: Bruce Davidson/
Magnum; Fig. 8–3: Magnum; Fig. 8–4: Edo Koening/Black Star; Fig.
9–1: UPI; Fig. 9–2: Monkmeyer; Fig. 11–1: Ron Benvenisti/Magnum;
Fig. 11–2: Bruce Davidson/Magnum; Fig. 12–1: Leonard Freed/Magnum;
Fig. 12–2: Adapted from J. Brown, "Principle of Intrapersonal Conflict,"
Journal of Conflict Resolution, 1 (1957), p. 137.

Index